HUMAN RIGHTS AND WRONGS

SLAVERY, TERROR, GENOCIDE

Helen Fein

Routledge
Taylor & Francis Group

LONDON AND NEW YORK

To Joyce Apsel and Rhoda Howard-Hassmann

Excerpt from the poem "Tortures" is reprinted from Wislawa Szymborska, *View With a Grain of Sand* (1995), edited by Stanislaw Baranczak and Clare Cavanagh. Reprinted by permission of Harcourt, Brace.

"The Vocabulary of Terror in Argentina" is reprinted from Marguerite Feitlowitz, *A Lexicon of Terror: Argentina and the Legacies of Torture* (1998), pp. 51–60. Reprinted by permission of Oxford University Press and Marguerite Feitlowitz.

"Training of State Killers in Guatemala" is reprinted from Jennifer Schirmer, *The Guatemalan Military Project* (1988), pp. 285–290. Reprinted by permission of the University of Pennsylvania Press.

First published 2007 by Paradigm Publishers

Published 2016 by Routledge
2 Park Square, Milton Park, Abingdon, Oxon OX14 4RN
711 Third Avenue, New York, NY 10017, USA

Routledge is an imprint of the Taylor & Francis Group, an informa business

Designed and Typeset by Straight Creek Bookmakers.

ISBN 13: 978-1-59451-326-8 (hbk)
ISBN 13: 978-1-59451-327-5 (pbk)

Contents

Acronyms

AI	Amnesty International
AID	Agency for International Development
ANCD	Argentine National Commission on the Disappeared
CEDAW	Convention on the Elimination of All Forms of Discrimination Against Women
CEH	Commission for Historical Clarification
CERD	Committee on the Elimination of Racial Discrimination
CIA	Central Intelligence Agency
CIIDH	Centro Internacional para Investigaciones en Derechos Humanos (International Center for Investigations of Human Rights)
COPREDEH	Guatemalan Human Rights Commission
CSI	Christian Solidarity International
DOPS	Social and Political Police
DPU	Dispositif de Protection Urbaine (Department of Urban Protection)
DRC	Democratic Republic of Congo
ERP	People's Revolutionary Army
EU	European Union
FGM	female genital mutilation
FLN	Algerian Front for National Liberation
FRY	Federal Republic of Yugoslavia
GAM	Group of Mutual Support
GDI	Gender Development Index
GDP	Gross Development Product
GNP	gross national product
GOS	Government of Sudan
GVHR	Gross Violation of Human Rights
HDI	Human Development Index
HPI	Human Poverty Index
HRNGO	human rights nongovernmental organization
HRW	Human Rights Watch

Acronyms

ICC	International Criminal Court
ICCPR	International Covenant on Civil and Political Rights
ICP	Iraqi Communist Party
ICTJ	International Center for Transnational Justice
ICTWC	International Criminal Tribunal for War Crimes
IFHR	International Federation of Human Rights
KGB	Komitet Gosudarstvennoy Bezopasnosti (Committee for State Security—former USSR)
KLA	Kosovo Liberation Army
KR	Khmer Rouge
LIVA	Life Integrity Violation Analysis
MDC	Movement for Democratic Change
NATO	North Atlantic Treaty Organization
NED	National Endowment for Democracy
NGHRO	nongovernmental human rights organization
NGO	nongovernmental organization
NGV	not gross violators
NIF	National Islamic Front
NKVD	Narodny Kommisariat Vnutrennikh Del (People's Commissariat for Internal Affairs)
OAS	Organization Armée Secrete
OAU	Organization of African Unity
OE	Ottoman Empire
PEN	National Executive Power
PHR	Physicians for Human Rights
PPP	Purchasing Power Parity
PRT	Revolutionary Workers' Party
PUK	Patriotic Union of Kurdistan
RCC	Revolutionary Command Council
RPA	Rwandan Patriotic Army
RPF	Rwandan Patriotic Front
RTLMC	Radio Télévision Libre de Mille Collines
SARS	severe acute respiratory syndrome
SPLA	Southern People's Liberation Army
SPLA	Sudan People's Liberation Army
UDHR	Universal Declaration of Human Rights
UNAMIR	United Nations Assistance Mission in Rwanda
UNDP	United Nations Development Programme
UNGC	United Nations Convention on the Prevention and Punishment of the Crime of Genocide
UNICCPR	United Nations International Covenant on Civil and Political Rights
UNICESCR	United Nations International Covenant on Economic, Social, and Cultural Rights
UNSC	United Nations Security Council
USDOS	U.S. Department of State
WMD	weapons of mass destruction
WVS	World Value Survey

Preface and Acknowledgments

The impulse to write this book began two decades ago after almost two decades of studying genocide and massacres. My approach and design have changed several times over these decades, years that have been characterized by profound political changes. Many, I am sure, recall the past fifteen years as a roller coaster from exuberance to pessimism, fear, and anxiety. Presently, judgments and punishment of perpetrators of crimes in the countries discussed herein continue—a dictator on trial dies before judgment, another is hanged after judgment, and a former head of state is indicted. The tape of judgments of twentieth-century crimes continues rolling.

However, it is not my aim herein just to describe those times but to understand the persisting and recurrent gross violations of human rights that occurred. Basically, I view the sociological imagination as a lens to understand the social organization of good and evil. This quest implies that could we understand, we might transform the world. Like virtually all genocide and human rights scholars I know, I want to stop genocide and crimes against humanity. My aim is not to create a utopia but to avoid dystopias. Several dystopias were instigated by utopian dreams in the twentieth century.

My book is based on an approach to sociology that focuses on developing grounded theory, showing how such theory is illustrated in specific situations. My aim is to use sociology to clarify the concept of human rights and show how the human condition and the assumptions with which we begin produce human wrongs: slavery, terror, and genocide. It is not a chronology or a comprehensive survey of human wrongs. Last, I consider the contemporary practical implications to help avoid or stop crimes against humanity and to assist the victims of such situations.

I am grateful to all of my colleagues in different disciplines (see the following acknowledgments and references in different chapters) for how their research has helped me and for their moral support. This book is intended to help students, teachers, and citizens to understand the underlying causes (dilemmas, preconditions, and precipitants) of particular and chronic atrocities and consider alternative resolutions. This is very different from the current concentration and historical exegesis of particular situations that perplex us in 2007.

Many readers, I suspect, will be people who would like to change the world. Although this is not a "how to" book, I discuss in my last chapter the many nonviolent ways citizens in more powerful and affluent countries can aid others in less powerful and poorer countries, along with the question of military intervention. It is not the best of all possible worlds, but it is our world, and we are responsible for continuing to try to mend it. Rabbi Tarphon said in year 132 of the Common Era (*Pirke Avot, Sayings of the Fathers*): "It is not necessary for you to complete the work, but neither are you free to desist from it." I have tried to live by his injunction.

Acknowledgments

Many organizations and individuals have made this book possible. The American Sociological Association supported my research on violations of life integrity by two grants in 1992 and 1998 from the Fund for the Advancement of the Discipline. I am grateful to the International Security Program of the Belfer Center for Science and International Affairs of the Kennedy School of Government (Harvard University) for the seminars in which I participated as a member of BCSIA between 1997 and the present.

Organizations whose staff were helpful include the Dalit Freedom Network, Freedom House, the International Labor Organization, the National Security Archive, Scientific American, the United Nations Development Programme, and the United States Holocaust Memorial Museum Research Division. The generous contribution of Frank Chalk, illustrating war crimes, crimes against humanity, and genocide (in chapter 6) enhances these concepts for readers.

For statistical analyses, I am indebted to Anthony Savoie and Herbert Spirer. Savoie responded with ingenuity at all times. Spirer has also during two preceding decades enabled this research with his acute criticism and unflinching support for projects leading to this book. Research assistants employed in coding human rights reports include David Richards, Robert Hancke, Tom Scotto, and Jason Wittenberg. Paul Adamides, Jennifer Birk, and Steven Oakland facilitated this project by transforming (and enabling me to convert) my computer files for this research.

Readers of all or part of the manuscripts preceding this book and experts whose criticism and suggestions were invaluable include Joyce Apsel, Kevin Bales, Peter Black, Marjorie Crow, Kate Doyle, Craig Etcheson, Richard Fein, Marguerite Feitlowitz, John Gay, Jaime Malamud Goti, Ted Gurr, Barbara Harff, Robert Hayden, Rhoda Howard-Hassmann, Steven Jacobs, Mark Kramer, Milton Leitenberg, Rene Lemarchand, Kanan Makiya, Ellen Messer, Michael McClintock, Kate Raworth, Nancy Ricks, Romesh Silva, Robert Smith, Roger Smith, and Steven Shulman. Needless to say, the final decision (including parts with which they might not have agreed) was mine.

I am especially indebted to Deborah L. West who edited the manuscript over several years for her continuous patience and perspicacity. Dean Birkenkamp, Jennifer Knerr, and Melanie Stafford of Paradigm Publishers have provided me with a singular publishing experience. They have been generous and supportive throughout this process.

This book is dedicated to Joyce Apsel and Rhoda Howard-Hassmann, colleagues and friends, whose support in bleak times enabled me to conclude this project.

Helen Fein
Cambridge, Massachusetts

I
Distinguishing among
Human Rights and Wrongs

Of all the animals with which this globe is peopled, wrote David
Hume [1739–1740], "there is none towards whom nature seems, at
first sight, to have exercised more cruelty than towards man, in the
numberless wants and necessities with which she has loaded him,
and the slender means which she affords to the relieving of these
necessities." … [Thus] the idea began to develop that human beings also possess invisible things called "rights" that morally protect
them from the aggression of their fellow men, and especially from
the power of the governments under which they live.

—Kenneth Minogue,
"The History of the Idea of Human Rights," 1989

In the first decade of the twenty-first century, people concerned with
human rights still must wrestle with the fact that the denial of critical
human rights continues to be the norm in many countries. Denial
continues despite the wave of declarations and treaties after 1945
proclaiming universal human rights and criminalizing genocide,
torture, and apartheid, even after the breakdown of the communist
bloc in Eastern Europe and the end of apartheid in South Africa in
the 1990s.

I argue herein that such denial has been normal because it serves
distinct social functions not only for rulers but at times for many
citizens of societies in which gross violations of human rights—persistent human wrongs—are the rule. This book asks what explains

critical human wrongs, beginning with violations of life integrity (defined later in this chapter), and what might prevent or block their use.

The transformation since 1945 of the ideal of universal human rights—rights owed to all persons because of their humanity—from laws of particular states into international law is a major contribution whose promise remains unfulfilled. There are many different ways of justifying rights, but they begin in Western civilization with the idea of natural law expressed by John Locke (1690) and embodied in the Declaration of Independence of the American colonies (1776) and the Declaration of the Rights of Man and Citizen (1789) passed by the French National Assembly. Both asserted that men were created free and equal and assumed white men the subject—they became citizens.

The framers of these declarations upheld slavery and racial, property, and gender discrimination for two centuries. The consensus on the roots of rights did not extend to other persons and groups who might enjoy them. In the United States, the excluded African slaves had to get the backing of the federal government after the Civil War for emancipation and voting rights. The latter were later denied and not reliably secured until the passage of the Civil Rights Act of 1965. Both African-Americans and women in the United States (as did women elsewhere in the West) had to mobilize through social movements in the nineteenth and twentieth centuries in order to wrest such rights. Rather than focusing on how human rights can be justified, my aim is to show, through selected case studies, how and why they were denied from the middle of the twentieth century to the present and what effect that has had on people and nations. In this chapter, I sketch the basis of a social theory accounting for why and how groups sustain or deny basic rights. I start with a constructivist approach and focus on violations condemned in the modern era of rights consciousness and earlier. This era began after World War II with the extensive agreement among countries that was affirmed in the Universal Declaration of Human Rights (UDHR) passed by the UN General Assembly in 1948.

Human rights were constructed by people, principally in relation to the state, itself an organization evolving through history. As Jack Donnelly and Rhoda Howard argue, the rights that were wrested several centuries ago in the West and began "as a tactic of the bourgeoisie to protect its own class interests ... [have] long since broken free of these origins" and are indispensable now to protect peoples throughout the world (Donnelly 1989, 70). Their origin has no more bearing on their universality or usefulness today than the origin of polio or smallpox vaccine has on the benefits of such inoculations to people in other lands.

Constructing and Distinguishing among Human Rights

Human rights can be viewed as a way to resolve certain basic human dilemmas, stemming first from human vulnerability as observed by Hume in the eighteenth century. Humans need protection to grow from infancy, to survive hunger and drought, environmental assaults, and a scarcity of resources. Both cooperation and competition between and within groups for resources—as well as for status (honor), position (rank and class), and power—are pervasive in social life. Competition for such goods often triggers conflicts between groups and states.

Such conflicts have led to wars and justifications for despotism or unlimited authority. Although the state, an "association that claims the monopoly of the legitimate use of violence" (Weber 1946 [1919], 34), is supposed to protect its citizens from the violations of invaders, crime, and internal chaos, it is also a leading violator of rights. The practice of violence, intimidation, and terror by many states continues to be accepted by many people who apparently believe that the need for security justifies state violence; we ask why and how that happens herein.

In a classic statement of the justification for an absolute state, Hobbes accounted for (1651) the state as an institution to protect man from a state of nature that had produced anarchy or virtual war of all against all in which life was "nasty, solitary, poore, brutish, and short" (1961, 98–100). This account is often reconfirmed today in failed states and those torn by civil war. Regardless of whether we regard Hobbes's explanation as an allegory, a myth, or an ideology to justify seventeenth-century despotism, concentrated state power arouses another need: to protect people from the state and from authority. Lord Acton's dictum that "power tends to corrupt, and absolute power corrupts absolutely" still remains true (*Encyclopedia of World History* 2000, 3). Rights can be viewed as social constructs to check the state and fulfill human needs for protection, participation, expression, and subsistence. Rights protect human dignity, but dignity and honor—values in many traditions—do not necessarily imply rights or universal human rights (Donnelly 1989, chs. 3 and 4; Howard 1995, 4). Rights are claims (wrested, ceded, or promised), implying an acknowledgment, obligation, and duty by one party to another. The claim has been most often addressed to the state, which is today obligated by international law to protect all citizens but in earlier times had contracted to protect one group or class of citizens. Because rights were first developed and used against the state, and the state is usually the final guarantor of rights, I focus in comparison primarily on differences between states in respecting or violating rights.

How does one begin to distinguish among and rank priorities among rights? The UDHR had thirty articles, and since then rights of specific categories—women, children, the colonized—have been articulated and new rights have been proclaimed, such as the right to peace and the right to development (rights of states or collectivities rather than individuals).

Scholars and lawyers have divided rights in several ways. Some divide rights into generations of rights, viewing political and civil as first generation, social and economic as second generation, and collective rights such as development and peace as third generation. Some scholars see civil and political rights as being negative or cost-free rights, merely requiring the state to keep its hands off, whereas social and economic rights are positive rights, costly and dependent on the level of development. Others criticize this dichotomy as a false distinction (Cranston 1964, 40; Donnelly 1989, 31–34). We can conclude that the protection of civil and political rights is not primarily dependent on wealth or social investment but does demand political will. Economic and social rights, as they are conceived today, are more contingent on resources. But resources alone do not account for how well states do in fulfilling them. Chapter 8 presents evidence that poorer states that respect life integrity and political rights are more apt to develop and prosper with their citizens enjoying better health and longevity than are poorer states that are gross violators.

The difference between classes of rights is taken into account in international covenants protecting both classes of rights (further discussed in chapter 8). Many supposed debates over ranking rights argue over whether economic rights are really rights or are political goals or entitlements. These debates (which often barely conceal the advocate's motives of rationalizing regimes with dirty hands) have led some, such as Donnelly (1989, 34–37), to declare that rights are indivisible. Yet, we can only determine how different kinds of rights are related by making distinctions among them and observing indicators of states' practices—respect for or violations of rights.

My distinctions among rights did not come from any a priori theory but were devised after two decades spent studying human wrongs—especially genocide and massacres. I began in 1987 to analyze human rights reports of states across the globe with past incidents of genocide or present group conflict, focusing on a class of basic prepolitical rights I label life integrity rights (Fein 1988, 1995). Life integrity rights 1) are distinguished in this book from 2) civil and political rights and 3) subsistence rights, especially the right to food (among social and economic rights). This division, although the labels differ, corresponds to that of several other theorists (discussed in Donnelly 1989, 28–41). There is general agreement on the right to life and personal security, to liberty, and to subsistence.

Both life integrity rights and liberty preface the age of democracy. There is historical evidence that both life integrity rights and subsistence rights have been respected in some traditional and nondemocratic societies. The right to food was enforced in Europe in early modern times through bread riots (Rudé 1964). Indeed, the division between political and economic rights is recent. The leading question, often not noted, is which and whose economic rights. The right to property was one of the first rights in eighteenth-century natural rights that was justified by Locke and specified in the French Declaration of the Rights of Man and Citizen (1789) and the U.S. Constitution (1789). The right to life, liberty, and property, taken as a given in the eighteenth century, recast in the U.S. Declaration of Independence as "life, liberty and the pursuit of happiness," was amended in the twentieth century as the right to life, liberty, and subsistence (or the right to food). The modern emphasis on the latter can be viewed as a complement to property rights, a response to the fact that many people (often the majority in developed societies) work in organizations, factories, and farms that they do not own or personally control.

Many authors also agree on what constitutes human wrongs; these consistently include two classes of violations of life integrity (spelled out in table 1.1): (1) killings, torture, and arbitrary arrest and punishment and (2) slavery and apartheid.

Table 1.1 Life Integrity Rights and Their Violations

Rights	Violations	International Law and Date in Force
1. The right to life	Genocide, mass killing, summary/extrajudicial executions, and "disappearances"	UN Genocide Convention, 1951 *UDHR art. 3 **ICCPR
2. The right to personal inviolability/not to be hurt	Torture, rape, and sexual abuse; inhuman and degrading treatment and punishment	UN Convention Against Torture 1987 *UDHR art. 3 **ICCPR art. 9
3. The right to be free of fear of arbitrary seizure, detention, and punishment	No due process or any process, arbitrary detention, lack of fair trial	*UDHR art. 3 **ICCPR art. 9
4. Freedom to own one's body and labor	Slavery, forced labor, debt slavery, and equivalent institutions	Slavery Convention 1927 Supplementary Convention 1957; Convention Concerning Abolition of Forced Labor 1959
5. The right to free movement without discrimination	Group macrosegregation (apartheid), microsegregation, group detention, and forced resettlement	Convention on the Punishment of Apartheid 1976; Int. Convention on the Elimination of All Forms of Racial Discrimination 1969, **ICCPR art. 9, 13
6. The right to procreate and cohabit with family	No marriage or family formation by state policy; kidnapping and adoption or involuntary transfer of children	*UDHR art. 3 **ICCPR art. 9

Notes:

*UDHR—Universal Declaration of Human Rights (1948)

**ICCPR—International Covenant on Civil and Political Rights (1976)

Life Integrity Rights and Their Violation

My focus is on life integrity rights, because they protect the most basic values that transcend cultures and enable people to enjoy other rights. In order to rank these, I used a method derived from the work of John Rawls.[1] The violation of life integrity rights has been criminalized in international law over the past seventy years (see table 1.1). Looking backward through Western history, it is notable that life integrity rights were wrested before political rights and economic rights claimed in modern times.

I start with the physical right to be—to exist—followed by the right to be physically and mentally secure—not to be hurt or violated, to be free from arbitrary fear—and to own one's body and labor, to move freely, and to procreate and live with family (see table 1.1). Life integrity rights imply an integrated set of claims defending the biological and social integration of body and mind among all humans (denied by genocide, murder, and torture); of self-ownership, mobility, and social dignity (denied by slavery, segregation, and apartheid); of self and family (denied by prohibiting marriage and family development as under slavery and certain forms of totalitarianism); and of the reciprocal guarantees for protection of human groups (denied by genocide).

The right to life is the most fundamental among human rights. Although not absolute, the right to life is basic in both domestic and international law—indeed, "all other human rights become meaningless if the basic right to life is not duly protected" (Van Aggelen 1986, 742). In many civilizations human sacrifice and infanticide were approved social practices, practices that have been suppressed at different times and places over the last 2,600 years. The socially enforced suicide of widows (suttee) was common in India until the nineteenth century, and incidents of suttee still occur in that country. Recognition of the right to life as a universal human right is a recent achievement (in the last millennium) in human history.

Rights can be violated by states, societies, and organized nonstate and antistate actors. It became starkly evident in the United States (and around the world) on September 11, 2001, that transnational terrorist networks also threatened the right to life, committing crimes against humanity and genocidal massacres—a fact citizens of many conflict-torn countries who have experienced both antistate terror and state terror had known for some time.

Contemporary issues over the right to life revolve around universal human conditions and quandaries. Where does life begin and end? Whose life and rights should be protected? What are the limits to punishment?

Controversies continue in many countries over practices curtailing life of the born and the unborn that are not prohibited in international law: capital punishment (with due process and judicial safeguards), abortion, and euthanasia or assisted suicide. Many states view legislation on these issues as the exercise of democratic state sovereignty—there have been referenda within some states on several of these issues. Some citizens of different countries view their claims as advancing rights; for example, proponents of assisted suicide claim the "right to die." Similarly, proponents of unrestricted abortion claim "the right of free choice," the "right of privacy," or control over their bodies. But opponents of abortion advocate "the right to life" for all the unborn. Many people have more differentiated positions, depending on the motives for abortion and risks to mother and child. Herein, I exclude consideration of these issues on which there is no international legal consensus and much division among and within states over whether such practices are rights or wrongs.

In this book, I primarily review state violations and focus on the right to life as defined in international law. I start with the physical right to be—to exist—followed by the right to be physically and mentally secure— not to be hurt or violated, to be free from arbitrary fear—and to own one's body and labor, to move freely, and to procreate and live with family (see table 1.1).

Whose Rights? Evolving Conceptions and Controversies

Most of the violations discussed herein occur in the public domain. However, the primacy of the public domain as the arena of rights is increasingly attacked, as is the assumption that the notion of universal human rights is neutral, applying to all. Feminist critics often object to the division of the public and private domains, asserting that the traditional conception of rights benefits men, who are more likely than women to participate in the public domain, whereas women are more likely to be violated in the private domain or household (Bunch 1990; Thomas and Beasley 1993).

Domestic violence and gender equality (the issues of prime concern) have only been explicitly addressed in international law since 1979 with the adoption of the Convention on the Elimination of All Forms of Discrimination Against Women (CEDAW). Despite widespread reservations to CEDAW by states, recognition of women's rights as human rights expanded greatly in the 1990s and led to focus on them by international human rights nongovernmental organizations (NGOs) and international organizations. Resistance to implementing change in the name of cultural and religious values continues.

In international law, rape and sexual abuse by state agents (a widespread phenomenon) are stipulated as a form of torture and could constitute an international crime, including genocide (see chs. 4–6).

The International Criminal Court (established in December 1999) includes rape, enforced prostitution, forced pregnancy, and sexual slavery as crimes against humanity and war crimes if committed during armed conflict (Dauer 2001, 69).

The widespread incidence of violence against women—although its prevalence differs markedly (Dauer 2001, 73–74; Weldon 2002, app. A)—and our accumulating understanding of recent approaches to stop it (Penn 2003; Weldon 2002) indicate a reliance on international law, and the state alone is inadequate.

Such violence is often difficult to observe and is best tracked in attempts to stop it. In order to stop it, local social movements need to press for the redefinition of crimes against women such as "honor killings"—the murder of women because of their alleged violation of familial expectations of virginity—as both murder (under national law) and violations of international law.

Often in the last two decades both violence against women and women's inequality have been denied or justified by male leaders and religious authorities in Asia and Africa as expressions of cultural tradition or religion—in the name of Islam especially. But some outspoken women in the Islamic world—at times fleeing from their countries because of death threats—have denounced the latter as misinterpretations of Islam used to justify patriarchal dominance.

Women and men have been subject to all types of violations of life integrity in the twentieth century: genocide, torture (including state-inflicted or organized rape), arbitrary seizure and detention, slavery, segregation, and forced resettlement and state-imposed restrictions on family. Yet women and children are more likely than men to be subject to slavery, forced labor, rape, sexual abuse, and forced prostitution.

Some customs involving alteration and injury to the body without consent that are culturally sanctioned can also be framed as rights violations: for example, female genital mutilation (FGM) or female circumcision, widely practiced in Africa (Slack 1988). FGM is now illegal in nine of twenty-eight African states in which it is practiced. The Center for Reproductive Law and Policy estimates that 130 million girls and women have experienced FGM and "every year an additional 2 million face the procedure" (Chill and Kilbourne 2001, 159). It is viewed by physicians, health workers, and others as a cruel and hurtful bodily violation, an irreparable act undermining health, reproduction, and sexual feeling. Many international organizations—including the World Health Organization, the Vienna Declaration of the World Conference on Human Rights, the International Federation of Gynecology and Obstetrics, and Amnesty International—have condemned FGM as a violation of human rights or threat to health. "A UN-backed conference of ministers from nearly 50 Islamic countries and representatives of more than 20 international, Arab and Islamic organizations has called for an end to harmful traditional practices including child marriage, female genital mutilation, and gender discrimination in education" on November 17, 2005 (FGM Education and Networking Project, www.fgmnetwork.org, 2/22/2006). However, FGM is not cited in international law as a rights violation.

Defenders of tolerance of FGM observe that many parents (including mothers) who let this be done to their daughters view FGM as an expression of their rights and culture—an essential practice to safeguard their daughters' virginity and ability to attract husbands. FGM has spread to Europe with the influx of Muslim migrants and is generally deemed illegal there.

What is at issue here is not only labeling but who has the right to interpret what is a rights violation and what is the best strategy to end this practice. Some strategies and suggestions to end FGM include organizing social movements and education to promote social change, promoting new conventions pledging families not to practice FGM or to marry girls who have undergone it, criminalizing the practice locally, or labeling it a violation of international human rights. Thus, both interpretations and definitions of rights and strategies and tactics to rectify wrongs will continue to be debated.

Fundamental Questions and Assumptions Underlying Societies

For most of human history, life integrity rights have been violated—by governments, custom and cultures, and religious establishments—and reinforced by belief, cruelty, and the habit of obedience among ordinary people. If the denial of life integrity is viewed as being "normal" throughout history, one might ask: What characteristics, structures, and assumptions of societies determine whether life integrity is apt to be respected? I propose that these questions can be resolved by asking: 1) Who belongs? 2) Who rules? 3) How is labor recruited and work (and its products) rewarded and exchanged? How these questions are resolved will determine what rights are observed and what wrongs are tolerated.

If we were wandering anthropologists approaching a new tribe, group, or community, the first question we might ask is: "Who belongs?

Who is to be counted and protected?" This is the question of inclusion and solidarity. All societies define who is included within the universe of obligation, the range of people who must be taken into account, be protected and avenged when wronged, and by whom we can be held responsible (Fein 1977, ch. 1).

The victims of institutionalized violations of life integrity in the past were usually excluded from the universe of obligation of the powerful—strangers enslaved, women who were devalued or devoid of male protection, minorities, dissidents, social inferiors. The common conscience in societies based on class, racial, or religio-ethnic stratification—as were most empires and premodern societies—is constricted to one's own kind, excluding the Other from the universe of obligation—although less privileged Others must take the privileged into account for their own protection against violence by members of the privileged class toward them (Fein 1977, ch. 1).

In the modern state, the nominal answer to "who belongs?" is the citizen: All citizens are members. But there are different rules in different states as to who can become a citizen and how nonmembers join. Noncitizens are excluded from political rights and many legal guarantees. Although international law protects refugees—persons with fear of persecution—it cannot compel countries to accept and protect asylum seekers. International protection of refugees has become more problematic in the twenty-first century, as richer nations erect legal barriers against people fleeing poorer states without papers, many of whom are propelled for economic reasons.

Within the nation-state, inclusion is more than a matter of nominal citizenship, because states are characterized by different degrees and kinds of solidarity. Looking at this metaphorically, solidarity could be called the social "glue" that attaches members to society on the level above family and kin but below the state; it is widely observed under different names—"we-feeling," bonding, cohesion, and most recently, civil society and "social capital" (Eckstein 1966; Putnam 1993). The strength of such ties and the inclusiveness of bonds are generally regarded as positive. But there have also been societies based on exclusive solidarity—race, religion, class homogeneity—that have produced great suffering and death. Chapters 2 through 6 examine how exclusion is related to different forms of violation of life integrity. Exclusive solidarity can lead to ethnic discrimination, to rebellion and campaigns by minority groups for separation (uniting with another state or splitting), and to state leaders fomenting "ethnic cleansing" and genocide.

The second question concerns power, obedience, and legitimacy. Who decides who rules, and what are the rules and terms of obedience? How are rulers chosen, or how do they obtain power? How is power limited if it is constrained at all? What means do rulers have to induce and compel obedience? Beliefs (appeals to legitimacy and other norms), incentives (material rewards), and violence are the most common means of inducing compliance. Legitimacy is the belief that authority is justified. How is power justified and defended? Weber distinguished three different forms of legitimation. Power might be justified by charisma (divine grace), tradition (such as the belief in the "divine right" of kings), or rational legal authority, relying on constitutions and common law, as in modern democracy (Weber [1919] 1946, 78–79).

Different philosophical justifications of authority have been used to defend different forms of authority. Hobbes replaced belief in divine authority with a secular rationale based on human nature, which served to justify absolutism (1961 [1651]). Rousseau created the idea of social contract and the "general will," which justified the absolute power of the sovereign acting in the name of the general will, a sovereign power unchecked by freedoms and civil liberties such as the right of association (1989 [1762]; 1961 [1767]). Civil liberties and political rights later came to be viewed as essential components of democracy, the former protecting everyone (minorities and majorities), and the latter ensuring some form of free and regular choice—both imposing accountability and checks on rulers (Schmitter and Karl 1993, 39–45).There are many questions about how well democracy, often viewed as the best—or least bad—form of government, protects human rights. There are good reasons to expect that democracy should lead to belief in legitimacy and respect for life integrity as well as some doubts about the consequences of majoritarian rule and transitions to democracy, which are discussed in chapter 7. Democracy demands not only formal incorporation of all individuals as citizens, regardless of race and gender, but also inclusion of all citizens in the same universe of obligation. Ethnic discrimination and conflict are often signs that this has not been achieved. Even in societies in which all people are nominally included, there is, in many instances, a culture of contempt surrounding the Other who is socially excluded and more likely to be violated. The Others are varied: minorities, immigrants, strangers, untouchables in India, people of African descent in Europe and parts of the Americas, and indigenous peoples in all continents.

The third question all societies must resolve is how work and its rewards are allocated. Can human beings and their labor be forcibly extracted or owned and sold to others? Who controls resources (land, capital, labor), and what conditions determine who is in control? This is the question of exchange leading to some degree of equity or of exploitation. The question of exchange itself depends on inclusion, power, and politics.

Coercion, such as slavery—repressive or forced labor—and free exchange are two ways to recruit labor. Slavery and forced labor involve exploitation of the excluded and oppressed and usually are related to undemocratic forms of government or "herrenvolk democracy" (Van den Berghe 1967, 69). Slavery historically was not only a way to incorporate strangers but to exploit them to do what was considered dirty work—often backbreaking labor on plantations and latifundia—which wealthy owners disdained. Such owners and slaveholders often developed ideologies explaining why the slave class was uniquely deserving of and fit for such work. This forced exchange—of protection (negated by physical abuse and beatings) and food and shelter for lifelong work—is one to which strangers, especially conquered peoples, were most likely to be subjected, although in some societies debt might lead the poor to temporary or permanent slavery (Patterson 1982, 124–126).

The concept of free labor, considered by John Locke (1690) to be the basis of property rights and liberty, has often been criticized (Donnelly 1989, 93–100). Karl Marx made a trenchant attack on the notion of free labor under capitalism in the nineteenth century, believing all wage labor to be exploited, and derogated the idea of rights and parliamentary democracy as but an example of the superstructure of economic domination. However, Marx also accepted the need of the workers to organize to bring down capitalism, which he anticipated would reduce the working class to poverty so that they had no other options. Contrary to Marx's expectations, the campaign of workers for rights to organize and bargain collectively was ultimately successful in Europe and North America and led to the growth of trade unions, whose economic and political power led to greater equity in exchange, and the protection of workers through legislation regulating hours, conditions, safety, and wages. Political rights and civil liberties were essential to this achievement, enabling workers to assemble, organize, publish, and vote.

By contrast, capitalist and precapitalist forms of repressive labor (such as serfdom) have been shown not only to rely on violence but also to undermine the future conditions for democracy (Moore 1966). Noncapitalistic forms of repressive labor, such as the command economies of state socialism based on a Marxist-Leninist model, have produced neither equity in exchange nor equality of participation, as all terms of job tenure and salaries are fixed by the state, a state dominated by a "new class" based on political power—the new ruling class (Djilas 1957). The totalitarian state that this model produced, guided by a temporary "dictatorship of the proletariat" that lasted seventy years in the former USSR, negated any free organization.

Many modern economists and contemporary commentators view free labor as essential to a free market, which they view not only as being more efficient than command economies but to lead to or be required for a free (i.e., democratic) society. But a free market might not be free if the division of labor is based on arbitrary differences of race or caste or if free association is not permitted (so labor cannot represent itself collectively), producing conditions of exploitation that undermine wages (Dahrendorf 1959, 186–187; Durkheim [1893] 1933, 377; Gouldner 1960, 161–177). Therefore, both equality and the right to organize unions freely (and civil liberties permitting expression, assembly, and communication) should be positively related to equity in exchange and greater subsistence rights.

Chapters 2 and 3 consider past and contemporary severe exploitation—slavery and bonded labor—which annuls freedom and violates life integrity. It is more difficult to agree on how to define and measure less severe forms of exploitation and establish criteria for what is equity and what is exploitation.

However, one basic by-product of equity in exchange is the ability to survive—subsistence rights. "If one cannot obtain one's subsistence, one will die and thus be unable to enjoy any rights at all" (Donnelly 1989, 38). Since life depends on subsistence, one way to "test" this question (discussed in chapter 8) is to ask, "What kinds of states and state behaviors best maximize the chances of people to survive?"

Survival also depends on mutual caring. I suspect that many readers will ask: What is it about human nature that enables humans to inflict and ignore suffering?

Habits of the Mind and Heart

Commentators on the twentieth century have often remarked on the institutionalization of terror and genocide—doing evil became a job description. Recruitment of killers and torturers was not a problem.

History and experimental findings (Haney, Banks, and Zimbardo 1973; Waller 2002) show that ordinary men placed as prison and camp guards adapt to their role readily and brutalize inmates. Similarly, there are many examples of soldiers of different nations ignoring the rules of war and maltreating captives. Hatred of the victims can instigate mass violence but is not necessarily related to participation in state brutality. Further, people can learn to hate and be cruel simply by mistreating victims (Staub 1989, 80–85).

Social psychology, reinforced by experimental findings, suggests there are several cognitive habits that enable humans to injure and kill without guilt. There is a widespread readiness to inflict pain when ordered—"obedience to authority" (Milgram 1974). States can employ this readiness to provide "sanctions for evil" and produce "crimes of obedience" (Kelman and Hamilton 1989; Sanford et al. 1971). Waller points out that "Milgram's research demonstrates that it is *not* [italics in original] necessary to have a dehumanized victim in order to demonstrate destructive obedience to authority" (2002, 249). But it appears to make it easier for the perpetrators, because "blaming the victim" justifies the types of crimes that occur during genocides, pogroms, and lynchings (Waller 2002, 249–256).

But, I posit that there are necessary assumptions and conditions for authorities to blame the victims and for people to consider the orders of authority and the authority legitimate. Resistance as well as complicity and cooperation with authority is normal in certain contexts, even in the Holocaust (Fein 1979, ch. 6).

The role of the bystander is often critical. Several habits of mind enable humans to see people harmed and to harm people without becoming disturbed. Stereotyping "the Other" allows people to maintain social and moral distance from groups that might be injured (Fiske 1998; Staub 1978). Similarly, people who are injured are often devalued by others (observers and bystanders) in order to maintain the others' belief in a "just world" in which the innocent cannot be arbitrarily injured. For example, many observers say that "there must be something wrong with them [the victims]" (Lerner 1980). People who are not used to being cruel often devalue people whom they injure in order to avoid conflict between images of themselves and what they are doing. This is called "cognitive dissonance" (Festinger 1957).

Sociobiology and evolutionary psychology look at the toll of human slaughter and view it in a longer perspective, seeing it as a product of a universal human capacity or prehistorical habit, what Waller calls "our ancestral shadow," which leads to ethnocentrism, xenophobia, and a desire for social dominance, triggering aggression and violence (2002, 136–168). This leads to a mental "set of universal reasoning circuits [which] were designed by natural selection to solve the adaptive problems of intergroup relations faced by our hunter-gather[er] ancestors" (Waller 2002, 153). Such theorists posit that humans favor kin (because of common genes) and generalize this preference to identify with their kind—a nation, religion, race, or ethnic group. Given certain contexts, beliefs, and cultures, these predispositions enable humans to kill and hurt other kinds of people without any guilt in order to advance or protect their own kind (Nielson 1994; Waller 2002, 134; Van den Berghe 1981; Wilson 1978, 157).

But neither social psychology nor ethnology necessarily leads to hopelessness, the belief that these are intractable practices. Ethnological researchers have shown both the potential for aggression and the many ways humans and animals inhibit aggression and cooperate (Boyden 1987; Van der Dennen and Falger 1990). Such theories show that both altruism and aggression are natural responses, evoked under different circumstances. What we need to know (not considered by sociobiology) is why and how identification with others as kin or groups is constructed, reinforced, and transformed and how responses to outgroups change.

Nations that have been fierce and aggressive in one age can become pacific in another, for example the Vikings and the Danes. In the span of fifty years in the late twentieth century, nations that fought three wars in less than one hundred years—Germany and France—became allies in the European Union (EU) and the North Atlantic Treaty Organization (NATO). Understanding how we come to view others—outside and within the state—as enemies does not mean that the scorn, enmity, and hatred of today are eternal or intractable, but could imply hopefulness as well as caution. Human behavior cannot be explained just by generalizing from animal behavior or human prehistory; culture and institutions created by human design (e.g., the EU, NATO, the United Nations, and the new International Criminal Court) channel behavior.

Plan of This Book

Accounting for Human Wrongs—Slavery, Terror, and Genocide

Chapters 2 through 6 inquire when and why states institute and tolerate gross violations of life integrity—slavery and terror (torture, extrajudicial executions, and "disappearances" that instill terror)—and practice genocide (see definitions from international law in these chapters). Examples are based on twentieth- and twenty-first-century cases; it seems likely that such cases will continue to provide models for future use. These chapters will ask: What assumptions underlie the use of these violations, and what contexts, structures, and conditions propel perpetrators and societies to select and tolerate them?

In fact, the practices we seek to explain—slavery, terror, and genocide—are not "natural"; unlike war and combat, they have no analogy to practices of other species. Such uses of force can be viewed as rational choices of strategies to control people and organizations, chosen from the three possible modes of control: coercion (violence), persuasion (appeals to norms), and economic incentives (appeals to self-interest). Coercion has been used historically for political control, family control (now viewed as spousal and child abuse), and economic control. Neither ethnology, sociobiology, nor social psychology explains why the use of these practices varies so over time and among governments and why they are stopped, reappear, and spread. Given the evidence that these practices are purposeful institutions and approved crimes, routinized and accepted in particular times and places, I concentrate on explaining their origin and selection in terms of recurring social assumptions, habits, and problems as well as the particular circumstances that lead to their use.

The most apparent function of slavery is the exploitation of labor. It is an ancient institution transformed in the twentieth century by totalitarian states and global trends in trade. Torture, a common practice of terror regimes, serves as a means not only of interrogation (to get the information wanted) but also of humiliation, intimidation, and social control of the bystanders. Bystanders can observe the killing or disappearance of the tortured, some of whom are killed and their mutilated bodies displayed publicly, but others are returned to society. Both governments and antistate actors expanded the means of terror in the twentieth century to include not just killing, but also causing people to disappear, maiming, and severing body parts. Governments were more likely to incarcerate victims in concentration, labor, and extermination camps and to practice medical incarceration and psychopharmacological manipulation in mental hospitals. Nevertheless, peoples and groups often survive states of terror.

By contrast, genocide eliminates and decimates social groups and reconstructs the society, also driving out potential victims and subduing groups in rebellion. Ideological genocides, which reconstruct a society by eliminating a group (or groups) not included in the lead-ers' vision of the real or ideal people—Armenians in the Ottoman Empire (1915–1919), Jews and Gypsies in Nazi Germany (1941–1945), and several groups in Cambodia (1975–1979)—are not common. Late twentieth-century genocide was less often instigated by ideology than by state responses to group rebellion, usually itself a reaction to domination. Genocide has become almost the norm in some regions, and its use has spread to all continents. Chapter 6 discusses the use and causes of genocide.

For each type of violation, I ask:

1. Who are the victims, and how are they selected?
2. How do the victimizers differ from the victims?
3. What are the victimizers' purposes?
4. How did this practice evolve: What models, influences, and traditions lay behind it?
5. How is the practice acknowledged and legitimated? Do victims and bystanders concur in these processes?
6. What are the conditions or contingencies that triggered this?
7. What is the role of the bystander within the country and of other countries and organizations? Who might be bystanders or accomplices?

It is apparent that slavery, terror, and genocide are not isolated violations, and the same state might be mentioned in several chapters. States that employ genocide often employ torture and terror (see chs. 4–5), and both the Soviet Union and Nazi Germany have employed terror, slavery, genocide, and "ethnic cleansing." The institutions of control of totalitarian and authoritarian states—secret police, secu-rity services, concentration camps, prisons, training schools—can be adapted for different purposes.

Why do states choose one form of violation and not another? The answers might include threats, ideologies, exigencies, and op-portunities. Much research on torture, for example, shows torture has several preconditions, beginning with "a national emergency" or threat to state security. But such a threat can also be a rationalization of terror, as in Argentina (ch. 4), where terror continued after the threat was quashed. Frank Chalk (personal communication) theo-rizes that torture is a means of control over victims in groups that states want to keep or need within their society, and genocide is a

**Table 1.2 Assumed Preconditions and Issues
Underlying Types of Life Integrity Violation**

Preconditions and Issues	Slavery	Terror/Torture	Genocide
1. Solidarity/exclusion of victim from universe of obligation	YES	YES	YES
2. Victims constitute a group	YES	at times	YES
3. There is a conflict over legitimacy with victims' group	NO	yes	at times
4. There is a real threat from victims' group	NO	yes	at times
5. There is a perceived or symbolic threat from victims' group	NO	yes	at times
6. The violation serves to regulate terms of exchange coercively	YES	at times	no
7. The population from which the victims are drawn is expected to remain an enduring part of society	yes	YES	no

Note:
Responses in capitals indicate more certain expectations than responses in small letters. "At times" means that this is a questionable variable: it is not necessarily the case.

means of elimination of groups they want to exclude. This is consistent with research on Nazi Germany, which shows torture and terror were restricted to known and active enemies of the regime, seldom used against most Germans, and genocide was restricted to Jews and Gypsies, outside the state's universe of political and moral obligation after 1933 (Johnson 1999).

Given this hypothesis, research on these violations (discussed in chs. 2–6), and the theory that has been advanced, in table 1.2, I list expectations about each practice.

To clarify table 1.2, I shall reiterate the assumptions. Line 1: For all these practices—slavery, terror, and genocide—the victims must be excluded from the victimizers' universe of obligation: They do not have to be protected and can be enslaved, injured, violated, or killed with impunity and without guilt. All such victims suffer "social death" (Patterson 1982) and degradation; the victims of genocide are also targeted for physical death.

Such exclusion, however, is most problematic in the case of terror and torture, where victims might be drawn from the same groups as the torturer. In this case, the attempt to exclude the tortured from the societal universe of obligation can backfire, isolating the torturers. The victims might be defended by their kin and valorized as martyrs.

Line 2: Where victims constitute a group distinguished from the victimizer—a collectivity or class distinguished by race, religion, ethnicity, language, or social role—it is easy to view them as a collective Other. When they come from the same groups and classes as the perpetrator—often the case in regard to the tortured—they might be distinguished by social labeling as deviant, demonic, and dangerous: for example, an "enemy of the people," an "enemy of Christianity and Western civilization."

In the latter case, victims are generally selected as individuals who are suspected of doing or knowing something, although they are more likely to be drawn from certain groups than others.

Lines 3, 4, and 5: Slavery was most often imposed on conquered peoples—people who did not constitute a threat or no longer were a threat. But in the twentieth century, citizens in totalitarian states could also be enslaved by labeling them as criminals or enemies of the people, although they did not challenge the state. The victims of more conventional forms of enslavement are also pariah groups (such as untouchables outside the Indian caste and power structure) or strangers separated from their state, society, and kin: They are unable to defend themselves, threaten the victimizers, or challenge the legitimacy of the state.

By contrast, the tortured and (in some cases) certain victims of genocide do belong to or are viewed as part of groups threatening society, the state, or domination of the state by the ruling elite. They might overtly challenge the legitimacy of the state itself or have done so in the past. They might threaten the power of the elite that controls the state or of an emerging elite that seeks to take it over. However, terror can also be waged against persons who are not politically organized and do not threaten the state but are seen as deviant or undesirables—criminals, street people, homosexuals.

In some cases of genocide, the threat is purely contrived and symbolic, a product of ideology, such as in the Aryan ideology defining Jews as a nonhuman, demonic, and dangerous species, which was used to justify Nazi Germany's drive to annihilate the Jews.

Line 6: Slavery eliminates exchange, substituting total coercion. Slaves do not own themselves, their kin, or property. Slaves have no formal bargaining power, although there might be informal means by which they can shape their masters' sense of obligation (Genovese 1974). In some societies, individual slaves have risen to high social positions, but this does not mean they enjoy use of rights, rather that the masters have the latitude to treat them well or badly and to exploit their talents.

Planners of genocide who seek total annihilation are unconcerned with exploitation in any rational economic sense. The way in which genocide "trumps" exploitation was shown in how Jewish slaves were worked to death during the Holocaust in slave-labor camps (Ferencz 1979; Rubenstein 1975). Slave owners, by contrast, have an economic interest in preserving their slaves as capital.

Terror can alter exchange relationships indirectly if the kidnapped, tortured, or disappeared are leaders or organizers of a group that claims the right to organize to represent itself in exchange, such as peasants' organizations and workers' unions. In such cases, these disadvantaged classes use civil liberties and political rights in order to claim economic rights and improve their conditions of exchange. When leaders are tortured, followers are apt to be terrorized, and the organization might wither as people withdraw into isolated and fearful solitary existences.

Line 7: In both the cases of slavery and torture, the group or larger community from which the victims are drawn usually remains part of society, although individuals, kin, and social networks in which they are embedded might disappear or be disrupted. In the case of genocide, all or part of a group is eliminated. Both genocide in part and "politicide"—mass killing of groups who have demonstrated political opposition—can serve to terrorize the remaining members of the group (Harff and Gurr 1988).

Contemporary Questions: Wresting Rights and Arresting Wrongs

Chapters 2 through 6 focus on explaining wrongs committed against humans in the twentieth and early twenty-first centuries. Chapters 7 and 8 focus on the practice of rights and wrongs contemporaneously. Chapter 7 considers the relation between respect for human rights and freedom during and after the Cold War. Historical paths to democracy and the role of great powers in opening up and foreclosing options are also discussed. Chapter 8 considers the impact of freedom and respect for life integrity on subsistence rights in two regions (in Africa and the Americas), comparing rights respecters and gross violators, showing positive effects or a "virtuous cycle."

Last, in chapter 9, I examine how the findings herein agree with, modify, or expand the theory originally sketched and suggest an action agenda to consider how people can prevent and arrest gross violations of life integrity. My discussion considers results in cases discussed in this book and the opportunities as well as difficulties relating to new problems of the twenty-first century.

Note

1. My ordering of priorities is an example of John Rawls's (1971) "lexical method" of ranking, adapted by Rubin and Newburg (1980): "A lexical ordering is an ordering like that of words in a dictionary. The words are initially ordered by their first letter. Then they are ordered by their second letter within each group sharing the same first letter" (281–282). I started with the most valued priority (in this case life) in first place, followed by the value in the next place (not to be hurt), and so forth.

2
Twentieth-Century Slavery within the State

> Slavery is the permanent, violent domination of natally alienated and generally dishonored persons.... We may summarize the two modes of representing the social death that was slavery by saying that in the intrusive mode the slave was conceived of as someone who did not belong because he was an outsider, while in the extrusive mode the slave became an outsider because he did not or no longer belonged.
>
> —Orlando Patterson, *Slavery and Social Death*, 1982

It is widely believed that slavery ended in the nineteenth century with the cessation of the transatlantic slave trade from Africa to North America, but it continues in other guises. This chapter focuses on slavery within the state and the next chapter looks at global slavery and trafficking for the sex trade among countries. One must ask: What constitutes slavery fundamentally? Box 2.1 cites legal definitions of both slavery and trafficking.

The reader might note the broadening of the practices cited from 1956 to 2000 beyond the fact of ownership and the stress on motives of slaveholders and traffickers. Chattel slavery—holding slaves as movable property that can be bought or sold—is one of many forms of slavery, which include penal enslavement, state slave labor, and debt bondage. Slavery has an ancient history, as do other exploitative forms of labor.

The addition in the 1956 Supplementary Convention of "the sale or involuntary transfer of women for marriage 'without the right to

---

Box 2.1 Definitions of Slavery and Trafficking

The Slavery Convention of 1926 codified the object of European conferences and conventions of 1885, 1888–1890, and 1919: "Slavery is the status or condition of a person over whom any or all the powers attaching to the right of ownership are exercised."

The 1956 Supplementary Convention on the Abolition of Slavery, the Slave Trade, and Institutions and Practices Similar to Slavery elaborated protection to include a "person of servile status," which includes the following: a) debt bondage; b) serfdom; c) the sale or involuntary transfer of women for marriage "without the right to refuse" or inheritance of a woman on the death of her husband; and d) "any institution or practice whereby a child or young person under the age of 18, is delivered by either or both of his natural parents or by his guardian to another person, whether for reward or not, with a view to the exploitation of the child or young person or of his labour."

The 1957 Abolition of Forced Labour Convention of 1957 committed the members of the International Labour Organization not to use forced or compulsory labor: "a) As a means of political coercion or education or as a punishment for holding or expressing political views ideologically opposed to the established political, social or economic system; (b) As a method of mobilising and using labour for purposes of economic development; (c) As a means of labour discipline; (d) As a punishment for having participated in strikes; (e) As a means of racial, social, national or religious discrimination."

The 2000 Protocol to Prevent, Suppress and Punish Trafficking in Persons, Especially Women and Children, Supplementing the United Nations Convention Against Transnational Organized Crime Article 3 offers the following definition: "'Trafficking in persons' shall mean the recruitment, transportation, transfer, harboring or receipt of persons, by means of the threat or use of force or other forms of coercion, of abduction, of fraud, of deception, of the abuse of power or of a position of vulnerability or of the giving or receiving of payments or benefits to achieve the consent of a person having control over another person, for the purpose of exploitation. Exploitation shall include, at a minimum, the exploitation of the prostitution of others or of other forms of sexual exploitation, forced labour or services, slavery or practices similar to slavery, servitude or the removal of organs."

---

refuse'" is consistent with the implication of autonomy in the sixth right in our list of life integrity rights (see table 1.1, ch. 1), "the right to procreate and cohabit with family." The 1956 Convention focuses on slave traders, owners, and family members as violators. Violations by the latter include involuntary transfer of women in marriage for money, involuntary transfer of a wife to another person, and inheritance of the widow. Unfortunately, we do not have contemporary cross-cultural data that distinguish arranged marriage systems in which women have the right to refuse from systems in which they do not. It is also plausible to suppose that there might be voluntary agreement and involuntary exchange of women within the same system.

Gerda Lerner (1986) theorized that the successful enslavement of women in the ancient world marked the beginning of slavery. Both in the Hebrew Bible and epics and plays from the Greek world, we read of men being slaughtered and women enslaved (Fein 1999, 45–49). Patterson observed:

> that this sexual bias in favor of women [becoming slaves] holds true for the great majority of peoples ... before the Atlantic slave trade we rarely find more males being captured than females, and the practice of massacring male captives remained prevalent even where they were also enslaved.... It is obvious that women and children were easier to take than men; they were also easier to keep and to absorb into the community. (1982, 120–121)

Throughout history, individuals and groups usually became enslaved through capture in warfare, kidnapping, tribute and tax payment, debt, punishment for crimes, the abandonment and sale of children, or selling themselves—primarily to escape poverty (Patterson 1982, 105). Patterson, studying an anthropological survey of world societies from 1750 BCE to 1945 CE, concluded that slaves are usually persons separated from their kin; they are owed no protection and have no one with authority to protect them (Patterson 1982, 38–45). We shall consider how this applies to twentieth- and twenty-first-century slavery. At the beginning of the modern age, slavery was widespread, and the enslaved groups were usually drawn from other continents and other races and religions. Many slaves were imported to the west from Africa. The Arab slave trade spread throughout Africa and the Middle East.

Despite the nineteenth-century emancipation movements and abolition of the transatlantic slave trade, slavery persisted. The twentieth century opened with the exposé of slavery and mass killing in the Congo, a private fiefdom of King Leopold of Belgium. Edmund Morel documented these practices and successfully mobilized an international movement against them (Hochschild 1998). During the "rubber terror" and the aftermath of Leopold's rule, it is estimated that the population of the Congo declined by half—perhaps ten million persons—from direct killing, starvation, exhaustion, heat exposure, disease, and the refusal of the indigenous peoples to bear children (Hochschild 1998, 226–233). State-instituted slavery in the first half of the twentieth century was devised in peace and wartime by two totalitarian states. The Soviet Union and Nazi Germany had extensive systems of slave labor based on different classes and groups. The Soviet Union seized both ordinary criminals and the politically suspect during peace and war and exploited them for economic development (Applebaum 2003; Werth 1999). Nazi Germany employed both forced labor from workers seized from occupied countries and prisoner-slaves in extermination and concentration camps, including German Jews stripped of their citizenship (Borkin 1978; Herbert 1990). The German camps often were way stations to genocide; the Jews and Gypsies were slated for extermination if they did not drop dead first from the conditions of labor. High proportions of prisoners of Nazi Germany and the Soviet Union died from the conditions of forced labor.

Diverse Origins of Slavery

Since the end of World War II, many communist states have continued to exploit citizens and convicts for labor. When the Khmer Rouge (KR) ruled Cambodia (1975–1979), all citizens served as forced labor under KR cadres, and a significant number—about half of the 1.67–1.87 million killed under the Khmer Rouge, or 885,000 persons (Kiernan 1996)—died from starvation and diseases caused or aggravated by starvation and overwork in that service. Cambodia's policies raise the question of state responsibility for genocide and famine, which is discussed in chapter 6. The Loghai or "reform through labor" camps in the People's Republic of China, modeled after forced labor in the Soviet Union, have been estimated to enslave millions, many now Falun Gong—religious dissidents—rather than political prisoners. There are more than 1,000 documented sites, disguised as commercial firms, that sell the goods the prisoners make at a profit (Loghai Handbook 2003–2004). There are also between 150,000 and 200,000 people reportedly held in slave labor camps in North Korea (Hawk 2003).

Besides these forms of servitude, there are states in Southeast Asia with government forced labor and guerrilla armies in Asia and Africa seizing people for service in many countries. Both armies and rebels convert the enslaved into instruments of violence. Many contemporary rebels against the state recruit and forcibly seize children as soldiers and sex slaves. Sometimes such children are turned into victimizers—killing, maiming, and raping their own people—so that they cannot go home again (Amnesty International 1998; Machel 1996). Soldiers under eighteen years of age are used in thirty countries today, Human Rights Watch estimates (Human Rights Watch 2006). Ishmael Beah, a former child soldier from Sierra Leone, relates why he joined the army and how commanders drugged children to dull pain and energize them to fight (2007).

To examine contemporary slavery, I shall examine three states dependent on or engaged in enslavement. Sudan is a state in which government incentives during the civil wars (1983–present) revived traditional patterns of enslavement. The second and third cases occurred during peacetime: traditional slavery (Mauritania) and caste and bonded labor (India). These countries are high slave-labor states. (I am basing the following observations on my calculations from 2005 estimates of slaves and population [Bales 2005, app. 2; UN Human Development Report 2005, table 33].) There were more slaves in India than in any other country in 2005 (18 to 22 million); they constituted the second highest ratio of estimated slaves to population (1.87 percent) among all countries. Mauritania had the highest ratio of slaves to population in 2005—almost 10 percent of its population. The slave population in Sudan is smaller, and its size uncertain; the best estimate is 10 percent; however, Sudan actively expanded the number it enslaved in the 1980s and 1990s.

Some might question why two of these three states are predominantly Muslim and African. My research showed that slavery was more likely in predominantly Muslim states in Africa than in predominantly non-Muslim states. Three-fourths of African states with populations 70 to 100 percent Muslim in 1980 (Morrison 1980, 45) were at the highest level of slavery in 2002 as contrasted with the 75 percent of African states with a Muslim population of 19 percent or less, which were at the next to the lowest level (scaled by Bales 2002).

The selection of two African, predominantly Muslim states and a predominantly Hindu state (India) was consonant with my finding that non-Christian states were likely to be higher on slavery than Christian states. The examples were chosen on two bases: (1) the prevalence and toleration of slavery and (2) the extent and reliability of the documentation developed.

David Brian Davis observed the origin of racial slavery in medieval Islamic society (2001, 41). Although both Christianity and Islam professed belief in the unity of mankind, no religiously motivated anti-slavery movements arose in Islamic countries that were comparable to the antislavery movements that arose in the UK and United States in the nineteenth century, motivated by Christianity and Quakerism (Hochschild 2005).

Although the state always plays a role in guaranteeing slavery, it does not necessarily initiate slavery or maintain slaves. Recent data on the role of the state in attempting to stop interstate trafficking or its lack of a significant effort to do so are provided by the U.S. Department of State, as mandated by U.S. legislation, noted in table 3.1 in chapter 3.

What should be noted in the following analyses is how slaves are defined in contemporaneous and twentieth-century societies. Although throughout history, slaves have often been of the same race as their masters (as race was perceived by both), racial ranking and preferences are common in many systems. There is "a universal reluctance to enslave members of one's own community, hence the need to redefine them as outsiders" (Patterson 1982, 178). This tendency supports the assumption that slaves must be defined outside the universe of obligation (ch. 1): "the range of persons and groups toward whom basic rules or 'oughts' are binding ... people whom must be taken into account, to whom obligations are due, by whom we can be held responsible for our actions" (Fein 1977, 7).

Most patterns of enslavement take place within the nation-state. Exceptions to this include trafficking and transport of women across borders for domestic service and prostitution (discussed in ch. 3). This chapter will examine how exclusion, opportunity, and violence interact to trigger enslavement and to perpetuate slavery.

State-Instigated Slavery in Sudan

Slavery reemerged in Sudan during the second Sudanese civil war (1983–2005), a war challenging whether Sudan—divided by religion, race, culture, and history—is or can be one nation. Sudan has been torn by internal war for most years since its independence in 1956. Rebellion began in southern regions, where the British had suppressed rebellions in the 1920s. Central governments in Sudan now and in the past have relied on exploiting local divisions to divide and rule. The north and south of Sudan are divided by often coinciding lines of religion (Muslim versus Christian), culture (Arab versus African), and race (white versus black) as it is locally construed. This division was reinforced by historical trends, including colonialism and the slave trade.

Jok Madut Jok, a southern Sudanese anthropologist, observed:

> The factors that fueled the practice in the old days persist in Sudan.... The reemergence and increase in slave-raiding expeditions and the sale of victims in Sudan are build [*sic*] upon the racial construction of the country and the cultural ideologies that make up the identities of the Sudanese people. After all, the raiders of the new slavery are radical Muslims, self-perceived as racially superior, and they usually arrive in Nilotic (Nuer and Dinka) areas with no compunctions about killing non-Muslims and non-Arabs. (Jok 2001, 6)

Sudan was a trading center for the trans-Sahara-Mediterranean slave trade from the seventeenth through the nineteenth centuries; Arab traders transporting Africans were a linchpin of the trade. During the late nineteenth century, the Turko-Egyptian administration of the region, responding to Western pressure, attempted to suppress the slave trade, but their attempts were compromised by the bribery and evasion of the traders (Keen 1994, 26). The establishment of British colonial rule under an Anglo-Egyptian condominium at the end of the nineteenth century led to greater commitment to suppression of the slave trade (not slavery)—ending slavery was not the major interest of the British.

The British relied on the Baggara, nomadic Arab tribes of south-western Sudan, to raid rebellious peoples, such as the Nubians in the Nuba Mountains and the Dinka in the south. These predators burned villages and stole the cattle of their victims, which ultimately led to famine. Captured Africans were either incorporated into the army or used for cotton production or domestic work (Keen 1994, 28–30). The use of coercion for military recruitment and the government's fear of the social and economic consequences of abolition led to a great gap between the nominal official British policy of abolition and facts on the ground (Collins 1999, 12–14; Keen 1994, 30).

The British use of the Baggara reinforced Baggara-Dinka hostility. To the British, "the Dinka peoples were considered to be largely outside the political community and largely undeserving of government protection" (Keen 1994, 30). This changed in the 1920s as Dinka counterraids and the threat of widespread rebellion moved the British to find means to protect the interests of the Dinka. These included co-opting local Dinka leaders into a "Native Administration," monitoring and mediating land disputes between Baggara and

Dinka, suppressing raids, and promoting safeguards against famine that benefited both groups (Keen 1994, 32–34). These institutional means were fortified by the Dinka leadership's use and display of respect for Arab symbols, their pledges of common loyalty to the ruling government, charity toward members of neighboring tribes, and intermarriage (Keen 1994, 35–36).

The colonial transfer of power in 1956 (which can be related to the global postwar movement for decolonization) introduced a new political context. To the south, Sudan's independence in 1956 meant their subjection to a northern regime; they were again "outside the political community." This led to a civil war lasting sixteen years, which ended with the 1972 Addis Ababa agreement promising the south regional autonomy and integration of their army into the national army. But after a decade in which little cohesion was built between regions, President Numayri's tilt to the Islamic extremist movement (by legislating Islamic punishments) and his reversal of autonomy in 1983 triggered the second civil war.

The grievances of the south were exacerbated by economic exploitation and discrimination. The north obtained disproportionate resources from the union and redefined regional lines to ensure that revenue from oil (discovered in the south in 1978) went to the central government (Keen 1994, 66–68).

The government of Sudan, an authoritarian but multiparty regime between 1986 and 1989, was taken over in 1989 by the National Islamic Front (NIF), an extremist Islamic organization with ties to Libya and Iran. The NIF initiated a reign of repression of all democratic opposition, disappearance of opponents in "ghost houses," and ended the possibility of negotiations between north and south. The NIF government further transformed Islamic law into the law of the land, eliminating women's rights and purging dissidents from the military and the universities.

The NIF transformed the war against the Sudan People's Liberation Army (SPLA) not only into a war against the non-Muslims of the south but also a war against Muslims and non-Muslims in the Nuba Mountains who opposed the government. Progovernment imams in 1992 authorized "jihad against all those who defy the Call, whether Moslems or non-Moslems," and called for the imposition of Islam on all non-Moslems, isolation of Nuba Christians from international human rights and humanitarian or solidarity organizations, and resettlement of Nubians "in peace villages to help achieve objectives" (African Rights July 1995, 112–113).

Systematic rape of Nubian women in such peace camps has been reported. Rape is not only a war crime, but in this context could be a violation of the UN Genocide Convention, based on the Akezu decision by the International Criminal Tribunal on War Crimes in Rwanda (African Rights July 1995, 221–227; Fein 1997, 30; *New York Times* September 3, 1998, A1 and September 15, 1998, A24). The NIF government endangered the lives of foreign aid workers after 1989, labeling them as "neo-Crusaders," ousting non-Islamic aid organizations, and asserting that food aid administered and monitored by foreigners was an intolerable intrusion into Sudanese sovereignty. In 1989, government forces shot down a plane of Médecins sans Frontières (Doctors without Borders), killing everyone on board.

As Sudan joined the extremist Islamic bloc, Western states related to Sudan based on their own security needs, especially security from terrorism sponsored by Sudan and its allies against the United States and Egypt, its regional ally. The question of aid and starvation became secondary.

Sudanese government policies during the civil war reinforced famine and genocide by attrition (see ch. 6), which, along with civilian bombing, had taken the lives of at least 1.9 million southern Sudanese between 1983 and 1998, or one of five southerners (Burr 1998, 7–9). In the south, the government armed militias of nearby tribes that had been Dinka enemies in the past—such as the Rizeigat Baggara who were not paid in coin but in loot—that is, what they could snatch during their raids. Thus, these tribal militias were incited to raid, loot, and strip the Dinka of their assets, principally their cattle, which had prevented their starvation in the past. Raiders snatched women and children; children were sometimes sold ("pawned") by their starving parents to enable them (and other members of the family) to survive (Burr and Collins 1995, 114–115). The Rizeigat Baggara benefited most from obtaining cattle, land, and slaves.

Supply and demand led the market price for child slaves to drop from 60 pounds sterling to 10 pounds between February and April 1988, and age and gender elevated the price for young women to as much as fifty times that of old men and women (Keen 1994, 101, 105). The abundance of slaves depressed the local labor market when southerners, fleeing famine, sought agricultural labor on farms in the southern Darfur and southern Kordofan provinces; they often were forced to work for nothing (Keen 1994, 121–124). The provision of relief by nongovernmental organizations enabled some forced laborers to flee to the relief encampments, but others were sent there by their employers to supplement their meager rations and divert grain to their employers (Keen 1994, 161–164).

Southerners who have collected names estimated that at least 75,000 Dinka children were sold into slavery in the north (Burr and Collins 1995, 257). Although the total number enslaved is unknown, other estimates and surveys also suggest that it is very high (Keen 1994, 101). The UN Special Rapporteur, Gaspar Biro, observed in 1996 on the complicity of the government of Sudan: "It should be noted that all these practices have a pronounced racial aspect, as the victims are exclusively southern and persons belonging to the indigenous tribes of the Nuba mountains [i.e., blacks]. Among the latter group, even Muslims are enslaved" (Biro, February 20, 1994, 16–17).

Chattel slavery has usually included rape and sexual exploitation. Sexual abuse of the Sudanese captives is widely reported by human rights organizations and by ex-slaves who have escaped or been bought and freed by Christian activists (Human Rights Watch/Africa 1995, 32–32; Keen 1994, 101–102; Lewthwaite and Kane 1996). The women were raped, young girls were forced to endure female genital mutilation—not a practice of the Dinka but of the Arabs—and men were castrated (Ally 1996; Keen 1994, 247; Mahmud and Baldo 1987).

In many cases, human rights issues were not noted or stressed by the bystanders, foremost of which were the Western aid organizations that publicized the famine but not its cause—not the role of the government in diverting food, fomenting slavery, and other gross violations of life integrity, including killing and rape. The way in which slavery in Sudan became an issue in the West is a study of how contesting and cooperating religious and social movements frame definitions of problems.

In the beginning of Christian Solidarity International (CSI) expeditions to buy back slaves, the emancipated slaves were escorted by local people back to their family and home villages. The work of CSI has led television journalists and reporters to accompany the liberators to document the slaves' passage to freedom and their testimonies; these, in turn, have generated support for the antislavery movement.

The U.S. coalition involved blacks and whites and liberals and conservatives, and it was organized by diverse groups, including the Black Congressional Caucus, evangelical Christians, the American Anti-Slavery Group, and Freedom House.[1] The initial religious thrust, largely organized by evangelical Christians in the United States, spotlighted the persecution of Sudanese Christians as Christians (rather than as Africans or southerners) and successfully pressed the U.S. Congress to pass the 1998 International Religious Freedom Act and Sudan Peace Act in 2001. The expansion of the coalition led to a broadening of its goals, focusing on slavery and ending the war while recognizing the rights of the southern Sudanese. The antislavery abolitionists drew widespread grassroots support, publicizing drives by schoolchildren who were donating money to free the slaves.

As slave redemptions have expanded in the number of trips and persons freed, critics of buybacks charged that the money paid served as an incentive to enslave more people and that some exchanges have been fraudulent (with local people acting the parts of slave traders and slaves). There are no reliable current estimates of the numbers and location of slaves in Sudan. It is impossible to verify either the extent of slavery or the effects of the buybacks.

The Sudanese government has repeatedly denied the existence of enslavement and slavery, preferring the term *abduction,* which appears to have been used by some international agencies that want to continue working with the Government of Sudan (GOS). Yet slavery was first documented by two Sudanese university professors (Mahmud and Baldo 1987). Allegations made and questions and charges raised by UN organs and spokespersons since 1988—the UN Working Group on Contemporary Forms of Slavery, the UN Committee on the Rights of the Child, the International Labor Organization, and the UN Human Rights Commission's Special Rapporteur on Human Rights in Sudan—have been effectively foiled and stalled by the Government of Sudan.

Within Sudan, slavery is not an issue among citizens who oppose government repression. William Finnegan, a U.S. reporter, wrote:

Even most political liberals, Mahmud [author of a 1987 report documenting slavery] had warned me, "are in total denial." I had tea one evening in Omdurman, in a magnificent old house belonging to one of the leading Sudanese political dynasties. The lady of the house, a professor of mathematics, served me dates from her garden and spoke movingly of her dangerous work with other mothers in organizing protests against conscription.... But when I mentioned the slavery issue her manner changed. "There is no such thing here," she said sharply. "The Sudanese people are not that kind of people." When I cautiously mentioned Mahmud and his work, she said that he was a "bad man" and his work was "wrong." (1999, 71–72)

Mauritania: A Case of "Voluntary Servitude"?

"The name Mauritania itself reflects the political and social dominance of the Moors" (Geretzny 1967, 46). Its location in the Sahara
with its proneness to drought and desertification has led to increased
urbanization (although most of the country is sparsely settled), poverty, and unemployment. After independence from France in 1960,
the Islamic Republic of Mauritania was an authoritarian one-party
state until 1992 when it became an authoritarian multiparty state.
Principal internal conflicts focus on the struggles of black southern
ethnic groups, Afro-Mauritanians, against the Moors, while external
problems centered on control of the Western Sahara.

Investigations of slavery are constricted by the government's control
of information and heavy police presence. Government agents stage
charades by posing as freed slaves, and they are abetted by paid-off
freed slaves who parrot the government line and have even trans-
ported slaves outside the view of investigating missions (Bales 1999,
89; *Newsweek* 1992). Bales pursued his investigation by posing as a
zoologist (using hidden cameras) in order to avoid the police agents
following him continuously (Bales 1999, 83).

Estimates from the 1990s are that from tens to hundreds of thousands of black Africans are held in virtual slavery by Moor (Arab and
Berber) masters, employed in agricultural labor, domestic work, hauling water, and trade in the cities (Bales 1999; Burkett 1997). In 1984,
Jacob Oliel estimated before the Working Group of Experts on Slavery
(under the UN Sub-Commission on Prevention of Discrimination
and Protection of Minorities) that there were 250,000 chattel slaves
in Mauritania (Sawyer 1986, 14, 236).

Yet slavery has been legally outlawed three times in Mauritania. The
last time was in 1980 after a trial of ex-slaves, or *haratin* (a separate
stratum), aroused international disapproval. But although slavery
was then outlawed, holding slaves was not made illegal, and the law
specified that slave owners were to be recompensed, which was never
done, "so masters routinely consider the law null and void" (Burkett
1997, 58).

The economic problems of Mauritania have left many with limited
possibilities for finding arable land or work. Environmental problems
were compounded by the government's mass expulsion, or "ethnic
cleansing," of southern Afro-Mauritanians in 1989 in order to get
arable land (principally bought by Moor land buyers), which dis-
possessed many Afro-Mauritanians in the south. "By inciting hatred

against the Afro-Mauritanians the government diverts attention from the plight of the slave population and at the same time encourages the Black Moor ex-slaves to distance themselves from the 'traitorous' Afro-Mauritanians" (Bales 1999, 94).

Slavery continues to be comfortable and profitable for the slave owners. Bales found slaves working in the capital, Nouakchott (he estimated as many as 100,000 slaves there), involved in running grocery stores and in hauling and distributing water—an extensive service, because there is no running water (Bales 1999, 99–107). Bales calculated that the average monthly profit from one slave selling water was $93—after subtracting his food and other expenses. An owner with four slaves would get $371 monthly, or a 265 percent return on investment—a fortune in a country where the average annual per capita income then was about $480 (Bales 1999, 95, 104–105).

Although there are organized ex-slaves and movements to free slaves in Mauritania, the enslaved—especially women—often stick with their masters because of lack of clear legal right to leave with their children, intergenerational family links, uncertainty about paternity, lack of alternative jobs in the marketplace, and traditional attitudes justifying their status. "God created me to be a slave just as he created a camel to be a camel," Fatma, a slave who ran away after a beating she believed could have led to her death, said to a reporter. When the reporter inquired about rape, "she replied matter-of-factly, 'Of course they would come in the night when they needed to breed us. Is that what you mean by rape?'" (Burkett 1997, 56). Slavery is not only very profitable for the masters but ensures the Moors' retention of political power (they are a minority), because slaves are not part of the polity. If slaves were active citizens, they might form a coalition with the haratin and Afro-Mauritanians and displace the Moors.

Recognition of slavery is an issue for governments aiding Mauritania and governmental and nongovernmental organizations. There is an ideological and semantic disagreement among some governments and human rights nongovernmental organizations (HRNGOs) as to whether and how to define slavery. The U.S. State Department report-ed in 2006, as in previous years, that "a system of officially sanctioned slavery in which government and society join to force individuals to serve masters did not exist. However, there continued to be reports that forced and involuntary servitude persisted in some remote areas. Voluntary servitude also persisted, with some former slaves and descen-dents of slaves continuing to work for former masters in exchange for some combination of money, lodging, food, or medical care" (U.S. Department of State 2006). Such "remote areas" evidently include the capital and its environs where Bales, *Newsweek*, and *New York Times* reporters interviewed slaves.

Moctar Teyeb, an escaped slave from Mauritania who serves as the American coordinator for El Hor—freedom—(a Mauritanian antislavery organization) and outreach director for the American Anti-Slavery Group, charged at a hearing of the U.S. Senate Committee on Foreign Relations (U.S. Congress 2001) that the United States changed its line toward Mauritania in 1995 after Mauritania began to vote with the United States in the United Nations, retreating from Mauritania's previous support of Iraq.

In fact, the U.S. Congress in 1996 banned "economic and military assistance or arms transfer to the Government of Mauritania unless the President certifies to the Congress that such government has taken appropriate action to eliminate chattel slavery in Mauritania" (HR 4036, sec. 202), yet U.S. aid continued.

Support for Teyeb's charge also comes from comparison of the frank judgment in the U.S. State Department's 1994 survey of slavery in Mauritania, which noted that "credible reports indicate that there are from 30,000 to 90,000 people living in slavery" (1994, 185; see also Bales 2005, 97). De facto slavery in Mauritania has been reported repeatedly by the international London-based Anti-Slavery Society, Human Rights Watch, Amnesty International, and UN subcommittees. Within Mauritania, there are two independent NGOs—SOS Esclaves and El Hor—that bring court cases to emancipate the enslaved.

Outside pressure on Mauritania to change is virtually nonexistent. France and the United States, the major aid donors, have either ignored slavery or, as has been shown, claimed that it is vestigial. But assistance is essential to develop a plan and support to instigate the political will in Mauritania to end slavery and to develop jobs, despite desertification and a stagnant economy. Although many observers have noted that there would be a need to compensate slaveholders, there would also be a need for psychological and economic rehabilitation of slaves so that they could function in the economy.

India: Forced Servitude in the World's Largest Democracy

India is often noted as the second most populous state in the world and a parliamentary democracy (among the few in Asia) that has endured since its independence in 1948, only interrupted by the

State of Emergency declared by Prime Minister Indira Gandhi from 1975 to 1977. Before independence, Indians' capacity for self-rule was challenged by critics pointing to the eruptions of Hindu-Muslim conflict, potential discrimination against minorities, and the continuing discrimination against the untouchables (Dirks 2001).

Other critics countered that such conflict and discrimination were reinforced by British rule. The Indian National Congress and the non-violent movement led by Mohandas (Mahatma) Gandhi from 1919 to 1948 played an essential role in winning this independence and creating a secular democratic state. However, Gandhi's influence led to political arrangements that inhibited the ability of untouchables to represent themselves (McMillan 2005, 56–64; Omvedt 1994, 170–174). The untouchables (called by Gandhi *harijans,* "children of God," and known today as *dalits*) legally became members of Scheduled Castes after 1935, but generally their status and stigma did not change.

The untouchables are deemed not only socially inferior but outside the religiously validated Hindu hierarchy of *varna,* that is, caste. Social and ritual inequality is justified by millennia-old Hindu religious texts that depict the four major castes—*Brahmins* (priests), *Ksatriyas* (rulers and soldiers), *Vaisyas* (merchants and traders), and *Shudras* (laborers and artisans)—as arising from different parts of the creator. In practice, there are thousands of subcastes vying for status, so the system allows more mobility than a static description would suggest. But those outside this schema are considered unclean, polluting, and hence untouchable. This led caste Hindus to impose segregation, for example, preventing untouchables from drawing water from a common well, in many villages.

This institution led to cumulative discrimination of and disadvantage for the untouchables, who often incorporated a sense of inferiority as a result. By tradition and caste fiat, they have done the dirty work. Landlessness, the lack of credit, the dependence of the poor on moneylenders in a rural economy, and their need for protection by members of the upper castes also make the dalits more vulnerable to exploitation.

India has tried since its independence in 1948 to legally rectify the political, social, and economic inequities produced by the caste system, but there is a great gap between laws, decrees, and court rulings and their implementation. The Indian government enacted its own system of affirmative action after independence—a pledge of reserved places in government jobs and school openings for members of the Scheduled Castes and Classes (the latter include tribal peoples).

The effect of electoral reservations has become "a scheme of political trickledown, where the substantive interests of the socioeconomically disadvantaged are served by symbolic representation" (McMillan 2005, 327). The contemporary situation of rural dalits has changed the least; they remain relatively unaffected by government reservations, which principally assist the educated.

Further, the majority of reserved jobs in the federal government remain unfilled, according to recent reports by the National Commission for Scheduled Castes and Scheduled Tribes (1996–1997 and 1997–1998), which observe what "Dalit activists call 'an unacknowledged reservation policy' for upper castes, particularly Brahmins, built into the system" (Human Rights Watch 2001).

Resentment of reservations for Scheduled Castes and Tribes, perceived to reduce the life chances of caste members, is among the grievances that inspired support for a resurgent Hindu nationalist movement beginning in the last decade of the twentieth century. However, a dalit movement in support of their recognition and advancement countered the Hindu nationalist movement from the late 1990s. Such organizations include the Dalit Freedom Network, the National Campaign on Dalit Human Rights ("CastOutCaste"), and the National Federation of Dalit Women.

R. M. Pal observed (1994) that "the worst aspect of human rights violations in India is not custodial deaths and atrocities by state agencies (as highlighted by Amnesty International and other groups) but oppression and cruelty to classes and groups manifested by the caste system and religious intolerance fomented to hatred." He related the killings by upper-caste Hindus of twenty dalits, who were hacked to death while police sat by in Tsundur village in Andhra Pradesh on August 6, 1991, and asked, "Why did they kill the dalits? The immediate provocation was that the foot of a dalit boy (a postgraduate) touched the foot of an upper caste boy in a cinema. This incident gave the upper caste landlords, who did not tolerate the dalits walking with their heads erect, an excuse to teach the dalits a lesson."

When untouchables violate the etiquette of caste relations (called a version of apartheid or segregation by many), upper-caste Hindus often respond by violence—lynching, rape, or massacre. Human Rights Watch suggested that violence against dalits has risen because of growing activism by the dalit rights movement, ignited by "attempts to defy the social order; cases relating to land disputes and demands for minimum wages; and cases of atrocities by police and forest officials" (Human Rights Watch 2001). Despite intimidation and the reluctance of dalits to report, from 1995 to 1997 almost 91,000 cases of crimes and atrocities against dalits were reported, which included 1,697 for murder, 12,591 for injury, 2,824 for rape, and 31,376 for offenses under the Prevention of Atrocities Act (Human Rights Watch 2001). Social boycotts, ostracism, and systematic discouragement of children from learning and enrolling for more education also serve to keep the dalits in an inferior place.

Economically, the dominant way that servitude is perpetuated in the Indian subcontinent is through bonded labor. Wage earners and their families (including children) are forced to work without wages in order to "repay" a debt that usually keeps growing—because of usurious interest rates and the need for new loans to survive annual cycles of harvest and drought and emergencies such as accidents and illness. The Indian School of Social Sciences cites a not atypical case of a northern village farmer who was still working seventeen years later to pay off a debt of 500 rupees ($14) with its accumulated interest (Mehta 1997, 62). Such workers usually cannot check accounts, because the employer keeps the books, and the workers are illiterate and innumerate. The vast majority of these workers in bonded labor in India are from Scheduled Castes and Scheduled Tribes; the case is similar in Pakistan and Nepal (Human Rights Watch 2001).

Although the Indian constitution guarantees equal rights and there have been laws and court decisions outlawing bonded labor in 1976 and 1984—judicial activism to free bonded laborers has become normal since the 1980s—these laws are often not enforced at the state level because the states fail to identify bonded laborers (Prakash 1990, 78–80). State governments are likely to be controlled by elites representing dominant castes and economic interests who hold bonded laborers and dalits in contempt.

S. S. Prakash distinguishes types of bondage, many of which stem from traditional patron-client relationships: customary (traditional) bondage, intergenerational bondage, loyalty bondage, sharecropping cum bondage, and modern bondage (Prakash 1990, 51–53). In loyalty bondage, "the bonded labourer preaches his sons, i.e., the coming generations to serve faithfully the master and they feel that they are very fortunate to serve especially if the master is a little kindly towards them." When there is a familial connection over generations and personal bonds, there might be less violence employed against such workers—provided they stay in their place—than when they work in industry and quarrying.

By contrast, modern bondage is completely impersonal with no pretense of protection, and it might start out as a job. The worker might be recruited with the promise of a good wage, which vanishes on the worker's arrival. Some industries, such as stone mining and crushing and brick making, are dependent on bonded labor; bonded laborers have been repeatedly liberated at such sites (Citizens Commission 1995, 51–59; Jain 1997).

We do not know how many bonded laborers there are in India. Bonded laborers have been observed working in fields and factories, in quarrying, and in rug weaving. They are often subjected to personal violence, rape, unsafe working conditions leading to accidents, and deprivation of medical care and education for their families. Quarry workers surveyed had to pay equipment costs and were exposed to perilous conditions. The injured not only had no medical care on the job, but they also had to obtain "loans" from their employers so they could get to the hospital—loans that extended their servitude (Jain 1997, 95, 98).

Although children might be working alongside their parents, parents are powerless to protect them, and intergenerational bondage occurs regularly; a 1981 study estimated that it happened in 19 percent of cases (Prakash 1990, 50–52). Children's vulnerability to exploitation and violation stems from both inheriting their parents' debt and parents selling them to employers. Even the unborn can be pledged. In a match factory in the state of Tamil Nadu, "a child in the mother's womb is pledged to the factory owners, maternity leave and loans are obtainable to the pregnant workers on the undertaking that the child to be born would work for their factory" (*The Hindu*, August 17, 1986, 3, reported in Prakash 1990, 55).

Although the government of India mandates emancipation and rehabilitation of bonded laborers, this is often unenforceable. First, attempts to count and to emancipate bonded laborers meet with resistance. In a report of an attempt in 1988 by the Indian judiciary to monitor a 1983 court decision regarding the condition and status of quarry workers in the state of Haryana, Jain found that local political pressure often prevented the monitors from even identifying bonded laborers (1997, 135–136). Second, there were few alternate opportunities in the area. Jain's study only found 136 persons who had been released, many of whom had gone back to the quarries because of lack of other work opportunities. Third, the employers used violence and intimidation to keep the workers in place. "Musclemen" hired by the employers beat up escaped workers (Jain 1997, 99). Bales observed that although much has gone wrong—such as landlords forcing laborers to sign over government restitution grants to the landlords—the government of India is the only government that is committed to freeing bonded laborers and has developed some organization and methods to do so. In the state of Uttar Pradesh, 26,000 bonded laborers were freed between 1979 and 1989 (1999, 228–229). Indian government studies have pinpointed what economic and social changes are needed to make liberation work, beginning with involvement by the bonded laborers. All workers need education, jobs, and training; rural workers also need arable land, legal guarantees of title, reasonable credit, and emergency grants (Bales 1999, 229).

Some bonded laborers are children, but all child labor is not bonded labor. The Citizens Commission on Bondage and Child Labour estimated in 1995 that 60 million children were working in India in various industries, trade, and agriculture, but there is no consensus among child labor opponents as to whether immediate or staged abolition is desirable or possible. There is a widespread social attitude in India that children of the poor should work as soon as they can because they are an economic asset whose contribution to their parents cannot be taken away (Weiner and Noman 1991, 186–190). Critics (such as Weiner and Noman 1991) point out that child labor depresses wages and that education improves the children's life chances and leads to healthier, more prosperous, and smaller families.

Besides judicial attempts to liberate bonded laborers by intervention (Jain 1997; Prakash 1990, 100–114), there is increasing nongovernmental activism in India, including organizations to combat bondage.[2] The National Campaign on Dalit Human Rights (1998) organized a worldwide appeal with solidarity groups in different countries and a presentation at the UN World Conference Against Racism, Racial Discrimination, Xenophobia and Related Intolerance in Durban in September 2001.

The UN Committee on the Elimination of Racial Discrimination (CERD) decreed in 1996 and 2001 that caste discrimination based on descent is racial discrimination, falling within the scope of the International Convention on the Elimination of Racial Discrimination (1965). India contests this, labeling it a religious question.[3] Although many educated Indians repudiate caste verbally, caste gives meaning to many lower-caste Indians, providing them a comparison group to whom they may feel superior. Human Rights Watch notes: "Much of the conflicts take place within very narrow segments of the caste hierarchy, between the poor and the not so poor, the landless laborer and the marginal landowner," but the caste Hindus have more power over local police and district and state governments (2001).

Notes

1. African-Americans, who one might expect would champion the exposure of black slavery in Sudan, were divided for almost a decade, largely because of the opposition of the Rev. Louis Farrakhan, head of the Nation of Islam, who declared accusations of enslavement in Sudan were part of a Zionist plot against Islam. His denial spurred reporters to go to Sudan to document the case (Hentoff 1995).

2. These include the Dalit Freedom Network (founded in 2003), the International Dalit Solidarity Network (formed in 2000), the National Campaign on Dalit Human Rights (1998), and the Bandhua Mukti Moreha (Bonded Liberation Fund), founded in 1981.

3. A U.S. Congress investigation in 2005—"India's unfinished agenda: equality and justice for 200 million victims of the caste system"—attracted leading dalit activists and authorities from India. They testified that discrimination persisted even in the distribution of food and shelter after the tsunami that struck Tamil Nadu. They charged that the government of India was complicit in avoiding enforcement of constitutional provisions to protect dalits who had converted from Hinduism. Speakers testified that violence against dalit women reinforced caste oppression—rape and gang rape are common. Some observed that globalization and privatization did not benefit dalits who are educated (if in school at all) in regional languages that would not qualify them for modern employment. They recommended that there be reservations of jobs in private employment and that foreign aid should go to education for dalits along with preference for them in granting educational visas to the West.

3
Slavery, Trafficking, and Globalization

> 1783 marked the beginning of a boom in the British slave trade.... Slavery seemed as entrenched as ever. If pressed, some Britons might have conceded that the institution was unpleasant—but where else would sugar for your tea come from? ... No major thinker defended slavery, but few spent real effort attacking it.
>
> —Adam Hochschild, *Bury the Chains*, 2005, 85–86

> First, it is important to recognize that the consumers of trafficked people operate within a moral economy that allows them to rationalize this activity. This moral economy will not normally be the dominant cultural or legal context, but a subculture that defines trafficked people in a way that allows their exploitation.
>
> —Kevin Bales, *Understanding Global Slavery*, 2005, 156

Globalization and trafficking in persons are several centuries old. We must ask: What accounts for the differences in the extent of slavery in countries around the world and trafficking of persons (with and without their consent) today from some countries to others? Although most public attention has focused on trafficking girls and women for prostitution, other persons have been trafficked for domestic service, rural and industrial labor in many continents, and as camel jockeys in the Gulf states.

Kevin Bales, the preeminent student of what he calls the "new slavery" (in which slaves are not legally owned), relates this to the number of disposable people in the world, a function of the growth of population and extent of poverty throughout much of the world (Bales 2004, 2005). Both "push" and "pull" factors influence trafficking as they do legal and illegal migration. Bales concluded, based on statistical study, that "the most significant factors predicting trafficking in persons in a country, given in descending order of their power to do so, are the level of a country's governmental corruption; the country's infant mortality rate; the proportion of the population below the age of fourteen; the level of the country's food production; the country's population density; and the amount of conflict and social unrest the country suffers" (Bales 2005, 139). These are "push" factors explaining that people are most likely to leave poor countries for rich countries. Governmental corruption is observed in his statistical analyses in the "push" and "pull" factors. Bales deprecates the influence of ethnic and racial differences in selecting and enticing these slaves (Bales 2004, 8–13).

Tracking trafficking and slavery (see table 3.1, pp. 46–47) is problematic for several reasons, beginning with the fact that sources include trafficked persons among the enslaved. Estimated numbers are impossible to confirm. However, distinguishing patterns among countries enables us to get a perspective on who is going where and make some preliminary inferences as to the similarities and differences in the causes of trafficking and experiences of trafficked persons.

This chapter focuses on globalization and trafficking for prostitution, illustrated in two countries that are very dissimilar—Israel and Thailand. It draws on John Stuart Mill's "method of agreement" as a means for inductive or grounded theory (George and Bennett 2005, 153–160); specifically, I seek to probe whether another factor explains trafficking besides those specified by Bales, for example, gender and "otherness"—ethnicity, race, religion.

The states selected are at different levels of development, have a different dominant religious background—Israel is predominantly Jewish and Thailand Buddhist—and are on different continents, drawing women from different regions. Both are in Tier 2 of the U.S. State Department's ranking of countries (see table 3.1)—countries "which do not fully comply but are making significant efforts." They were also selected because of the availability of reliable documentation, largely drawn from activist feminist and antitrafficking movements in these areas.

Prostitution is an organized, public, visible, and highly profitable trade holding women (in brothels, clubs, massage parlors) in the shadows of the night world usually known by law enforcement (or

44

nonenforcement) workers as well as by clients. Although most people trafficked are workers to be exploited for the profit or surplus value from their labor, forced prostitutes are also a source of capital accumulation for their employers. "Trafficking does not require a large capital investment and it frequently involves little risk of discovery by law enforcement. In addition, trafficking victims, unlike drugs, can be resold and used repeatedly by traffickers" (U.S. Department of State Trafficking in Persons Report, June 2002, 2).

Another report of trafficking to the United States found that

> Overall profits in the trade can be staggering, as several cases indicate. Thai traffickers, who incarcerated Thai women and men in a sweatshop in El Monte, California, are estimated to have made $8 million over about six years. Thai traffickers, who enslaved Thai women in a New York brothel, made about $1.5 million over roughly a year and three months. In that case, the women were made to pay debts ranging from $30,000 to $50,000. The women were forced to charge $130 per client; the madam of the brothel would receive $30 and the smugglers would receive $100. (Richard 1999, 19)

Getting women and girls to work as prostitutes (by enticement, deception, and kidnapping) is not a new phenomenon—it goes back centuries. To be sure, there is debate among human rights workers and feminists exposing this problem as to the scope of forced prostitution, how to distinguish its victims, and types of reform needed. Herein, forced sexual servitude and trafficking are distinguished from ordinary prostitution. The former are forbidden not only by international conventions on slavery and slave trafficking but also by the Convention on the Elimination of Discrimination Against Women (1979), which requires states to "suppress all forms of traffic in women and exploitation of prostitution of women" (Article 6). The 2000 Protocol to Prevent, Suppress and Punish Trafficking in Persons, Especially Women and Children, Supplementing the UN Convention Against Transnational Organized Crime, stresses that "consent of a victim of trafficking ... to the intended exploitation ... shall be irrelevant where any of the means set forth in subparagraph (a) [threat or use of force or other forms of coercion, of abduction, of fraud, of deception, of the abuse of power or of a position of vulnerability] have been used."

The UN Special Rapporteur on Violence Against Women helped distinguish trafficking of women from voluntary prostitution by redefining the former in 1996 as "[a]ll acts involved in the recruitment

Table 3.1 Patterns of Trafficking and Rank of Slavery, 2005

Trafficking	Slavery Rank	
	Low (1 or 2)*	High or Highest (3 or 4)*
High into Country	Australia Czech Republic France Germany Hong Kong Israel# Italy Japan# Netherlands Portugal	Oman Qatar## United Arab Republic## Yemen#
High from Country	Albania# Bangladesh Belarus# Bulgaria# Cambodia## Colombia Congo# Croatia# Georgia Ghana# Laos# Macedonia# Togo## Turkmenistan Ukraine*# Uganda# Vietnam#	Afghanistan# Burma## Gabon# Guinea-Bissau Haiti*# Indonesia# Mauritania## Nepal Nigeria# Philippines*#
High to and from Country	Hungary# Malaysia# Mexico*# Moldova*# Poland Singapore# South Africa*# Turkey# Turkmenistan Serbia-Montenegro# South Africa*#	Benin*# Brazil# Burkina Faso# Cameroon*# China*# Côte d'Ivoire# Gambia*# Equatorial Guinea# India*# Niger*# Pakistan São Tomé and Príncipe# Saudi Arabia## Senegal# Sierra Leone# Sudan## Thailand#

Notes:

*Ordinal rankings (1–4) for slavery are from Bales (2005).

#, *#, ## These symbols are based on U.S. sources on the extent and response to trafficking: # indicates Tier 2 countries and *# indicates countries of special concern among Tier 2 countries; ## indicates Tier 3 countries. The U.S. Department of State defines the tiers as follows:

Tier 1: Countries whose governments fully comply with the Act's [Victims of Trafficking and Violence Protection Act of 2000] minimum standards.

Tier 2: Countries whose governments do not fully comply with the Act's minimum standards but are making significant efforts to bring themselves into compliance with those standards.

Tier 2 Special Watch list: Countries whose governments do not fully comply with the Act's minimum standards but are making significant efforts to bring themselves into compliance with those standards, and: (a) The absolute number of victims of severe forms of trafficking is very significant or is significantly increasing; or (b) There is a failure to provide evidence of increasing efforts to combat severe forms of trafficking in persons from the previous year; or (c) The determination that a country is making significant efforts to bring themselves into compliance with minimum standards was based on commitments by the country to take additional future steps over the next year.

Tier 3: Countries whose governments do not fully comply with the minimum standards and are not making significant efforts to do so.

Countries omitted from this table because they are not high on trafficking (according to Bales 2005) include: Armenia, Austria, Barbados, Canada, Costa Rica, Denmark, Dominica, Dominican Republic, Egypt, Estonia, Greece, Jamaica, S. Korea, Kyrgyzstan, Lebanon, Luxembourg, Panama, Puerto Rico, Spain, Sweden, Switzerland, Trinidad and Tobago, UK, and the United States. All ranked 1 (lowest) on slavery.

Algeria, Argentina, Armenia, Azerbaijan, Kazakhstan, Kenya, Peru, Tajikistan, Tanzania, Uzbekistan ranked 2; Gabon ranked 3 by Bales.

However, there are differences in judgment between the USDOS and Bales: Several countries not ranked high on trafficking by Bales are on the USDOS Tier 2 Watch list: Armenia, Azerbaijan, Dominican Republic, and Greece.

Sources: Kevin Bales, *Understanding Global Slavery* (Berkeley: University of California Press, 2005), appendix 2, "Rankings of Countries on Ordinal Scales for Slavery and Trafficking," 183–186; U.S. Department of State, *Trafficking in Persons Report* (Washington, D.C.: USDOS, 2005).

and/or transportation of a woman within and across national borders for work or services by means of violence, abuse of authority or dominant position, debt bondage, deception or other forms of coercion" (Kempadoo 2005, xii).

Trafficking thrives in the international marketplace not only because there are always women available seeking employment in richer countries and policemen who can be corrupted but also because the market has been deliberately expanded. The sex trade has become a specialized attraction for international tourism in the last decades of the twentieth century, complementing other global trends in pursuing the exotic, forbidden substances, and pleasure. Sex tourism attracts customers to foreign places of pleasure and must produce a staff to satisfy their demands (Opperman 1998).

What distinguishes sex trafficking from voluntary sex work is not whether or not enlistment is voluntary but whether sex workers are free to leave. When taken over international borders, these women and girls are trapped by their status as illegal migrants, alien and outside the law. They are then further dependent on the brothel owner to evade prosecution and deportation. This dependency is reinforced as the brothel owner or sex trader strips them of legal identity, taking their passports or papers (if they have any). Often, brothel owners use both violence and economic sanctions to keep them in place. Many become bonded laborers, forced to sign documents affirming their debt to the trafficker or brothel owner. Brothel operators use rape to break unwilling workers and physical force to punish them and prevent their escape. They threaten physical reprisals against a worker's family if she flees and warn her of her legal liability to repay the debt—a sum based on the money the trafficker gave the parents and the costs allegedly incurred by the woman.

Trafficked women and girls are usually drawn from less-developed poorer countries and politically chaotic areas and go to more developed, richer, more stable countries, but there is a wide range of destinations for global traffickers (see table 3.2). From the former Soviet Union, "substantial numbers" of women and girls have gone to Germany, Switzerland, Japan, Macau, and the United States. Others have gone to Australia, Belgium, Cambodia, Cyprus, Egypt, Finland, Greece, Israel, Italy, the Netherlands, the Philippines, South Africa, Spain, Switzerland, Tanzania, Thailand, Turkey, the United Arab Emirates, and Vietnam (Caldwell, Gallster, and Steinzor 1997, 3–10). From Bangladesh, Burma, and Nepal, they have been imported into Australia, China, India, Macau, Japan, and Thailand (Skrobanek, Boonpakdee, and Jantateero 1997). Some women are willing to migrate, pushed by pressures and pulled by opportunities, as are all migrants.

The women from the former Soviet Union are drawn by advertisements for dancers (or waitresses, nannies, hostesses, etc.) that promise good pay and good clothes, knowing or not knowing what is expected of them. "Russian women are in high demand in many countries because of their 'exotic' nature and relative novelty in the sex market" (Caldwell, Gallster, and Steinzor 1997, 5). The decline in living standards after 1991, increased unemployment, gender

Table 3.2 Estimates of Number of Slaves (Including Trafficked Persons) 2005

Country	Low	High
Over 1 million		
India	8.5 million	22 million
Pakistan	2.5 million	3.5 million
100,000–999,999		
Brazil	100,000	200,000
China	250,000	300,000
Mauritania	250,000	300,000
Nepal	250,000	300,000
United States	100,000	150,000
75,000 and over		
Haiti	75,000	150,000
50,000 and over	50,000	100,000
Burma		
20,000 and over		
Afghanistan	20,000	50,000
Benin	20,000	40,000
Italy	30,000	40,000
Ivory Coast	30,000	80,000
Nigeria	20,000	40,000
Thailand	30,000	60,000
Turkey	20,000	30,000

Source: Kevin Bales, *Understanding Global Slavery* (Berkeley: University of California Press, 2005), Appendix 2, 183–186.

discrimination, and sexual harassment at work in the former Soviet Union also push them to leave.

Trafficking and Sex Work in Thailand

Women from Southeast Asia (the Greater Mekong Subregion) are most likely to be attracted to Thailand. Phil Marshall and Susu Thatun observe the "push down pop-up effect ... whereby the problem is reduced or pushed down in one place, only to emerge somewhere else.... With notable but insufficient measures to reduce demand for children, there are reports that successful programs to prevent Thai children from Northern Thailand entering the sex trade are displacing the problem to ethnic minority children, and to the neighboring countries of Lao PDR and Myanmar" (2005, 44).

Where patriarchal attitudes and power prevail, female children have also been sold by their parents to work in brothels. In Burma, family members are reported to get $400–$800 from the trafficker taking the children over the border to Thailand (Human Rights Watch/Asia 1993, 3). In Burma, this sum is a fortune; $800 exceeded the average annual income in this area at that time. The estimated per capita income in Burma (Myanmar) in 1990 was $659 (UNDP 1993, 139).

In some cases, they may be physically snatched and kidnapped. In Thailand, young girls and children are especially desired because of their looks or their age. Clients are said to believe that virgins are free from AIDS and HIV. In fact, children are extremely vulnerable to AIDS, HIV, other sexual infections, and injuries, because the clients, often previously exposed to many prostitutes, are then carriers of these sexually transmitted diseases. When the girls get sick, they are sent home.

Thailand has a broad toleration of prostitution, which has made its sex trade a tourist attraction. Thousands of Burmese girls a year have been brought to Thailand, but in the early 1990s they constituted only 0.2 percent of the total female labor force, less than 3 percent of an estimated 800,000 to 2 million prostitutes in Thailand (Human Rights Watch/Asia 1993). Prostitutes made up 6 to 14 percent of the female labor force in Thailand at the time (UNDP 1993, 168, 180). Thus, prostitution was one of the leading occupations for women in Thailand. Thai women were also trafficked to debt bondage in Japan with the cooperation of Thai traffickers (Human Rights Watch 2000).

Within Thailand, prostitution is an important industry. In the early 1990s, the tourist trade was estimated to have contributed $3 billion annually, or 2.5 percent of the gross national product (Human Rights Watch/Asia 1993, 16). Three out of every four visitors were unaccompanied men (Human Rights Watch/Asia 1993, 16).

A web of Thai laws both outlaw prostitution (1960) and sanction it in "baths, massage or steam baths which have women to attend male customers" (1966). Laws also prohibit both trafficking in women and rape, but the laws are often not enforced.

The gap between law and condoned practice has given rise to widespread collusion (a protection racket), impunity for traffickers, and a pattern of prosecuting women, not brothel owners. In a case that became a public scandal in 1992, a Thai woman who fled from a brothel was brought to a local police station, where she was murdered. Although a parliamentary inquiry pointed to six suspects, including four policemen, nobody was charged, and twenty policemen were transferred to another station (Human Rights Watch/Asia, 1993, 80–81).

A recent U.S. State Department Report on trafficking concluded that the government of Thailand does not meet minimum standards, noting that enforcement was weak and corruption pervasive. The government had made "modest progress" in addressing trafficking-related corruption in 2004. There were 307 trafficking-related arrests, 66 prosecutions, and 12 convictions—most drew light sentences. However, there is now a National Committee on Trafficking in Women and Children that includes representatives of Thai and international nongovernmental organizations. The Thai government provides "commendable protection" to victims of trafficking, with ninety-seven shelters throughout the country.

Israel

Among the lands of the former Soviet Union that are targets for traffickers, forced prostitution in Israel is perhaps the best documented because of the efforts of the Israel Women's Network (Vandenberg 1997). Neither prostitution nor sex trafficking across borders was illegal in Israel, but solicitation, pimping, and forced prostitution could be prosecuted. It is notable that it was the prostitutes who were usually arrested, not the pimps or brothel owners (Vandenberg 1997, 22–26). The brothel owners and traffickers were usually Israeli citizens, often

Jews of Russian origin who were labeled locally as the Russian Mafia. "Traffickers in Ukraine reportedly have begun exploiting an Israeli law that allows all Jews to immigrate to Israel by providing victims with false Jewish identity documents" (U.S. Department of State Trafficking Report, 2005).

Unlike Thailand, Israel is not a regional magnet for sex tourists, and prostitution is not a major avenue of female employment. Prostitutes constituted only 1 percent of the female labor force in Israel in 1996 in contrast to Thailand, in which prostitutes constituted 6 to 14 percent. But prostitutes from the former Soviet Union then constituted 20 to 25 percent of the 8,000 to 10,000 prostitutes in Israel (Vandenberg 1997, 5) as contrasted to the 3 percent of prostitutes from Burma in Thailand. Although prostitution in Israel is not a major source of employment or of national income (estimated to be 0.6 percent of total income in 1993 using international data sources), it is a highly lucrative industry for the traffickers and brothel owners. "Estimates vary, but some experts believe that the prostitution mafia in Israel generates a turnover of $450 million annually" (Vandenberg 1997, 18). Prostitutes were unlikely to go to the police because they could be deported, and the debt follows them home as well as do threats against their family if they defect.

Young women were lured from their homelands by newspaper advertisements and local recruiting offices promising good jobs in Israel. They were smuggled in by various means—forged documents, tourist visas, and fictitious claims of relationship—and on some occasions real tourists were kidnapped (Vandenberg 1997, 6–9). An Israeli study revealed that most of the trafficked women work in the 300 to 400 escort agencies and brothels in Israel, most of which are in Tel Aviv. The Labor and Welfare Committee of the Knesset reported that more than 1,000 minors around the country were involved in prostitution with their parents' encouragement, because of their dire economic situations (*Ha'aretz* 2004).

On entering Israel, the women were told that they had a bond to repay both for the trip and for false papers—up to $20,000—which was to be taken from their nominal wages. So in effect, they received virtually nothing (Vandenberg 1997, 15–16). Women from ex-Soviet countries also went to agencies set up to secure employment for them abroad. The agencies advanced costs of documents and airline tickets, causing the women to incur debts of $1,500 to $30,000 (Caldor, Gallster, and Steinzor 1997, 14).

An Israeli Knesset report in 2005 estimated that between 3,000 and 5,000 women had been smuggled into Israel in the previous four years to work as prostitutes. The report told of the sale of women for as much as $10,000. They were forced to work up to eighteen hours a day. "On average the women receive only three percent of the money they earn from prostitution, the report said" (BBC News, March 24, 2005). An earlier report to the Knesset Committee estimated that "one million 'visits' are made by clients every month to brothels in the country who channel some $450 million annually into the local sex industry" (*Jerusalem Post,* March 17, 2004; March 24, 2005).

Amnesty International and the U.S. Department of State "have also reported an alarming increase in prostitution rings in Israel" (BBC News, March 24, 2005). Amnesty International testified (before the UN Committee on the Elimination of Discrimination Against Women) in 2005 "that the smuggling of individuals or groups of foreign workers, including sex workers, is tolerated, so long as the smugglers are known not to bring into the country individuals who may pose a threat to Israel's security."

Trafficked women are viewed by Israeli authorities as illegal immigrants and are subject to deportation. Although the government established a shelter for trafficked women in 2004, it was also reported in 2004 that unless they agreed to testify against their traffickers, such women were still held in detention facilities. The Parliamentary Committee on the Trafficking of Women said in its report of April 2005 that the women should be referred to shelters. However, in March 2006, the Israeli Interior Ministry offered an incentive to trafficked women who were willing to testify by giving them Israeli work permits for a year and residence in a new shelter offering support services that enabled them to find new occupations (*Jerusalem Post,* March 31, 2006). Enforcement efforts by the government appear to have raised the sales price of such women (*Jerusalem Post,* March 31, 2006; August 18, 2006; November 15, 2006).

As expected, police corruption and cooperation with pimps as sources of information on crimes were noted in Israel as in Thailand. In both countries, forced prostitutes of alien origin are politically and numerically invisible—although they can be readily observed on the streets and in the brothels.

In May 2000, Amnesty International (AI) charged that hundreds of young women who had been bought and sold by organized crime rings were held in debt bondage in Israel, and the government had "failed to take adequate measures to prevent, investigate, prosecute and punish human rights abuses committed against trafficked women" (Motro 2000, 22). The U.S. Embassy in Tel Aviv sponsored and convened a conference that year in Tel Aviv on trafficking. The AI critique and U.S. pressure led the Israeli Knesset in July 2000 to pass a law, "lingering in Knesset committee for years," that penalizes traffickers with ten to sixteen years' imprisonment (Motro 2000, 22).

Israel was in the third tier of the U.S. Department of State's first report on trafficking in 2001, but was elevated to the second, or middle, tier in 2002 (see table 3.1) for "making significant efforts" to comply (U.S. Department of State 2002, 63). That same month, a reporter wrote of a "sting" operation that led to eighteen arrests of traffickers who brought in Ukrainian women (sold for about $7,500) smuggled by Bedouins from Egypt into Israel. U.S. pressure instigated the raids; Israeli sociologist Chaim Nardi complained about the lack of citizen support for suppression of the trade in women (Gutman, June 28, 2002, A8). Other attempts to protect women from the Russian federation from being trafficked stem from nonprofit organizations in Europe.

The pattern of arrests and prosecutions of traffickers in 2004 was much higher in Israel than in Thailand (as reported by the U.S. Department of State Trafficking Report 2005). In Israel, 28 cases out of 103 arrests (or 27 percent) resulted in convictions, whereas in Thailand, 12 of 307 arrests (or 4 percent) led to convictions. There are many more shelter facilities in Thailand than in Israel. Conservative estimates are that there are at least ten times more prostitutes in Thailand than in Israel. Police corruption has been observed in both countries. In neither country were patrons prosecuted.

However, the Knesset in October 2006 passed comprehensive legislation prohibiting trafficking that provides compensation for victims of trafficking. "The new law was supported by Knesset members across the political spectrum ... in the wake of the U.S. State Department downgrading Israel's rating in this area, [which] could have resulted in a cut-off of U.S. government aid to Israel" (NIF News, October 20, 2006).

Explaining Contemporary Slavery

Slavery, whether in camps, brothels, or homes, depends on violence against the powerless who are excluded or cut off from protection of kin, community, and religious or secular authority. In the past, enslavement was a result of capture in war, kidnapping, tribute and tax payment or debt, punishment for crimes, abandonment and sale of children, or selling of self (Patterson 1982, 105). In the twentieth and early twenty-first centuries, slavery was still a result of capture in war, kidnapping, debt bondage, and sale of children. Enslavement as punishment for crimes has also been observed in communist countries. Contemporary enslavement in capitalist states in which slavery is illegal is usually based on some contract leading to debt bondage. Most often in these states, it is maintained by criminal networks and occupies a small niche in the labor market.

Is modern slavery new? Bales (1999, 2004, 2005) contrasts the "new slavery" with the old slavery of the nineteenth-century slave owner of Africans in the Americas, who owned, imported, and sold slaves. In continents and countries where bondage is most prevalent in the twenty-first century, it is not new. Bonded labor in India and Pakistan and slavery in Mauritania are continuing phenomena going back to before the nineteenth century. Thailand has a continuing socially sanctioned tradition of volunteering and selling women, which undoubtedly expanded in the 1960s with the influx from Vietnam of U.S. soldiers. Brazil, which continues to deny the impact of race and slavery on its social structure, was "the last country in the Americas to abolish legal slavery"; indeed, "It is hard to know if slavery ever completely disappeared in Brazil" (Bales 1999, 124).

Looking at slavery in countries with high prevalence, one might ask: Can slavery be explained primarily by poverty? Bales relates the "new slavery" of slaveholders with no legal claim but nominal contract relationships to the existence of millions of "disposable people," driven by overpopulation, rapid and unequal development, and landlessness, to be lured into servitude or to sell themselves (1999, 12–18). Since poverty makes people more likely to accept exploitation because they have no or few alternatives, this seems to make sense.

I probed this question by starting with a more general hypothesis: The greater the economic development, the less prevalent slavery will be. My statistical analyses (not shown herein) of the prevalence of slavery in the 183 countries in the study of life integrity violations in 1997, employing Bales's scale of contemporary slavery (2002) and the 1997 level of economic development, showed that slavery was highly and negatively related to economic development (indexed by gross national product). It is not clear from an investigation at one point in time what is cause and what is effect. It could be that extreme poverty leads to slavery or that slavery undermines development. Slavery reinforces exploitation without risk-taking or entrepreneurship.

Bales's proposal is plausible: Extreme poverty predisposes people to become or to remain slaves, but that is not the only factor. There is something else mediating the prevalence of slavery besides the characteristics and condition of the victims—the context and beliefs of the enslavers and bystanders.

Findings reveal that slavery is less likely to be high in Christian states than in non-Christian states (see also the discussion in chapter 2). Because one might correctly note that Christian states are more likely to be states of high development, the prevalence of slavery can also be related to the economic development of the states classified by different dominant religions.

Among non-Christian states, twenty-one of thirty-seven (56.8 percent) at the lowest level of development are high (levels 3 and 4) on slavery; among Christian states at this level, eight of twenty-two (36.4 percent) are high. Slavery is more likely to decline among Christian countries as development increases than it is in non-Christian countries.

The non-Christian countries are predominantly African and Asian, regions of historic enslavement, exploitation, and subordination. Slavery was and is associated with beliefs linked to hegemonic religions in these areas. Religion often defines who is excluded from the universe of obligation, and religious civilizations have been involved in the slave trade and in the abolition of the slave trade. Condemnation of slavery on religious grounds among Christians ignited the abolition movement in England and the United States, a movement that succeeded in extinguishing slavery in the Americas and Europe in the nineteenth century, despite the intense opposition of Christian slaveholders (Davis 1984; Drescher and Engerman 1998; Fredrickson 1981, 152). To examine the impact of religion, states were classed by the dominant religion—the religion of the majority—in 2000.

The largest group of non-Christian countries is the majority Muslim countries. The prevalence of slavery is also related to religion in the seven Southeast Asian states that are predominantly Hindu and Buddhist (the latter also affected by caste) as compared to other states. Five of these 7 states (71.4 percent) are high on slavery. All these states are at the lowest level of development, except Thailand and Sri Lanka, which are at the low-intermediate level.

The Indian subcontinent accounts for the majority of slaves today. Among the 27 million slaves in the world today, Bales estimates that 15 to 20 million or 56 to 74 percent are in bonded labor in South

Asia—India, Pakistan, Bangladesh, and Nepal—states with present or supposedly past caste systems (Bales 2004, 4).

In Africa, the differentiation between Arabs and non-Arabs has been reinforced by the expansion of Islam as a result of conquest. The self-interest of dominant ethnic groups is conventionally rationalized by attributing inferiority to the enslaved group. Racism did not lead to slavery but was a result of slavery itself in the Islamic slave trade, as it was in the Christian slave trade (Davis 1984, 38–45). Arab slavers demonized and stereotyped black Africans, as did Christian slave traders. "The similarity between Muslim and later Christian racial imagery tells us less about black Africans than about the common pressures felt by a 'white' ruling race intent on celebrating its own progressive civilization while keeping slaves or an underclass of freedmen in a state of permanent subordination" (Davis 1984, 45).

The antislavery movement was a foreign import in the Islamic world, and slavery was only formally abolished in many Muslim states in the twentieth century after independence (Lewis 1990, 78–80; Lovejoy 2000, 292–293). The modern victims of de facto slavery in Sudan and Mauritania are inhabitants of states justifying their rule as Islamic states. Islamic nationalism and radical Islam today seem to have idealized a premodern state. Yet, Koranic law is an inadequate explanation of Sudan's instigation of enslavement of the Dinka (usually Christian) and Mauritania's toleration of the continued enslavement of black Africans (usually Muslim).

Rather, it is the caste-like notion usually labeled as racism that explains slavery; their belief that some people are intrinsically inferior enables Arab masters (who also might be dark-skinned) to exploit black Africans. In both Sudan and Mauritania, slavery is sanctioned by Islamic authorities, and many of the enslaved in Mauritania appear to believe their condition is the will of Allah. But the victims do not concur in Sudan, where the enslavers are Muslim and the victims are non-Muslim. How Islamic slavery rested on race is manifested in language change: "the Arabic word for slave, 'abd, had come to mean only a black slave and in some regions, to refer to any black whether slave or free" (Davis 1984, 33).

Similarly, the Indian word for caste, *varna*, originally denoted color. N. K. Dutt believes that it arose from a "racial struggle between the fair-skinned Aryans and the dark-skinned non-Aryans" (1968, Vol. 1, 29). There are different interpretations of the origins and perpetuation of caste, and sometimes interpretation reflects caste or group interests of the interpreter (Dirks 2001, 235–249).

Like the '*abd*, the *dalits* (untouchables) in India are seen as essentially inferior. They are below the caste hierarchy of Hindu society (defined initially by Aryan conquerors), a system that defines the degree of dignity and vocation of different strata. It is seen by many Indians to be natural that dalits enact their duty to do the hard and dirty work, that they are deprived of dignity, and that they have no protection.

The vulnerability of the victims of slavery often depends on social and religious stigma and powerlessness related to race, caste status, and gender as well as poverty. The enslavers are heirs to doctrines of inferiority of non-Aryans, noncaste Hindus, non-Muslims, non-Arabs, and nonwhites. There still is, as Orlando Patterson observed about premodern slavery, "a universal reluctance to enslave members of one's own community, hence the need to redefine them as outsiders" (Patterson 1982, 178).

The transmission of belief in inferiority to such groups also enables them to be good slaves. Females, children, the poor, and untouchables are generally expected to be submissive and usually comply. "Cultural norms have prepared these young women for control and compliance" (Bales 2002, 86). We might view this as a culture of abasement.

Women in poorer and unstable societies are particularly vulnerable to trafficking because of sex discrimination (reducing their choices within their society) and the culture of abasement. The sex trade exists to satisfy taken-for-granted conceptions of male needs. East and West concur in the belief that women can be bought and sold.

In the case of Thai and Burmese women, patriarchal attitudes and cupidity have allowed fathers and male relatives to sell women, turning them into a commodity. "A recent survey in the northern provinces [of Thailand] found that of the families who sold their daughters, two-thirds could afford not to do so but 'instead preferred to buy color televisions and video equipment'" (Bales 1999, 40). The sellers are driven not by need but by greed. We cannot understand the "new slavery" just by taking into account the predictive factors Bales adduces (2004, 8–13), but, rather, we must focus on the attitudes and values that frame the perception of certain people as suitable for enslavement.

Women, however, are not always simply victims of the exploitation of male relatives but might be implicated in their plight, especially in the states of the former Soviet Union where there are few opportunities for work; it is estimated that 70 to 80 percent of the unemployed in the Russian Federation are women (Richard 1999, 43). Although they might have expected to become prostitutes, they did not expect to become slaves—beaten, raped, unpaid, and stripped of passports, documents, and dignity. Such trafficked women are usually far from home, outsiders who are unable to flee or protest because they know that the authorities would not listen or would deport them. Strangers and foreign workers are outside the political community. This often is one of the prerequisites for trafficking overlooked by Bales (1999, 2004).

The other precondition is the impunity of the buyers. This might decline as countries of origin of the male tourists warn them that they can be prosecuted at home. The United States has not only warned travelers but has prosecuted men for molesting children—boys and girls—abroad (Farrell 2004). The impunity of the customers—a prerequisite of prostitution that is taken for granted—is now an international condition that can be changed. Globalization can be used to reform the moral economy, promoting intolerance rather than toleration of trafficking and sex tourism. The moral economy has changed before: The English did emancipate their slaves without threat of a civil war (Hochschild 2005). The twenty-first century offers another opportunity to end slavery.

4
States of Terror in the Late Twentieth Century: Algeria and Argentina

Nothing has changed,
The body is a reservoir of pain;
it has to eat and breathe the air, and sleep;
it has thin skin and the blood is just beneath it;
it has a good supply of teeth and fingernails;
its bones can be broken; its joints can be stretched,
In tortures, all of this is considered.

Nothing has changed,
The body still trembles as it trembled
before Rome was founded and after,
in the twentieth century before and after Christ.
Tortures are just what they were, only the earth has shrunk
and whatever goes on sounds as if it's just a room away.

—Wislawa Szymborska, "Tortures,"
in *View with a Grain of Sand* (1995)

The images of the historic instruments of modern state terror still persist: the guillotine from the French Revolution, the camps in the Gulag Archipelago and show trials from Stalinist Russia, the German concentration and death camps, and rampaging mobs humiliating and torturing enemies of the day during China's cultural revolution. They are enduring archetypes of terror, genocide, and state power unchecked—usually in the name of some utopia.

Terror can emerge from the people, from the state, and from antistate movements—and these can interact. However, the state had the greater capacity for organized, lasting, and pervasive terror in the twentieth century. Terror states endured in the twentieth century for up to half of the century. Successors of the initial terror regime might become convinced that terror no longer works and is unnecessary or dysfunctional. The Soviet Union showed stages of evolution from a terror state to a bureaucratic authoritarian state before the USSR disintegrated. China relied on mass participation in terror and intimidation rather than state control from the top, a mode of control invalidated by the successors of Mao. Nazi Germany (whose terror was relatively constrained against its "Aryan" citizens) only changed because it was defeated.

This chapter considers the origins of modern terror and how it arose in the contemporary period in Algeria and Argentina. Chapter 5 considers Guatemala and Iraq and some conclusions from chapters 4 and 5.

Torture, Cruelty, and Punishment

Although people in many states have experienced state terror, collective terror, and transnational terrorism—murders by antistate actors—up to the present day, it can be easy to forget its essence. Terror results from extrajudicial execution, torture, disappearance, bombing in public places, maiming, and public humiliation and condemnation. Regardless of its source, terror terrifies. Unlike punishment, which, however harsh, is a response to violation of a rule, which one could avoid by obeying the rule (Walter 1964), there is no way to avoid terror.

Terror has often been linked to cruelty, sometimes not only as a means of punishment but as entertainment for the masses. The Roman Empire's spectacles, which included humans pitted against animals in the arena, amused citizens and disposed of religious minorities and other expendable people—slaves. Emperor Tertullian recalled the shouts, "'Christians to the lions'" (Tertullian ca. 160–230 B.C.E., cited in Sider 2001). Mass participation in cruel punishments has not disappeared, but the predominant strategy of modern terror—especially torture—is to diminish visibility, to hide the process.

Torture is not just cruelty for its own sake but is an instrument of control, used throughout history primarily to gain information. Torture was used in ancient Greece and Rome first against slaves and then against debased freemen (Peters, 1985, 11–39). For more than two millennia, Rome, the Roman Catholic Church, and Western states maimed, pressed, punctured, and otherwise tortured suspects under interrogation to induce them to give information, to name names, and to confess to the charges of the Inquisitor or prosecutor. However, in England, torture declined after 1166 and was outlawed in 1215 for a simple reason. The English system of law was distinctive in that conviction did not depend on confession as in other parts of Europe; juries determined guilt or innocence (Langbein 1976; Peters 1985, 58–59).

Punishment as well as interrogation relied on physical invasion of the human body in premodern Europe. Two hundred years ago, European states routinely physically marked and maimed the bodies of criminals (Foucault 1977). Within the last 250 years, there has been in the West a revolution in law and consciousness requiring respect for the bodies of the accused and relying on other means of discovery and punishment. Torture was prohibited or formally abolished in many states in the eighteenth and nineteenth centuries after the revolutions in the United States and France in the late eighteenth century, in Russia in 1801, and in Japan in 1879. (This is not to say that torture was never used after those dates, but abolition was a step toward doing away with routinized practices and making instances of torture subject to prosecution.) Yet there is no lineal progress in abolishing torture; after 1917 the Soviet Union and Nazi Germany used and justified torture and terror, setting the guidelines for the practice of many states after 1945.

Twentieth-Century Models and Diffusion of Terror

In the twentieth century (after 1919), states that repudiated the democratic model were the greatest employers of terror. In Europe, new regimes based on communism and fascism revived the use of terror but with distinctive differences. Both the Soviet Union and Germany created specialized secret police agencies (the Cheka and

NKVD in the Soviet Union and the Gestapo in Germany) and security and intelligence services to spy on and control their populations. But propaganda and participation, partly manipulated by mass parties and party-controlled organizations (free associations were banned), also created support for these regimes, forming the basis of a model Hannah Arendt and others after her called totalitarian (1966). The totalitarian models based on fascism spread in the interwar years.

The uses of terror reflected the differences between the Soviet Union and Nazi Germany, were inspired by very different ideologies, and faced varying internal support and threats. The Soviet Union was based on an ideal of a classless state embracing all the people. Nazi Germany frankly proclaimed its end was a racial state. The Soviets most often created victims within their society, millions of victims by arbitrary labeling—"enemy of the people"—victims of all classes and nations (Werth 1999). Nazi Germany restricted itself to victims outside its idealized Aryan community—*Volksgemeinschaft*—excluding Jews and Roma—except for Aryans challenging its rule, communists, and dissidents. Germans who did not fall into suspect categories had little to fear (Johnson 1999, 485):

> The overwhelming majority of ordinary German citizens, however, never became targets of the terror and were usually left alone to control their own lives. The terror was therefore not the blanket, indiscriminate terror of popular myth.… Most Germans may not even have realized until very late in the war, if ever, that they were living in a vile dictatorship.… The great majority of ordinary Germans had believed that they had little reason to fear the Gestapo or the concentration camps.

Terror and torture (now defined by international law) expanded from totalitarian states to colonial and authoritarian states after the Cold War began, especially after 1970 in Latin America—see box 4.1. "Disappearance," a practice begun by Nazi Germany in occupied Europe under the "Night and Fog" decree (1941), spread to Latin America and elsewhere and was accompanied by torture and secret incarceration.

The Latin American military and torturers were aided (and sometimes trained) by the U.S. Army and intelligence agencies who had analyzed German practices and learned from German and East European "experts" in counterguerrilla war who emigrated to the United States (as well as to Latin America) after World War II. These experts were enabled by official complicity to evade U.S. immigration laws

Box 4.1 International Law on Torture and Some Accounts

Convention Against Torture and Other Cruel, Inhuman or Degrading Treatment or Punishment (Adapted by the United Nations General Assembly on 10 December 1984):

Article 1.

1. For the purposes of this Convention, the term "torture" means any act by which severe pain or suffering, whether physical or mental, is intentionally inflicted on a person for such purposes as obtaining from him or a third person information or a confession, punishing him for an act he or a third person has committed or is suspected of having committed, or intimidating or coercing him or a third person, or for any reason based on discrimination of any kind, when such pain or suffering is inflicted by or at the initiation of or with the consent or acquiescence of a public official or other person acting in an official capacity. It does not include pain or suffering arising only from, inherent in or incidental to lawful sanctions.

Testimony of a Victim: Jacobo Timerman (Argentina)

> In the year and a half I spent under house arrest I devoted much thought to my attitude during torture sessions and during the period of solitary confinement. I realized that, instinctively, I'd developed an attitude of absolute passivity. Some fought against being carried to the torture tables; others begged not to be tortured; others insulted their torturers. I represented sheer passivity. Because my eyes were blindfolded, I was led by the hand. And I went. The silence was part of the terror. Yet I did not utter a word. I was told to undress. And I did so, passively, I was told, when I sat on a bed, to lie down. And, passively, I did so. This passivity, I believe, preserved a great deal of energy and left me with all my strength to withstand the torture. I felt I was becoming a vegetable, casting aside all logical emotions and sensations—fear, hatred, vengeance—for any emotion or sensation meant wasting useless energy.

Source: Jacobo Timerman, *Prisoner without a Name, Cell without a Number* [New York: Knopf, 1981], 34–35.

An Account about a Tutor of Torturers, Dan Mitrione

> This testimony by a former Cuban double agent, Manuel Hevia Cosculluela, who served with the CIA in Uruguay's police program, tells of a conversation with Dan Mitrione, a U.S. advisor who was later shot to death after being kidnapped by the Tupamaro guerrillas. According to Hevia, Mr. Mitrione said:
>> When you receive a subject, the first thing to do is determine his physical state, his degree of resistance, through a medical examination. A premature death means a failure by the technician.
>>
>> Another important thing to know is exactly how far you can go given the political situation and the personality of the prisoner. It is very important to know beforehand whether we have the luxury of letting the subject die....
>>
>> Before all else, you must be efficient. You must cause only the damage that is strictly necessary, not a bit more. We must control our tempers in any case. You have to act with the efficiency and cleanliness of a surgeon and with the perfection of an artist.

Source: A. J. Langguth, "Torture's Teachers," *New York Times,* June 11, 1979, A19.

barring Nazi collaborators (Langguth 1979; McClintock 1992, 59–99, 258–262; Simpson 1988; Wechsler 1990). The readiness of Latin American ruling elites and classes to use such methods was evidenced by earlier decades of repression, cruelty against indigenous people and peasants, and authoritarian traditions.

In the bloc of states that developed communist regimes (or spoke in the name of Marxist-Leninist rhetoric), the Soviet model (relying after the death of Stalin in 1953 more on economic sanctions and incentives than on terror) was emulated in Eastern Europe (occupied by the Soviet Army after World War II), Cuba, Africa, and Asia. In the latter regions, it was more likely to lead to bloody purges and executions, such as in Ethiopia, North Vietnam, and Afghanistan, the latter invaded by the Soviet Union in 1979 after a communist coup in 1978 triggered a civil war (Bolouque 1999). The Maoist model of the People's Republic of China employed mass participation to punish and shame, periodic purges of party leadership, "reeducation," and labor camps. A variant of this was emulated in Cambodia, with disastrous results (see chapter 6).

Since World War II, terror has increasingly come to be used as a means of control, instigated by reasons of state and by the fears of leaders. Despotic leaders tend to view all opposition (which they create by their methods) as a plot against them (Fein 1991). Some characteristic means of state terror include extrajudicial execution (without charge or trial), "disappearances" (abduction and incarceration or killing without acknowledgment), and torture. Although some bodies are hidden, others are purposely exposed. The display of dead, tortured, and dismembered bodies in public places creates further terror and degrades the victims' humanity in death. Other means of intimidation include death threats against political activists, human rights lawyers, witnesses of targeted persons, officers of human rights groups, and relatives.

Prevalence of Torture

Among contemporary gross violations of human rights, the most common institution detected is a pattern of torture used by police and jailers, a threshold practice that can escalate to terror—see box 4.2 for definitions and justifications of torture. Torture is monitored by many human rights nongovernmental organizations (HRNGOs) and some governmental and intergovernmental organizations. Such HRNGOs, along with health professionals, former victims, and others

---

Box 4.2 Vocabulary and Justifications of Terror

The Vocabulary of Terror in Argentina

Boleta (n. ticket) "You've got your ticket," prisoners were told when they were about to be transferred.

Desaparecido/a (n. Something that, or someone who disappeared).

Huevera (n. egg carton). Torture chamber in the ESMA (prison camp) whose walls were lined with egg cartons to muffle the sounds.

Parrilla (n. traditional Argentine grill for cooking meat). The metal table on which *chupados* ("those who have been sucked up" [i.e., disappeared]) were laid out to be tortured.

Picana (n. electric cattle prod). Main instrument for torture. Invented in Argentina in 1930 and routinely used in police stations ever since.

Quirófano (n. operating theater). Torture chamber.

Rectoscopo (n. rectoscope). Anal torture device invented by Julio Simon, the extremely sadistic anti-Semite known as Julian the Turk.

Submarino (n. submarine; traditional Argentine children's treat consisting of a chocolate bar slowly melting in a cup of warm milk). Form of torture in which the prisoner's head was held under water befouled with urine and feces. When the victim was on the verge of suffocation, his head would be raised and then dunked again.

Trabajo (n. work). Torture. In some camps, "work cards" were filled out after every session. Arranged horizontally were the following headings: Interrogator, Group, Case (prisoner's number), Hour Begun, Hour Finished, State (i.e., "Normal" or "Dead").

Trasladar (v. to transfer, to move). To take prisoners away to be killed.

Traslado/a (n. one who has been transferred, one who was a transfer, one who "got his ticket").

Vuelo (n. flight). Death-flight. Death-flight duty was rotated to virtually all naval officers, who were ordered to load *desaparecidos* onto planes, undress them, and throw them into the sea.

Source: Marguerite Feitlowitz, *A Lexicon of Terror: Argentina and the Legacies of Torture* (New York: Oxford University Press, 1998), 51–60.

---

concerned, have established clinics for rehabilitation of victims of torture and codes of ethics to deter medical participation and to prevent torture, have instituted lawsuits to hold perpetrators accountable, and have organized conferences, journals, and publications to document torture.

Unlike the brutality of much contemporary civil war, which is crude, with untutored, repetitive, and improvised atrocities—rape, cutting off limbs, burning homes—state torture is carefully crafted, justified by

---

Box 4.2

Explanations by Brazilian Torturers

We worked as if at war. We were patriots, we were defending our country, we were proud of that, so they were adversaries, the enemy. We were proud of what we did ... working in DOPS [Social and Political Police] ... ridding the country of a threat, of a Communist regime.... We [were] people doing a patriotic job, a big job, an important job.... We were a religious people, a Christian people.

Brazil is a Catholic country. In Brazil they are used to this kind of behavior—like torture, for example, because Catholic churches tortured people for years and years, centuries and centuries.

Living in an aggressive environment affects you, contaminates you little by little, without you feeling it.

[Torture] is used on thieves and assailants because ... sometimes the evidence is so obvious and they deny things so cynically that if a policeman working with him doesn't have a certain balance, he'll slap him around a little [on the "parrot's perch," where the victim is suspended with legs bent above and arms below].

Torture is zealousness in trying to discover, unravel a crime. [The police] handle a lot of work. [But] we don't have the resources to work on an investigation ... [so] the shortest route is by torturing.

Source: Martha K. Huggins, Mika Haritos-Fatouros, and Philip G. Zimbardo, *Violence Workers: Police Torturers and Murderers Reconstruct Brazilian Atrocities* (Berkeley: University of California Press, 2002), 198–201.

---

doctrine, and routinized. Specialized agencies develop: secret police, centralized intelligence agencies, paramilitaries, and death squads. These are usually coordinated by authoritarian and military regimes, which have learned from the past, from present patrons, and from their neighbors.

Although democratic states have at times sanctioned the use of torture and agents of the state sometimes initiate torture when it is not state policy, the victims do not usually disappear; they retain a legal and social identity. During the last two decades of the twentieth century, in democratic states in which torture or ill treatment (governments consistently refuse to label their practices as torture) was government policy, torture was more likely than in authoritarian states to be checked by constitutional means or regional courts.

Chapter 4

Strategy of Inquiry

In this chapter and in chapter 5, we probe how and why terror was selected or evolved in four cases: French Algeria (1954–1962), Argentina (1976–1981), Guatemala (1966–1996), and Iraq (1968–2003). These cases include poor states (Guatemala, Algeria) and upper-middle-income states (Iraq and Argentina); Christian (France and Latin America) and Muslim states (Algeria and Iraq); a state colonized until 1962 (Algeria) and independent states (Argentina, Guatemala, and Iraq); and states allied with the West (France, Argentina, Guatemala) and Iraq, originally affiliated with the Soviet bloc. They include an ethnically homogenous state (Argentina) and ethnically diverse states (Algeria, Guatemala, Iraq). They are states with political rebellions (French Algeria, Guatemala) and states in which opposition was suppressed (Argentina and Iraq) before the terror. They were selected because of both their diversity and the extent of documentation. The political diversity and economic range of these states are consistent with evidence that the superpower (Soviet-American) rivalry and use of proxies did not explain most cases of political terror. The evidence also points to the fact that "a country's level of economic prosperity does not seem to be related in an obvious way to political terror" (McCann and Gibney 1993, 10).

States of terror such as Guatemala and Iraq can become states of genocide (to be discussed in chapters 5 and 6). Genocidal massacres by both sides were observed in Algeria. Many Argentineans consider what occurred there during the so-called Dirty War a case of genocide (Braylan et al. 2000, 5–8; Feierstein 2006; Feitlowitz 1998, 142). Although this does not conform to international law, some genocide scholars would expand the notion of a group to include political victims or any victims as defined by the perpetrator (discussed in chapter 6).

This chapter and chapter 5 ask:

1. How are the perpetrators and victims related? How are the perpetrators selected, trained, and desensitized? What is the role of other citizens, leaders, and bystanders? Do they support the state?
2. How does the type of government affect, enable, or accelerate its use of torture and terror? What was the form of government before and after their use?
3. What is the role of foreign patrons and models?

4. What are the justifications for terror and torture?
5. What is the context, crisis, or problematic situation in which torture and terror arose?
6. How did it end?
7. What were the effects?

Algeria

The Algerian war (1954–1962) was the first major post–World War II example of collective terrorism and revolutionary war within a state. Algeria was formally not a colony but a part of France for more than a century, although the majority of Algerians who were Muslim were not French citizens. In Algeria, both sides developed doctrines and practices that were repeated in succeeding decades. Revolutionary war and counterinsurgency became accepted euphemisms for collective terror and antistate terrorism (on the part of the ruled) and state terror by the rulers.

Algeria was conquered and annexed by France (1830–1842), defined as a department of France with its deputies included in the French Parliament. Much of the political history of Algeria preceding and during the Algerian War (I have relied on Horne [1987] herein unless other sources are cited) can be understood by the conflict and confluence of interests among three parties: (1) the government and public of France, (2) the indigenous Algerians and their movements, and (3) European Algerians and their movements. Until 1959 all parties in France from left to right considered "Algérie Française," that is to say, an integral part of France.

The people of Algeria were divided by religion, nation of origin, and ethnicity: Muslims (89 percent)—of whom the majority were Arabs with a minority of Berbers—and Europeans (11 percent) known as *pieds noir*. The latter included Christians of French, Spanish, and Italian descent, and Jews. Jews constituted one-fifth of the non-Muslim population and were usually classed as Europeans, although many had lived in Algeria for hundreds of years, predating the French conquest.

Regardless of the class and educational differences within both Muslim and non-Muslim communities, political rights of the pieds noir trumped those of the Muslims. Europeans were French citizens, whereas Muslims were French subjects. To become a French citizen, Muslims had to renounce their rights under Islamic law, which meant virtual apostasy.

However, the Jews of Algeria had been granted French citizenship by the Cremieux Decree (1870), although their citizenship rights were stripped during World War II, when the collaborationist Vichy government of France passed many antisemitic measures discriminating among French citizens before the German occupation (Fein 1979, 110–113). Jews in Algeria were then expelled from European schools and menaced with the threat of deportation to detention and extermination camps.

Postwar French offers of reform to Algerian Muslims, such as promising them two-fifths of the seats in a local assembly (although they constituted nine-tenths of the population), were foiled by the opposition of the pieds noir. Muslim liberals became increasingly marginalized in their own community, as their moderation reaped no rewards. Both economically and socially, their community lost ground. Although there were class and social differences within both the Muslim and European communities, the Muslim community had become increasingly pauperized because of rising population, a decline in their landholdings, and high unemployment, which led to increased urbanization and an exodus of the Algerian working class to France.

Despite (or because of) the wide income gap among the pieds noir, most shared a uniform disdain for Muslims. "Analyzing the various degrees of disdain in Algeria, a pieds noir journalist, Albert-Paul Lentin, observed how 'the Frenchman despises the Spaniard, who despises the Italian, who despises the Jew; all in turn, despising the Arab'" (Horne 1987, 58).

Violence among French troops, European Algerians, and Muslim Algerians preceded the Algerian war. Genocidal massacres on both Muslim and non-Muslim sides followed a 1945 celebration of the end of World War II, which became a riot in Setif, with Muslims indiscriminately "killing, raping, mutilating, pillaging, burning" Europeans and French—including Senegalese—troops. The latter responded with summary executions and reprisal massacres. The Muslim dead (by estimate of the French authorities) outnumbered the Europeans by 15 to 1 (Kuper 1981, 60–61).

As in other instances of collective violence in ethnically stratified societies, violations by each side were used as a justification by the other to punish the perpetrators collectively for their crimes. Each side viewed its violence as a just punishment for a group outside its universe of obligation, a member of which had violated their group. The other group saw it as a crime, which, in turn, justified their collective punishment or vengeance (Fein 1977, ch. 1).

In the decade after the Setif massacre, the Algerian Front for National Liberation (FLN) was formed by Algerian Muslim leaders who believed that their existing moderate parties were ineffectual. The initial proclamation of the FLN in 1954 called for "revolutionary struggle" to attain "National Independence through restoration of the Algerian state, sovereign, democratic, and social, within the framework of the principles of Islam [with] preservation of all fundamental freedoms, without distinction of races or religion," promising that French citizens in Algeria would have a choice between French and Algerian citizenship.

The FLN at first attacked military targets (French troops and police) with little impact. The government of French prime minister Pierre Mendes-France (which had recently evacuated from Indochina) depended on support from the pieds noir bloc and reiterated that Algeria would continue to be French. Its policy of "integration ... [was] viewed with distrust by Europeans and Muslims alike" (Horne 1987, 116). Jacques Soustelle, appointed governor general of Algeria by Mendes-France, forbade collective punishment and indiscriminate reprisals against Algerians, but his order was undermined by his subordinates, who ordered Algerians to supply collective labor in response to FLN destruction of telephone poles. Soustelle himself promised revenge at the funeral of a murdered French administrator.

The FLN escalated the conflict by authorizing a policy of collective terrorism—"total war on all French civilians, regardless of age and sex"—in June 1955. "'To colonialism's policy of *collective repression* [author's italics] we must reply with collective reprisals against all Europeans, military and civil, who are all united behind the crimes committed upon our people. For them, no pity, no quarter!'" (Horne 1987, 119). The FLN also executed Muslim moderates who stood in its way.

The most notorious collective execution (organized by special squads) was in the mining town of El-Halia, in which a minority of 130 Europeans worked with 2,000 Muslims "who for years had coexisted amicably ... with a rare degree of equality" (Horne 1987, 120). The Muslim mineworkers either disappeared before the FLN squads came, turned away, or collaborated with the attackers as four groups of fifteen to twenty men each went from house to house killing, slitting throats, and disemboweling the inhabitants. This attack provoked a French Army massacre in reprisal, and the remaining settlers established "vigilance committees." By French estimates, there were about ten Muslims killed for each European killed in these massacres; by FLN estimates, it was closer to one hundred to one (Horne 1987, 121–122).

The FLN turned from mass participation attacks on Europeans to bombings (secretly plotted by a few), later trying to restrict the targets to European civilians after being criticized for indiscriminate urban attacks, which also killed Muslims. This strategy instigated the French government to bring in French paratrooper units commanded by Gen. Jacques Massu, who took over command in Algiers in 1957 during the Battle of Algiers. Interrogation and torture became routinized under General Massu's command and seemed to succeed in breaking FLN cells in Algiers and winning the battle—but not the war. As bombing became the FLN strategy against Europeans, torture (principally to get information from Muslim Algerians) became the strategy of the French state.

The use of torture was penalized in the French criminal code and abhorrent in France not only because of the tradition of the Enlightenment and the French Revolution, but also because of the French experience with interrogation by the Gestapo during World War II. Although torture was believed to have been used sporadically in Algeria before 1954, Horne observes that it became so pervasive after 1954 that it instigated criticism from across the French political spectrum—from influential Catholics to leftists. Investigations by a committee of French citizens showed that torture was used under three French cabinet ministers, and General Massu transmitted the orders (Vidal-Naquet 2002 [1962]). Repudiation from different sectors of French public opinion and a resignation within the military in Algeria led the French government to authorize an investigation by its inspector general in the Algerian government, Roger Wuillaume.

The Wuillaume Report in 1955 acknowledged the widespread use of torture and recommended institutionalizing certain methods: "[T]he water and electricity methods, provided they are carefully used ... do not constitute excessive cruelty" (Horne 1987, 197). The report opposed prosecution of perpetrators of torture. General Soustelle "'categorically refused' to accept the Wuillaume conclusions" and filed them away (Horne 1987, 197; Maran 1989, 49–50).

The debate about French methods in Algeria was part of a larger debate about the values, identity, and influence of France as a nation in the world. How could France preserve its rank, power, and prestige in the world? France had retreated from Indochina, planned to give independence to Morocco, and could foresee the end of empire. It increasingly became clear that France was a minor player in the Cold War and that the United States did not support the French desire to retain full control in Algeria.

The United States had guaranteed the maintenance of the French empire after World War II but pressed it to decolonize its black African possessions, refused to support France's retention of Algeria, and, under two presidents (Eisenhower and Kennedy), diplomatically intervened to end the Algerian war. The United States had forced France, Britain, and Israel to get out of Egypt in 1956, ending their expedition to reverse Nasser's nationalization of the Suez Canal. "France was too important to the Americans, indeed the key to much of what happened in Europe, Africa, and Asia from the American perspective, to be allowed to run amok" (Wall 2001, 264). The United States would make no concessions to General de Gaulle on any other issue—the French president had made many demands that were rejected—before the Algerian War was settled (Wall 2001, 261–268).

But simply pulling out of Algeria or granting full autonomy (as in Tunisia and Morocco) was not possible for France because of the claims of French citizens of Algeria—the pieds noir—who regarded Algeria as their homeland and had caused the apartheid-like structure of governance to be created in the first place. There was no guarantee that any of their rights would be respected if France gave in to the demands of the FLN.

This dilemma is in the background of French justifications of torture. Maran ascribes the French use of torture to their belief in their "civilizing mission" in Algeria (1989). However, military and other sources justifying torture cited several rationales, most focusing on its use as a defense against terror.

The most vocal advocate of the civilizing mission was General Massu, who wrote fourteen years later (1971/1972) citing four rationales: First, the objective of the Army was not only to protect the Algerians but to improve their life in all ways—it depended on "this trusting and reciprocal fraternalism." Maran views this as the "mid-twentieth [-century] version of the civilizing mission.... Doubts about Massu's genuine affection for the people of Algeria can only fade on viewing the Massu family's two adopted Muslim children, Malika and Rodolphe" (Maran 1989, 94). Second, Massu observed that it was the Muslim population that was primarily threatened by the FLN, and the job of the French was to protect them from assassinations, mutilations, and burnings organized by the FLN.

Similarly, Père Delarue, chaplain of Massu's paratrooper division, explained that the end justified the means when combating terrorism. "When dealing with recalcitrant prisoners from whom information was urgently needed, it was imperative, Delarue said, to find 'effective methods, even if they are unaccustomed methods, and apply them without weakness'" (Maran 1989, 98). Third, there was moral equivalence in retaliation: "'an eye for an eye, a tooth for a tooth'" (Massu, cited by Maran 1989, 101). These arguments relied on equating FLN atrocities with torture, justifying torture as deserved retaliation. Last, there was the utilitarian moral calculus—injuring one or a few to save the many—which deemed it immoral not to use torture on an individual who might possess knowledge of a bomb, endangering many lives (Maran 1989, 101–102). The "ticking bomb" case is the paradigmatic example cited in many countries to justify torture.

Going beyond justifying torture as a defense, its advocates developed an ideology and methodology for counterinsurgency, best expounded by Col. Roger Trinquier, a member of Massu's paratroopers and a fellow veteran of Indochina. Trinquier asserted in 1961 that "the goal of *modern warfare* is control of the population.... Terrorism then, is a 'weapon of warfare'" that demands an unconventional response to an unconventional situation in order to control the population; "'we must not trifle with our responsibilities ... by refusing interrogation specialists the right to seize the truly guilty terrorist and spare the innocent'" (cited in Maran 1989, 99–100).

Thus torturers became modern professionals—"interrogation specialists." Trinquier was head of a new bureau in Algiers, Dispositif de Protection Urbaine (DPU), which controlled the city by dividing all locales—from sectors to buildings—and appointing local trustworthy men ("generally a Muslim *ancien combattant*") to oversee the population and report on suspicious activity. The DPU drew in an estimated 30 to 40 percent of the male population of the Casbah, using its "interrogation specialists" (Horne 1987, 198–199).

On the Algerian side, FLN terror was calculated by advocates and analysts of terror to be a low-cost strategy, given their resources. Terror was aimed at all Europeans and at Muslims who did not share FLN goals or methods. The FLN could anticipate that its collective terrorism would provoke collective revenge, instigating the French to kill Algerians indiscriminately and thus converting Muslims to the FLN cause.

Frantz Fanon, a psychiatrist from Martinique who came to Algeria in 1953, is often said to have justified collective violence against the colonizer as a "cleansing force" to liberate indigenous people (Fanon 1968 [1961]). But Fanon's work, ended by his early death at age thirty-seven in December 1961, was more complex. He advocated full citizenship for all residents in Algeria, respect for Algerian minorities, and the necessity for fraternal relations with democratic sympathizers among Algeria's European minority and Algeria's Jews who had supported the revolution (Fanon 1963 [1959], 148–157). He also stressed the need to observe the international laws of war, and he criticized the FLN use of terror and collective punishment (Maran 1989, 156–158). He looked forward to a secular democratic state for Algeria—actually the official FLN position in 1956 and 1962—rather than an official Arab Muslim state, such as the state, that actually emerged (Gendzier 1973).

French liberals, such as Germaine Tillon and Albert Camus, condemned both French torture and FLN terror and hoped for a negotiated solution. Further on the left, Jean-Paul Sartre and Simone de Beauvoir turned decisively against the French official position and argued for withdrawal, condemning French torture while becoming partisans of the FLN, accepting an ends-justify-the-means argument for FLN terror (Maran 1989, 158–160; Horne 1987, 124–126, 235–236). Tillon, an ethnologist and Algerian government social planner who had endured torture during the German occupation, once negotiated with FLN leader Yaced Saadi to break the "'attack-tortures-executions cycle'" by going to the French government to stop summary executions (after the FLN had stopped attacks) but did not get its cooperation (Maran 1989, 159).

Fears on the part of the pieds noir led to the formation of a secret army, Organization Armée Secrète (OAS), its attempted putsch in Algeria in 1961, and the spread of OAS and FLN terror tactics to France. The war and growing reaction against General Massu's forces led to antiwar activism in France. Gen. Charles de Gaulle came to power in 1958 and ruled by decree for six months. De Gaulle was determined to pursue peace and extricate France from Algeria. Taking heed of the French defeat in Indochina, he attempted to create a new role for France in the world and tried to maintain the support of the French Army in Algeria in this process. In Algeria, the OAS began massacring Muslims and Europeans working for the government or accused of sympathy with the FLN—executing pharmacists, postmen, tram workers, railway workers, school principals, and inspectors, among others.

France agreed to total independence in 1962, conceding to all of the FLN's original demands. The war, summing up military losses and atrocities on all sides, had cost the French 21,744 deaths (their estimate) and Muslims in Algeria—subject to both French and FLN atrocities—from 300,000 to 1,000,000 lives: a minimum of fourteen Muslims to one European (Horne 1987, 538). Independence led to the exodus and expulsion of virtually all the pieds noir and the Algerian Jews. It also led to the postwar humiliation, torture, and massacre of the *harkis*—Algerians working for the French military. Fewer than 15,000 of the 250,000 harkis had escaped from Algeria because France did not negotiate to give them refuge (Horne 1987, 537–538).

The genocidal massacres in Algeria are seen by genocide scholars as rooted in the ethnic class division of the polity before the conflict (Fein 1977, ch. 1; Kuper 1981). Kuper observes that "where there were two tiers of domination [such as the pieds noir and Algerian Muslims] in the colonial structure, decolonization was particularly charged with genocidal potential" (Kuper 1981, 61).

Neither France nor Algeria (confronted with Islamic terrorism and state counterterror since the 1990s) has overcome the memories and history of the Algerian War. French behavior in Algeria still provokes division and bad feelings in the twenty-first century. In 2001, France prosecuted Gen. Paul Aussaresses (aged eighty-three), whose memoir (*Services Spéiaux Algérie 1955–1957*) told without any repentance how he had used torture and summary executions in Algeria. He was convicted for the crime of trying to justify war crimes. Witnesses against him included a former Algerian activist, Louisette Ighilahriz, who was tortured and raped, and tied to a bed for two months. Other Algerians who had fought for the French and were abandoned and massacred went to court to charge the French government with crimes against humanity. Even the origin of a person's existence could raise charges: "[A] man born because of the rape of his teenage mother by French soldiers won the right to a war victim's pension in a historic ruling by a pensions court" (Daley 2001).

French and Algerian memories were tangled in a web of bloodshed, atrocities, and shame. French doctrine and methods in Algeria influenced Argentina during its "Dirty War." "In fact, *la guerra sucia* is a direct translation of DeGaulle's *la sale de guerre,* or Dirty War in Algeria" (Feitlowitz 1998, 11).

Argentina

Argentina, one of the most economically developed of all states in the Americas, before 1976 was ruled by the military, taking power by coups, through most of the twentieth century. The military had never been checked by civil power in Argentina preceding 1979. Argentina experienced only a short period of democracy in the second half of the century during the tenure of Gen. Juan Perón (1946–1955) before he was overthrown by the military. Perón came into office with the strong support of organized labor but not of the military or the church, key pillars of power. Perón adopted a variant of populist fascism, instituted the basis of a police state, and encouraged mob violence against right-wing targets on several occasions (Marchak 1999, 60). The 1976 coup in Argentina has been compared to other military coups in key Latin American countries before periods of terror: Brazil (1964), Chile, and Uruguay (1973). However, the victims (numerically and their ratio to population) in Argentina greatly exceeded those of these other states. If we take the maximal estimate of "disappearances"—30,000—11.5 Argentines per 10,000 vanished between 1976 and 1982.

Wolfgang Heinz (1997) found three commonalities behind these coups. First, there was an economic crisis because the traditional model of import-substitution industrialization no longer worked, and opening up to the world market was necessary but controversial. This required control of labor, intensifying income inequality, and checking protest (such as that of the left-wing peronistas). Second, there was a political crisis and a lack of legitimacy when the welfare state could no longer be sustained. Third, the coming to power (1959) of Fidel Castro in Cuba and his turn to the Soviet Union "sent shock waves to Latin American and U.S. Governments." The U.S. government was actively involved in training of police and the military (for instance at the U.S. Army School of the Americas) until checked by Congress in the 1990s.

Heinz attributes the differences among these Latin American countries to the strength of the guerrillas and decentralization of responsibility for repression in some countries, so that there was much room for improvisation, leading to "abuse, corruption, theft, and even abduction and blackmail for ransom by military officers, especially in Argentina" (1997, 22).

Perón was brought back from exile to power in 1973 and died in 1974. He was replaced by his wife, Evita, by all accounts a charismatic figure but an inept ruler. She was unable to check either the inflation or the terrorism of revolutionary organizations (the Montoneros and ERP [People's Revolutionary Army])—in part inspired by Ché Guevara. Right-wing terrorist bands, including the military and policemen, killed left-wing leaders, and an undeclared civil war began on the streets of Argentina's cities.

By 1976, inflation had climbed to 700 percent annually, and the guerrillas had killed at least 800 persons (ANCD, 1986, xii). More than 4,000 Argentineans were imprisoned under the law authorizing detention without trial (PEN or National Executive Power) after a state of siege was declared in November 1974, but they did not disappear. Indeed, in January 1976, the Supreme Court held the state of siege unconstitutional, a ruling that might have led to the release of the prisoners had the coup not occurred on March 24, 1976 (Amnesty International 1976, 83).

Although the disorder and fear created by guerrilla violence are said by many to have been instigated and justified by the 1976 coup, there is controversy over who the guerrillas were, how strong they were, and what might have been in part the hidden hand of the military. Guerrilla movements attracting middle-class youth included left-wing movements (the Revolutionary Workers' Party [PRT] and People's Revolutionary Army [ERP]) and right-wing *peronistas,* drawn from Catholic youth movements from which originated the Montoneros. The tactics of both left-wing and right-wing groups were similar: assassinations, robberies, and kidnappings.

Evidence strongly suggests that the Montoneros were infiltrated, and the assassination of a former president (General Aramburu in May 1970), which was attributed to them, was not their idea. They "were essentially set up as an enemy and were used by the military to justify repression of 'the left'" (Anderson 1993, 117–118; Marchak 1999, 100).

In Argentina, the military took over on March 24, 1976—after the left-wing guerrillas had been virtually eliminated—and the junta (commanders of the army, air force, and navy) assumed power and declared the Statute for the Process of National Reorganization. The coup and aims of the new government were said to be supported by most Argentineans, who were fed up with the disorder, unpredictability, and violence of daily life. Argentines' frustration and desire for stability were reiterated by influential people, including Jorge Luis Borges, Argentina's greatest writer, and Jacobo Timerman (director of the newspaper *La Opinion*). Timerman was later kidnapped and tortured in 1977—but was ultimately released and expelled from Argentina because of international protest.

Timerman recalled that prior to the coup, not only were there left-wing and right-wing guerrillas, right-wing Peronist death squads, and terrorist groups of labor unions, paramilitary army groups, and Catholic rightists, but there were also "hundreds of other organizations involved in the eroticism of violence . . . small units that found ideological justification for armed struggle in a poem by Neruda or an essay by Marcuse . . . and a hazy interpretation of Mircea Eliade might be perfect for kidnapping an industrialist to obtain a ransom that would make possible a further perusal of Indian philosophy and mysticism to corroborate the importance of national liberation" (Timerman 1981, 13–14).

The generals who had assumed power stated that the aims of the Process of National Reorganization were to radically restructure Argentina, to set limits to free thought and change, "'to eradicate subversion and to promote economic development based on the equilibrium and responsible participation of the various sectors of society,'" and to "'join the Western, Christian concert of nations'" (Feitlowitz 1998, 22–23). Marguerite Feitlowitz also observed that

> in the junta's analogies to cleanliness and health, we hear echoes of the Nazis. "These are difficult days," said [Navy Admiral] Massera, "days of cleansing, preparation. . . . This country has been ill for too long for a sudden recovery. That's why we must understand that we have only begun our period of convalescence . . . our recuperation of the nation's health . . . [and to do so] we must cleanse the country of subversion." By the time the junta seized power, it had its whole Neo-Nazi "germ theory" in place . . . articulated by Rear Admiral Cesar A. Guzzetti for *La Opinion* on October 3, 1976: "The social body of the country is contaminated by an illness that in corroding its entrails produces antibodies. These antibodies must not be considered in the same way as [the original] microbe. As the government controls and destroys the guerrilla, the action of the antibody will disappear. . . . This is just the natural reaction of a sick body." (1998, 33)

Nazi ideology was hardly a foreign import in Argentina in 1976. Known perpetrators of genocide and war crimes, such as Adolf Eichmann, had been given sanctuary there after World War II with the aid of government and church officials, and their identity was known by the U.S. Central Intelligence Agency (Goni 2002; National Security Archives [www.gwu.edu/~nsarchiv/NSAEBB/NSAEBB/150/INDEX.htm]). Besides Nazi ideology, there were contemporary multinational sources for the doctrine of the generals. The Doctrine of National Security drew on U.S. policies that justified repression in Latin America to bolster U.S. goals during the Cold War and French counterrevolutionary doctrine (developed during the war in Algeria), as well as on German intelligence agents who found refuge in Argentina after World War II

(ANCD 1986, 442; Feitlowitz 1998, 12). But Argentinean officers interviewed later "vehemently deny" that they "were implementing lessons
learned through U.S. training" as some academics suggest (Osiel 2001,
110).

Many Argentinean military men had gone to the U.S. School
of Americas, which stressed using all possible means to eliminate
guerrillas, including torture (Feitlowitz 1998, 9–10). However, Feitlowitz makes clear (see box 4.2) that torture had a long history and
indigenous roots in Argentina. U.S. Department of State documents
released in August 2002 reveal that the new government of Argentina
understood that they had U.S. approval "for its all-out assault on the
left in the name of fighting terrorism." Whenever the U.S. Embassy
raised complaints on human rights grounds (such as the ambassador's
démarche in response to the kidnapping of the Argentinean coordinator of U.S.-funded Fulbright scholarships), the new government
relied on Secretary of State Kissinger's reassurances. Kissinger told
the generals in 1976: "If there are things that have to be done, you
should do them quickly. But you should get back quickly to normal
procedures" (National Security Archive Electronic Briefing Book No.
133, August 27, 2004).

Although reinforcement was given by U.S. support, the governing
junta and its supporters drew on older and continuing sources: the
right-wing traditional Catholic negation of liberalism and modernity,
perspectives that not only negated Marxism but assumed a medieval
conception of unanimity (Malamud Goti 1996, 52–53). "The country
was now embarked, 'with the help of God,' on a quest for the common
good, for the full recovery of '*el ser nacional*' ... [which] translates as
'the collective national essence, soul or consciousness.' ... It arises
from and speaks to 'the delirium for unanimity,' in the apt phrase of
Argentinean historian Juan Jose Sebreli" (Feitlowitz 1998, 21).

Although there were many examples of doublespeak by the junta
regarding its aims (Feitlowitz 1998), in practice it prescribed weeding
out and "disappearing" of persons who had "subversive" thoughts—
such as liberalism, improvement of social conditions and public
health, and psychoanalytic theories—or actions tending to energize
any group. The practice of "disappearance" drew on the German
precedent, Hitler's "Night and Fog" order of 1941, which authorized
the disappearance of persons from occupied countries who were arrested and taken out secretively, usually in the early morning, so as
to arouse generalized fear but not opposition.

We do not know much about the strategy and organization of the "process" because official files on the disappeared are missing, hidden, or destroyed (ANCD 1986, 263–264). Yet, we have evidence of the roles of different organizations, the sites where people were incarcerated and tortured, types of torture, and places of killing and body disposals. Sources include contemporary investigations of international human rights organizations, from the official report of the Argentine National Commission on the Disappeared (ANCD) *Nunca Mas,* first published in 1984, prior reports of international human rights organizations, and subsequent testimonies of released victims and their parents. The great majority of disappearances occurred from 1976 to 1979. All details on the course of the disappeared are taken from *Nunca Mas* unless otherwise noted.

A decade later, some voluntary testimonies of perpetrators surfaced. The latter began with the confession of a guilt-ridden and anxious retired navy captain, Adolfo Scilingo, who on March 2, 1995, confessed to dropping prisoners from airplanes (Feitlowitz 1998, 193–255; Verbitsky 1996). Scilingo was moved to talk publicly both because he perceived his superiors (whose orders he trusted and acted on) as being hypocritical in denying their responsibility and because of his recurring anxiety and sleeplessness. His anxiety stemmed initially from an incident in which he almost slipped out of a plane from which he was ejecting drugged prisoners in midair.

The process began with armed men in unmarked black Ford Falcons blindfolding people and snatching them from their homes at night; a minority were taken on the street or detained at work or school. This phenomenon was not entirely new, as the army had set up secret detention centers in 1974. At the same time or later, the perpetrators looted the houses of the "disappeared." Some officers' wives were disappointed at the loot their husbands brought home when comparing it with other wives' booty. "Why confine oneself to a hair drier when somebody else got an air conditioner or a refrigerator?" (Malamud Goti 1996, 51).

Although victims had disappeared socially—relatives applied for writs of habeas corpus, which were torn up—the disappeared were registered and filed in the underground world of Argentine state terror. They were subsequently sent to secret detention centers (about 340 throughout Argentina) and tortured; sexual torture and rape of women were common. Pregnant women were usually killed after cesarean section, and their babies were given to Argentinean families (presumably favored by the junta) for adoption. No racial theory prevented Argentines from incorporating the children of the victims into their families. There were "at least 500 reported cases of appropriation of minors, of which slightly more than 70 have been returned to their original families" (Feierstein 2006).

The destinies of prisoners were decided in secret prisons and military barracks. The ANCD compiled a list with information on 8,960 people "but clearly the list is not exhaustive" (ANCD 1986, 284). The Mothers of the Plaza de Mayo estimated that 30,000 people have been disappeared and executed (Feitlowitz 1998, 257). About 12,000 political prisoners survived, says Mabel Gutierrez, director of Relatives of the Disappeared and Political Detainees (Rohter 2002). If the maximal estimate of survivors and victims executed is taken, 71 percent were killed. The difference between the 8,960 listed by the ANCD and the estimated 30,000 disappeared indicates the extent of intimidation and fear that existed at the time the list was compiled.

"'You've got your ticket,' prisoners were told when they were about to be transferred" (Feitlowitz 1998, 53)—see box 4.2. They were killed and their bodies burned, or they were drugged, shoved into airplanes, and dropped into the sea.

Who were the victims, and why were they selected? The governor of Buenos Aires province, Iberico Saint Jean, put it explicitly: "*First we will kill all the subversives, then we will kill their collaborators, then ... their sympathizers, then ... those who remain indifferent; and, finally, we will kill the timid*"—emphasis in the original (Feitlowitz 1998, 32).

There appeared to have been three rings of disappeared: (1) potential or perceived opponents of the regime; (2) their friends, colleagues, and contacts (some were detained because they were listed in telephone books of those in the first ring); and (3) sheerly random victims and victims of opportunity. For example, "At the height of the terror ... bored junior officers in the torture squads roamed the streets looking only for pretty girls to take back to camp to torture and rape and then kill" (Simpson 1985).

The great majority (69 percent) of victims documented are between sixteen and thirty years old (most between twenty-one and thirty) and are male (70 percent). There are also instances of the disappearance of entire families, although this does not appear to have been the rule. Some prominent occupational categories among the victims include agrarian labor representatives, architects (associated with progressive social change), critical clergy, journalists, and trade unionists.

Feitlowitz notes that "it has been proven that workers were 'marked' for disappearance by their supervisors and employers" (1998, 166). Several cases of disabled people—blind, paralyzed, in a cast—who were taken were also noted by the ANCD.

Most of the victims were probably Catholic. Jews were overrepresented as victims and especially vulnerable. Jews were subjected to especially sadistic tortures and to antisemitic taunts, curses, and threats. Guards painted Jewish prisoners' bodies with swastikas, used Nazi terms, and interrogated them about Zionism, the Argentinean Jewish community, and an imaginary Jewish plan to occupy Patagonia (ANCD 1986, xvii, 67–72; Braylan et al. 2000; Feierstein 2006; Feitlowitz 1998, 90; Marchak 1999, 254; Rapaport 1981; Rosenthal 1978; Timerman 1981). Some cases of kidnapping for profit were reported in instances of Jewish businessmen who were picked up and tortured but released a short time later after their property had been seized (Braylan et al. 2000, 17–18). The Argentine-Jewish community was intimidated by hate crimes, government-sponsored antisemitic propaganda, and Timerman's disappearance. Most prominent Jewish figures and Jewish community institutions were silent about the abductions (Feitlowitz 1998, 97–109).

Who were the torturers? Almost anyone in the military or police, it seems. Malamud Goti (a lawyer who prosecuted perpetrators under President Alfonsin's administration) estimated that there were about 1,000 to 2,000 persons involved in torture and disappearances (1998, 13). There were torturers known as sadists, torturers known as 9 to 5 organization men, and a few torturers known for trying to establish a relationship with their victims, marrying a former victim, or later sending Christmas cards. Most of the torturers seem to have believed that they were acting in conformity with the moral climate of Argentine society (Osiel 2001).

Most Argentineans were silent bystanders who managed to overlook, deny, and justify what was going on around them. Feitlowitz said (in personal conversation) that many people she interviewed later denied knowing anything at the time, but incongruities in their recollection and remarks contradicted their claim to have known nothing. Robert Cox (a British-born journalist and editor of an English-language newspaper in Buenos Aires), who fled Argentina in 1979 after an arrest and death threats, recalled: "The way people respond to this situation is to deny it.... I remember the absolute pain I felt when I realized what was happening and nobody would believe me or talk to me about it. They thought I was mad. It's like waking up in the morning and finding that one has been transformed into a beetle" (quoted in Anthony Lewis, 1981).

"*Por algo será*"—"there must be a reason"—said the aunt of a former Argentinean political prisoner who told me in 1998 of his family's reaction. Similarly, Amos Elon wrote in 1986 how a woman he met at a luncheon asserted: "'They deserved their fate....' 'Did they deserve to be tortured?' I asked, pointing down the mountain, 'and thrown into that lake?' 'This I did not know,' she said quickly. 'This I only learned later.' After a while, she added, 'They probably had to use torture. You see, the courts in Argentina were always so lenient'" (Elon 1986, 79).

Surveys taken in 1979 after reports of disappearances were widely reported showed that most Argentineans approved of the regime (Osiel 2001, 98). Marcela Scilingo, the wife of Captain Scilingo, said that she had talked about the death flights in 1986 or earlier to everybody in order to unburden herself, and no one blamed her husband—everyone understood (Feitlowitz 1998, 198).

Both denial that atrocities occurred and their justification are at work here. Denial enables people to maintain their belief that this is a just world, to persuade themselves of their innocence, and to suppress fears that might arise if they acknowledged that their neighbors and relatives were being kidnapped, tortured, and killed (Cohen 2001; 16, 71–72, 96; Lerner 1980). Yet, in some cases, the bystander's willingness to rationalize torture and execution recalls active complicity.

The victims were defined and labeled by the regime as noncitizens. "'The repression is directed against a minority we do not consider Argentine,' said [General] Videla, '... a terrorist is not only someone who plants bombs, but a person whose ideas are contrary to our Western, Christian civilization'" (Feitlowitz 1998, 24).

For Argentineans deemed citizens, life was richer than before, full of affordable consumer goods and amusements. Argentineans were enjoying prosperity during this period, attributed to new economic policies of the regime, which enabled them to travel and shop abroad. To divert them, the government organized international book fairs, and art and music festivals. To eliminate discordant images, it also organized urban beautification projects, destroying shantytowns.

The major institutions and press collaborated with the regime. The response of most of the highest prelates of the Roman Catholic Church was justification of the regime and denial that anything wrong was occurring (Feierstein 2006; Verbitsky 1996, 30). Most citizens initially approved of the new regime, by all accounts. Newspapers were silent, except for the English-language *Buenos Aires Herald* and Jacobo Timerman's *La Opinion,* which published lists of the disappeared—before Timerman's disappearance, torture, and release to Israel.

Scilingo's confession (published in 1995) implicated church and military authorities. He recalled that after his first "flight" to drop victims from airplanes, the "next day I didn't feel very good and I was talking with the Chaplain of the school, who found a Christian explanation for it ... [that] made me feel better ... he was telling me that it was a Christian death, because they didn't suffer, because it wasn't traumatic, that they had to be eliminated, that war was war, and even the Bible provided for eliminating the weeds from the wheat field" (Verbitsky 1996, 301).

After the confession's publication, the Conference of Bishops disassociated itself from institutional responsibility for approving these crimes. However, the conference was itself denounced by Bishop Miguel Esteban Hesayne, who had previously condemned torture. The bishop charged that the conference had failed to repent. The Vatican was also charged with complicity (Verbitsky 1996, 144–146).

The only visible civic dissent during the generals' reign was that of the Madres (Mothers) de Plaza de Mayo, who petitioned weekly for an explanation of what happened to their children on the plaza—the place in which "the Assembly of 1813 resolved that all instruments of torture had to be burnt" (Mellibovsky 1997, xiv). The Plaza de Mayo was established in 1580 for executions by the Inquisition and served as a place for public punishments for 230 years. The demonstrations, organized by about fourteen mothers of the disappeared in October 1977, were repeated regularly. The mothers continued even after twelve of them were abducted; the group had been infiltrated by a government agent (Simpson 1985, 152–170). Looking at the probable number of mothers of the registered disappeared (nearly 9,000), the numbers of the Madres demonstrating were "always small," usually less than one in a hundred of mothers of the disappeared (Simpson 1985, 167). The fathers, who sensed that they would be killed instantaneously if they protested, hung around to be the watchdogs and witnesses for their wives (Feitlowitz 1998, 94).

Most Argentineans appeared satisfied with their government and only began protesting when the economic consequences of the junta policies threatened their newfound prosperity with unemployment and inflation. Mass strikes began in 1982. The trigger for the downfall of the junta was the defeat of the Argentinean military in the Falklands War with Britain, which Argentina instigated in April 1982. Although the disappearance of their countrymen could not bring them to their feet, the loss of a small island, chiefly occupied by sheep, stirred mass protest. The generals agreed to call elections, after adopting an amnesty for themselves.

They elected a liberal government, headed by Gen. Raoul Alfonsin, which pledged to try perpetrators for human rights abuses. The trials were impeded by a December 1982 deadline for prosecution set by the Argentine House of Deputies. Ten leading members of the governing juntas were tried and jailed until they were pardoned and set free by President Carlos Menem in 1989 and 1991. Political changes, several military revolts, and the fears of disorder undermined the will of the government to continue with more trials, and it passed a "Punto Final" (Full Stop) law in 1986, which limited charges to sixty days. Malamud Goti, a prosecutor under President Alfonsin, changed his mind about the effect of the trials on Argentina, believing it was negative because "by depicting the world as consisting of the innocent and the guilty, the trials reproduced the authoritarian view that the world is split into allies and enemies," and absolved the many responsible by "direct or indirect participation in creating or setting the grounds that led to state terror." Further, "they reinvented history by pinning the blame almost entirely on a single social group—the military," using them as scapegoats while exonerating others who were responsible (1996, 7–8). He argued for victim-centered rather than retributive justice.

Responsibility for tolerating the Dirty War belonged not only to the Argentineans but also to the governments that recognized the junta, allowed its practices to continue, and conspired with it. The U.S. Congress sometimes pursued a different course than the U.S. administration and military. The U.S. Congress passed a law in 1973 curtailing military aid to gross violators of human rights and cut off military aid to Argentina in 1978 (during the Carter administration) after a two-year struggle led by liberal Democrats. The campaign and law were a response to a report by Amnesty International and requests by a dozen other human rights groups to take action to stop the disappearances. The aid ban was lifted in 1981 on the request of President Reagan (Guest 1990, 101, 152, 155, 166, 248). President Carter's administration was distinguished by his emphasis on human rights; that of President Reagan repudiated his predecessor's focus.

The United States was also implicated in condoning, and sometimes assisting, Operation Condor, a military network created in the 1970s by Chile, Argentina, Uruguay, Bolivia, Brazil, and Paraguay (later joined by Peru). Operation Condor coordinated actions to abduct and kill political opponents outside their country of origin and sometimes outside Latin America—for example, the assassination of Orlando Letelier (former Chilean foreign minister under President Allende) and Ronni Moffitt (an American colleague) in Washington, D.C., in 1976. The United States' principal contribution may have been the establishment of a secure telecommunications network for the countries involved operating out of the former U.S. military headquarters in the Panama Canal Zone. CIA agents and foreign "assets" were involved in the Letelier-Moffitt murders (McSherry 2001).

U.S. concerns and interests were divided. While U.S. human rights groups exposed and attacked Argentina and the *desaparecidos* were publicized in the U.S. press, U.S. business interests in Latin America and U.S. conservatives in the United States defended the Argentine terror and that of other states (Barber 1985; Buchanan 1977; Falcoff 1981; Hoeffel and Montalvo 1979; Levin 1982). President Reagan's ambassador to the United Nations, Jeane Kirkpatrick, articulated a doctrine distinguishing authoritarian from totalitarian countries. It justified overlooking disappearances and terror in the former, which tended to be U.S. allies such as Argentina (Kirkpatrick 1979). However, by 1979 few totalitarian countries existed, and fewer—apart from the communist states of Asia in which the United States had little influence—were disappearing and killing as many people as was Argentina at that time.

After the fall of the junta in Argentina, the Scilingo revelations and other confessions and denials roiled memory and caused some to reappraise the past. The younger generation is said to be more aware. Children of the disappeared ("*hijos*") organized and still meet periodically, despite threats, and *Nunca Mas* became part of the official high school curriculum (Feitlowitz 1998, 247–249). The mothers of the disappeared are now joined by grandmothers of the disappeared, seeking identification and custody of their grandchildren and great-grandchildren with the aid of new methods of genetic identification.

Positive changes in the army toward a human-rights-respecting force included the appointment of Gen. Martin Balsa as chief of staff, subordination of the military to civilian control, a new code of military justice, downsizing the army, and broadening the bases for inclusion, now accepting non-Roman Catholics (banned before) and women (Potash 1998). In 1995, General Balsa took the unprecedented step of repudiating the past and making it clear that the rules had changed. "*It is a crime to give an immoral order; It is a crime to execute an immoral order; It is a crime to employ unjust, immoral means to accomplish even a legitimate objective*" [emphasis in original] (Feitlowitz 1998, 223–224).

The final point for prosecution turned out not to be final because of a legal breakthrough in international human rights law, expanding the time and place where alleged violators could be prosecuted. This change was provoked by national and international reaction to the 1998 request of a Spanish judge, Baltasar Garzon, to arrest and extradite the former Chilean head of state, Augusto Pinochet (then in London), on charges of torture and genocide (the latter dismissed). The "Pinochet Effect" expanded the boundary of prosecutions of persons accused of crimes against humanity (Roht-Arriaza 2005). Responses to this led to prosecutions in Chile and Argentina (and of Argentineans by other states), which had not been possible before under the political settlements in these countries.

Prosecutions in Argentina began in 1995 for trafficking in babies of mothers who were disappeared and killed. New prosecutions for kidnapping proceed, as do foreign requests for extradition of prominent perpetrators. Argentina extradited (from Chile) and arraigned a former army chaplain, Christian Von Wernich, on charges of arbitrary detention and torture; the trial is still pending. Alfredo Astiz, the naval officer responsible for the disappearance of twelve of the mothers of the Plaza de Mayo and two nuns (French and Italian citizens), was convicted in absentia in France (leading to several international arrest warrants against him), rearrested in Argentina in 2003, and released there. Capt. Adolfo Scilingo was arrested in Spain and convicted on April 19, 2005, of crimes against humanity for the deaths of thirty people. He was sentenced to 640 years in prison and will serve a maximum of thirty years; an appeal has been lodged.

Authoritarian tendencies continue to be expressed in Argentina. Former president Menem justified the past repression and dismissed Captain Scilingo's confession (Feitlowitz 1998, 171–172, 187, 197). Menem was charged in August 2002 with involvement in the 1994 bombing of the Jewish cultural center in Buenos Aires by Iranian agents and accepting a payoff for his silence.

By 2002, Argentina confronted the devaluation of its currency and high unemployment, forcing many into poverty and leading to popular mobilization, such as demonstrations of hundreds of thousands against the government, and continuing social movements for change. Yet the military did not intervene or threaten intervention, and democratic government continued, with President Eduardo Du-halde in June proposing direct parliamentary democracy.

Traditions and habits of misuse of power persisted. There have been many allegations of torture and ill treatment in police stations and prisons and police killings "in disputed circumstances," and threats and intimidation of journalists persist (Amnesty International 2002, 34; 2005). But there was also judicial protest against police use of excessive force and an important decision by federal judge Gabriel Cavallo (March 2001) ruling that the Full Stop and Due Obedience Laws (which prevented prosecution of violations during the Dirty War) were illegal. Other judicial decisions mandated the arrest of former head of state Jorge Rafael Videla and officers involved in disappearances and extrajudicial executions during Operation Condor. General Galtieri was placed under house arrest for kidnapping. Impunity ended for the architects of terror, murder, torture—and the kidnapping and secret adaptations of children—during the "Dirty War."

5
States of Terror Turn to Genocide: Guatemala and Iraq

Today [1918], however, we have to say that a state is a human community that (successfully) claims the *monopoly of the legitimate use of physical force* within a given territory.

—Max Weber, "Politics as a Vocation,"
From Max Weber 1946 [1919]

Ethnic cleansing in the twentieth century is a product of the most "advanced" stage in the development of the modern state.... The modern state takes the census ... counts, measures, weighs, categorizes, and homogenizes.... [It] has little use for minority rights.

—Norman M. Naimark, *Fires of Hatred,* 2001

In this chapter, we consider two states that used terror against the whole population and turned to genocide when facing opposition from a distinct community differing ethnically from that of the ruling elite. The communities targeted in Guatemala and Iraq were also geographically isolated. The significance of the differences between these victims and the victims of state violence in Algeria and Argentina will be further discussed in chapter 6.

Guatemala and Guatemalans have used and been victims of both terror and genocide on a scale greater than any other country in Latin or Central America in the second half of the twentieth century. Since the 1996 peace agreement ending a thirty-six-year civil war, the violations from that period (previously reported by human rights organizations) have been authoritatively documented by the UN-sponsored truth commission, the Commission for Historical Clarification (CEH), which began its work in 1997. Documentation of the pattern of terror and genocide is provided by the report of the Centro Internacional para Investigaciones en Derechos Humanos (CIIDH).

The CIIDH study drew on an extensive database of violations and victims culled from newspaper citations—better at some times and places than others—and the archives of the Guatemalan Human Rights Commission (COPREDEH) and the victims' Group of Mutual Support (GAM), publications of religious and human rights group, and testimonies it collected. However, it is not a complete inventory of victims. The authors say that the almost 37,000 cases surveyed constituted only 19 percent of the total they estimated were killed and that the data were more complete for later regimes (Ball, Kobrak, and Spirer 1999, 8).

More information on the organization of the terror comes from the extensive interviews with the military compiled by Jennifer Schirmer (1998). Documents released by the United States, available through the National Security Archives to which we later refer, also reveal the political conditions at the time.

The CEH estimated that there were more than 200,000 deaths—mainly of civilians—and declared that the slaughter of the Mayan population in the countryside from 1981 to 1983 was genocide.[1] However, terror began in Guatemala twenty years earlier and was estimated (subtracting group massacres) to have taken 85,000 to 110,000 lives of targeted individuals. The CIIDH study showed that more than 99 percent of the killings were by agents of the state (Ball, Kobrak, and Spirer 1999, 8). Killings escalated from selective to collective slaughter—genocide—between 1978 and 1984 under the regimes of Gen. Lucas Garcia (July 1978–March 1982) and Gen. Rios Montt (March 1982–August 1983). Thus, the Guatemalan experience might yield insight into why and how a regime escalates from terror with individual victims to genocide against a distinct and previously subordinated group.

Since the Spanish conquest, there has been a persistent pattern of repression, resistance, and revolt in Guatemala (McClintock 1985, ch. 1). Both race and class (often reinforcing each other) divided the nation, producing policies and attitudes that have led to greater conflict than in other Central American countries. The racial division between the elite (and foreign-born entrepreneurs) and the indigenous majority justified to the elite the pattern of coercion they imposed on the indigenous people. Ernest Duff and John McCamant observe that the "labor relations that developed as a result of the subjugation of Indian workers in Guatemala ... have come to characterize labor relations with the *ladino* (mestizo) workers as well" (1976, 85).

The indigenous population had been incorporated into forced labor systems since colonial times. The encomienda system was replaced in the nineteenth century by debt bondage and laws making work obligatory and penalizing "vagabonds." Some indigenes assimilated culturally and became *ladinos,* and others maintained their identity as Indians.

The Guatemalan elites' perception of the natives as a hostile and inferior race led to both social and moral distance, making coercion a habitual method for labor control. By contrast, in neighboring Costa Rica, racial homogeneity (there were few indigenous people) and kinship patterns led to "relatively congenial relations with rural workers [in the nineteenth century] to prevent the latter from leaving" (Yashar 1997, 60).

Generalized racism and contempt toward the Indians have been noted often in Guatemala, sometimes in the name of development. Gen. Justo Rufino Barrios (Liberal politician and ruler of Guatemala 1873–1885) said in 1877—seeking to promote economic growth through encouraging foreign capital investment—that "'one hundred foreign families were worth as much as 20,000 indians [*sic*]'" (Yashar 1997, 39). Indian resistance to punitive policies in different periods had led to state reprisals and state massacres in retaliation (McClintock 1985, 5; Yashar 1997, 264). In the twentieth century, Guatemala had one of the two most "exploitative and coercive rural class structures" in Central America, with high rural poverty, inequality, and concentrated landownership. The other was El Salvador (Brockett 1991, 62–70).

The social and moral distance between races reinforced inequality and cruelty. The percentage of indigenous people in states of Latin America (1960–1970) was found to be highly correlated to state repression in that decade (Duff and McCamant 1976, 81–86). The percentage of people classed as nonwhite in Guatemala—two-thirds of the nation in the decade between 1960 and 1970—was higher than in any other Latin or Central American country at the time.

Guatemala's concentration of economic power, its coercive labor practices, the lack of division within the elite, the lack of an independent middle class, and its legacy of repression were conditions inimical to democratization, Yashar argues (1997, 7–23). However, foreign intervention from the United States was against change toward democratization in the 1950s and decades following (McClintock 1985; Schlesinger and Kinzer 2005). Popular mobilization for social change and a backlash against it appeared in Guatemala in the 1940s and 1950s. Discontent among the elite as well as striking workers led to a decade of presidents who initiated democratic reforms between 1944 and 1954: Juan Jose Arevalo (1945–1950) and Col. Jacobo Arbenz (1950–1954). Unfortunately, the reformers "simultaneously sought to appropriate [the] Mayan heritage as the essence of the Guatemalan nation ... [but] they also sought to destroy the existing Mayan people, which many, including reform politicians, feared and which ladinos admittedly did not understand" (Yashar 1997, 160–161).

The oligarchy feared that the Indians who joined in rural organizations and supported organized labor would "initiate race wars," leading to more class conflict and civil war. The elite charged that the movement was a communist plot (Yashar 1997, 195).

By the 1950s, bananas, marketed by the United Fruit Company, had become Guatemala's second largest export, following coffee (McClintock 1985, 24–25). The demand for labor discipline and intervention of foreign capital rose after the establishment of commercialized agriculture. At the same time, the military was becoming more independent and able to pursue its own agenda. During President Arevalo's tenure, the army began receiving U.S. military assistance and was constitutionally endowed with the right to elect a Supreme Council, giving it a new institutional autonomy (McClintock 1985, 20–21).

There is some debate about whether the well-documented U.S. intervention to overthrow President Arbenz in 1954 can be primarily attributed to the U.S. fear of communism in Central America or to its economic interests (Hey 1995, 32; McClintock 1985, 27; Schlesinger and Kinzer 2005, 107–146). The failure of Guatemalans to defend Arbenz has been attributed to his government's failure to reform the country, to divisions among and between ladino and Mayan elites, to the opposition of elites to land reform, and to the political passivity of the poor who were believed to support him (Grandin 2000, 211–217, 232–233; Hey 1995, 32; Schlesinger and Kinzer 2005, 198; Yashar 1997, 231).

More information about the coup (authorized by President Eisenhower in 1953) became available in 2002 and after, when the U.S. government released selected declassified documents of its Central Intelligence Agency (CIA) relating to Guatemala. The CIA authorized release and declassification of 1,400 pages out of 100,000-plus in its archives (NSA 2002).

The CIA compiled lists of persons in Arbenz's government "to eliminate immediately in event of [a] successful anti-Communist coup," another "final list of disposees" (including but not limited to Communist Party leaders), and "A Study of Assassination," advising that the "simplest local tools" are often the best. The coup was full of blunders, barely succeeded, and its CIA planners lied to President Eisenhower about the numbers killed (at least four dozen, not the one reported), according to a 1994 CIA analysis by Nicholas Cullather, a diplomatic historian.

Kate Doyle and Peter Kornbluh, analysts of the National Security Archive, tell us that the documents released by the CIA include its assassination manual for the 1954 coup (reprinted in part in the *New York Times* as an op-ed May 31, 1997) and the lists of Guatemalan communists to be disposed of "'through Executive Action'—murder—or through imprisonment and exile." "The 'A' list of those to be assassinated contain[s] 58 names—all of which the CIA has excised from the declassified documents" (Doyle and Kornbluh, NSA Electronic Briefing Book No. 4, May 23, 1997, www.gwu.edu/nsarchiv/NSAEBB/NSAEBB4.index.html).

The new junta of Gen. Castillo Armas and his supporters killed about 300 persons, mainly peasants leading agricultural unions (McClintock 1985, 29–30). The government incarcerated up to 9,000 Guatemalans and created an official Black List of 70,000 persons alleged to be members of the Communist Party and suspect political parties, unions, peasants', or teachers' associations. Still, the security system, dominated by the National Police, used the conventional methods of control, denying persons political participation—political imprisonment, exclusion, and exile—rather than denying them life.

Internal conflict in the army resulted in an unsuccessful coup against General President Miguel Ydigoras Fuentes on November 13, 1960. The coup was led by dissenting army officers, in part a response to U.S. use of Guatemalan territory to train Cuban exiles for the future Bay of Pigs invasion (Ball, Kobrack, and Spirer 1999, 13; McClintock 1985, ch. 1). Officers who escaped capture (trained in the United States, as were other officers) started the MR-13 guerrilla movement and were welcomed by ladino peasants previously organized by Guatemalan communists (Schirmer 1998, 15–16). The guerrillas (as well as the army) looked down on the Indians, considering them primitive and backward (Brockett 1991, 71; Hey 1995, 35; Schirmer 1998, 16).

Protests and strikes against U.S. actions triggered a reaction. The United States feared the spread of revolution from Cuba and responded to this conflict by modernizing Guatemala as a counterinsurgency state. A new coup in Guatemala in 1963 led to the restructuring of the security forces and the institution of a central intelligence agency and a paramilitary force of 20,000 in 1965 and 1966. The United States advised the Guatemalan military in detail and advanced the doctrine that communist subversion was the enemy across Central and Latin America, an enemy to be countered by counterinsurgency strategy.

Yet political competition reappeared in 1966, and Guatemalans elected a university professor, Julio Cesar Mendez Montenegro, with widespread support. Just before the election, the security forces detained at least twenty-eight members of the banned communist party and other underground groups, who then were "disappeared," signifying the escalation of violations (Ball, Kobrak, and Spirer 1999, 15–16; McClintock 1985, 82–83).

The new pattern of repression after 1966 was known as "counterterror"—terror to fight terror—and in practice it meant that suspects were killed out of hand. There were no more political prisoners, only political murders. This change led to an unprecedented state of siege in 1967–1968, which is estimated to have killed 2,000 to 8,000 people (Ball, Kobrak, and Spirer 1999, 16). During this period the war escalated and clandestine death squads appeared; some were security forces in civilian dress, and others were independent. "They converted murder into political theater, often announcing their actions through death lists or decorating their victims' bodies with notes denouncing communism or common criminality. Their secret nature not only provoked terror in the population, it also allowed the army and police to deny responsibility for a systematic campaign of extrajudicial killing" (Ball, Kobrak, and Spirer 1999, 17). Only one protest of U.S. policy appears in the CIA's declassified records, that of Viron Vaky, former U.S. deputy chief of mission in Guatemala in 1966, who was back in service with the State Department's Policy Planning Council in 1968.

Vaky argues that the Guatemalan government's use of counterterror is indiscriminate and brutal, and has impeded modernization and institution building within the country. Furthermore, he writes, the United States has condoned such tactics. "This is not only because we have concluded we cannot do anything about it, for we never really tried. Rather we suspected that maybe it is a good tactic, and that as long as Communists are being killed it is alright. Murder, torture and mutilation are alright if our side is doing it and the victims are Communists." Vaky urges a new policy in Guatemala that rejects "counter-terror" as an accepted tactic and represents a "clear ethical stand" on the part of the United States. (doc. 5, unclassified 4/14/1998, www.gwu.edu~nsarchiv/NSAEBB/NSAEBB111/docs)

Although there is limited documentary evidence for the years between 1961 and 1979, the CIIDH estimated that between 61 and 410 (usually below 300) state killings and disappearances occurred annually during those years. The numbers rose precipitously from 1980 to 1983 under the regimes of Gen. Romeo Lucas Garcia and Gen. Efrain Rios Montt. If the numbers of state killings and disappearances recorded in later years are compared with those in 1961, they were 3 times more in 1971, 28 times more in 1981, and 135 times more in 1982.

Before the 1980s, the overwhelming majority of victims were male peasants, and labor, university, and urban activists targeted for their individual opposition. How individuals were selected can be inferred from a death squad log of 183 persons "disappeared." It lists the name, organizational affiliation, profession, date of abduction, government agencies involved, and date of death—along with photographs that appear to have been torn from passports, driver's licenses, and official identity cards (Doyle 1999).

Yet political resistance (strikes, protest marches, land disputes) and guerrilla war continued leading the regime to escalate to what Rachel May calls "reactionary terror ... to halt or prevent demands for reform" (May 2001, 147–164). Repression created new grievances and incentives to resist and altered the mode of resistance in Guatemala at different periods (Brockett 2005, ch. 9). The workers' persistence in a sit-in strike at the Coca-Cola plant for a year, beginning February 17, 1984, was a case of nonviolent resistance.

Although murders increased in the cities from 1978 to 1981, they were still fewer and more targeted individually in the cities than in the countryside. The terror in the countryside dissolved communities, as the indigenous people were massacred by soldiers often from their own groups.

The use of rape as a weapon was observed by U.S. evangelical missionaries friendly to the regime, who were allowed to travel to the Mayan highlands in 1982 because their denominations had ties with

President Rios-Montt (Manz 2004, 25–27). The Guatemalan Army was a "total organization" (Goffman 1961), resocializing recruits to be alienated from their people of origin, beating them up and demeaning their origins, and teaching them to brutalize their countrymen and rape women (Jonas 1984, 240–241; Simon 1987, 85–87). "A certain Lt. Morales disliked the Indians and their customs. He demanded that we trade in our relatives for machine guns and our girlfriends for prostitutes. He taught us how to rape women.... In this way I came to be first a soldier, later a corporal, and then a sergeant. They promoted me because I had the courage to beat my own *compañeros* and I had the stomach to watch anything that was done" (Jonas 1984, 240–241).

How the capacity to murder, torture, and rape was redefined as evidence of masculinity is illustrated in box 5.1, in which a state killer explains the strategy of training as a method to show the recruit has "sufficient courage to torture and kill a person." In 1980, General Gramajo (the most vocal and perhaps most astute of the military strategists) and other generals believed that the situation was declining rapidly into an unwinnable war. Jennifer Schirmer observes that "arbitrary slaughter—paramilitary activity, summary executions, kidnappings, and forced disappearances, leaving eight hundred bodies a month on the streets—was becoming increasingly counterproductive" (1998, 18). Gramajo said about this period: "'Our country was on the verge of collapse—a polarized, intolerant society with decadent political institutions, an economy debilitated by capital flight, and isolated internationally'" (Schirmer 1998, 18).

Corruption and exploitation of economic links by the generals aggravated the situation, along with U.S. president Carter's new human rights policy, a credit scandal, and a rise in the popular movement against the military spreading to the indigenous population (Schirmer 1998, 20). To counter this collapse, elite army planners constructed a National Plan of Security and Development, which called for a return to guided democracy with military oversight and coordination after pacification, setting out a different agenda for the cities and the countryside.

Most urban victims were killed individually or in small groups in the 1980s. The regime sought to make the murders less visible in the cities. According to one informant (a torturer under G-2), the order was given under Gen. Rios Montt "that we could no longer assassinate people in public view nor assassinate them and leave them thrown onto the streets" (Schirmer 1998, 291). Herbert Spirer, a coauthor of

Box 5.1 Training of State Killers in Guatemala

To become an *elemento* of the G-2 [Government Intelligence agency], one must go through a course, to be trained. So one goes but [he hesitates], [it is a] training course in which one is taken to one of the cells ... where they have people destined to be killed, okay? The major or captain (never a colonel) takes you to the cell, gives you a knife and throws you together to see how, how you react against that person, while he watches.

Q: As a kind of training exercise?

Yes, in other words, it is to prove your tolerance for such things, to prove that you are cold-blooded, if you have sufficient courage to torture and kill a person.

Q. With a knife?

With a knife, with whatever [they give you]. But there [in the cell], the only thing they give you is a knife, nothing else, and one has to figure out for oneself how to torture that person, how to kill that person and if you have enough courage to do so. ... And then, from there, you begin to do your work, making pieces of that person, to do it like one cuts up an animal. And if one does [the job] well and they think you have enough courage to do these things, then they give you a position. ... This lasts only one or two hours. It makes me uneasy at times to relate this. I have always asked God's forgiveness and the forgiveness of some of the people I've killed for what I've done.

Q. What do they tell you about these people in the cells? Who are they?

Frankly, when one is doing this [work], one isn't interested whether the person is a *guerrillero* or not.

Q. It doesn't matter?

It doesn't matter because you must demonstrate your courage in how one kills a person. So one goes to the General Barracks ... in Guatemala City, to prepare oneself [for this work]. ... When you arrive at this section, they tell you that if they ordered you to kill your mother, you would have to go and kill her. Or your father, or your uncles, or your brothers, or any friend or relative—you couldn't refuse. You must go and kill them.

Q. As a G-2 *elemento,* did torturing a woman include raping her?

Yes, this is normal. But it depends on the women, too. Because there are many women who aren't worth the effort to look at. Some even make you sick. But at times, the opportunity arose to be able to kidnap a young woman, to investigate a young woman, or for a young woman combatant to be wounded in combat, or an excellent woman. ... Well, that woman couldn't escape.

Q. By everyone?

Yes, everyone. Ay! *El jefe* is the first [laughs]. And then the lieutenants or *el commandante* of G-2 or *el jefe de la patrulla,* then it would be my turn. Ay! This woman I like and so I would tell them, "Leave her over here" or "Cover me." [laughs] Yes, the rapes occur [as normal procedure].

Source: Jennifer Schirmer, *The Guatemalan Military Project* (1998), 240–244.

the 1999 CIIDH study, observed that there were urban Guatemalans who said that they were unaware of the massacres in the countryside between 1979 and 1983—a credible claim "because scarcely any rural killings were reported in the press during 1980 and much of 1981 due to lack of access, government pressure and intimidation through killings of journalists, and self-censorship' (Ball, Kobrak, and Spirer 1999, 44–47; ISG 1999). By her own account, Helen Mack—sister of slain Guatemalan anthropologist Myrna Mack—did not realize that terror was practiced in Guatemala until 1990, when her sister was stabbed twenty-seven times (*New York Times,* September 21, 2002).

In rural areas, most of the victims were targeted as members of a group or community; the names of many can no longer be recalled or were not identified at the time of their death. Protests by Quiche and Ixil Indians in Guatemala City in January 1980 incited the Lucas Garcia regime to target the indigenous people of the Mayan highlands, particularly the Ixil triangle, who the government believed were supporting the guerrillas. Before that time, the Mayan Indians had generally been outside politics, excluded from the political community.

Operation Ashes was the first of the five phases of the National Plan: Military orders were given to eliminate the Indians categorically in certain villages. The CEH reported that "in 1981 and 1982 it was heard from [indigenous] Army specialists ... about the order that had gone out ... to kill all the Indians. Some pilots and commanders' guards got their own relatives out of Quiche to safeguard them" (CEH, para 848). In Operation Ashes, many whole villages were burned, "draining the sea which the fish swam in," according to Gen. Rios Montt (Ball, Kobrak, and Spirer 1999, 27). Often, women were raped before being killed as part of a deliberate policy to destroy families. This was a centralized and highly coordinated campaign, in which villages were color coded on military maps according to their perceived state of loyalty.

Was it the fear of Indian insurrection, often voiced earlier, that incited the military to escalate from selective killing to genocide? Most likely the decision stemmed not just from the threat but from the prior exclusion and contempt for the Indians. "The government could kill Maya peasants [Indians] indiscriminately because there was little political price to pay.... It was also the result of the historical absence in Guatemala of any sense of common humanity by non-Indians towards Indians" (Ball, Kobrak, and Spirer 1999, 90). The genocide against the Indians ended because the army substituted another strategy, forcing the Indians to police their own villages to deter and apprehend guerrillas. Schirmer reports that the generals estimated that they killed 85,000 to 110,000 people in the Mayan highlands in this period.

The indigenous population was promised "Beans and Bullets"—a 70 percent to 30 percent ratio—in place of the 100 percent reliance in the past on bullets (Schirmer 1998, 23–24, 62–102). The United States' role was succinctly summed up by McClintock (1999):

> Certainly the U.S. military doctrine adopted and adapted by the Guatemalans did not contemplate genocide, although the murky line between selective murder and mass murder in counterinsurgency was acknowledged. The training exercises of the 1966 Army Handbook of Counterinsurgency Guidelines for Area Commanders (U.S. Dept. of the Army Pamphlet no. 550–100) admonished commanders that in pre-paring counterinsurgency programs: "You may not employ mass coun-terterror (as opposed to selective counterterror) against the civilian population, i.e., genocide is not an alternative." The fine line between "selective" and "mass" counterterror may have been missed by some trainees—and shrugged off by American advisers in Guatemala who were concerned only with defeating insurgency at any cost. In noting blandly that the Guatemalan military was destroying whole indigenous villages, a 1982 CIA report declassified by the Clinton administration explained uncritically that: "The well-documented belief by the army that the entire Ixil Indian population is [proguerrilla] has created a situation in which the army can be expected to give no quarter to combatants and noncombatants alike." Meanwhile the Department of State put its considerable muscle behind a campaign to discredit and silence human rights groups then struggling to make public what the CIA confirmed privately. (McClintock 1999, 76–77)

The National Security Archives documents on U.S. policy in Guate-mala from 1963 to 1993 confirm that both the U.S. Department of State and the CIA were well informed of Guatemalan Army massacres (www.gwu.edu/~nsarchive/NSAEBB/NSAEBB73/index3.htm). What McClintock calls "the Counter-Terror Smokescreen" is exemplified by United States Department of State [USDOS] Country Reports on Human Rights, an annual report, which equate the extent and responsibility for terror: "Kidnappings and assassinations by both the extreme right and left continued at about the same level as dur-ing 1978" (U.S. Department of State 1980). Even true facts can gloss more horrific realities: "There are no reports of political prisoners" (U.S. Department of State 1981). Manz, an anthropologist who docu-mented the effect of the terror on a Mayan village, also showed how the U.S. Department of State and the U.S. Agency for International Development reports censored, glossed over, and denied murders there (Manz 2004, 27–29).

Although many Americans believe that U.S. aid was cut off in 1978 during the administration of President Carter because of human rights violations, aid continued at the same level from 1978 to 1980 because of previous commitments. U.S. documents in the National Security Archives also reveal that "in 1995, U.S. press reports revealed that although overt U.S. military aid was indeed halted in December 1990, millions of dollars of secret CIA funds continued to flow to the Guatemalan armed forces during the ensuing years. Those funds were finally cut off after they became public" (www.gwu.edu/~nsarchive/NSAEBB/NSAEBB73/index3.htm).

Changes from the 1980s have been attributed to many causes: the end of the Cold War, the yielding of power by the military in Latin America to civilian and elected governments (including Guatemala), and the enervation of the guerrillas themselves. There is evidence demonstrated from time to time in assassinations and extrajudicial killings that there are still organized forces behind the scenes representing the generals.

The democratization strategy articulated in the generals' National Plan worked to restore the reputation of the government without endangering the autonomy of the military. The generals' decision to change might have been reinforced by a thrust in the U.S. administration (under President Reagan) to counter congressional and other criticism of U.S. policy in Central America by promoting transitions to democracy—through specific grants from the United States Agency for International Development (AID) and the U.S. National Endowment for Democracy (NED).

Critics charged that this "was window dressing, subordinate to the military thrust," a charge Carothers said "had considerable validity" in the early 1980s. However, U.S. policy in the late 1980s "gradually moved from the simplistic equation of elections with democracy to more substantial exertions on democracy's behalf" (Carothers 1999, 34).

In Guatemala, elections for a national assembly were held in 1984 and for a president in 1985. Clean elections were guaranteed by the continued control of the army on the basis of a pact with newly elected president Cerezo. The agreement prevented prosecution of members of the military for war crimes and genocide. The government and principal guerrilla group agreed to a UN Verification Mission in Guatemala in 1994 and to a peace agreement at the end of 1996.

The guerrillas were defeated. Yet the Thesis of National Stability, articulated by General Gramajo in 1989, still identified opponents as operating "outside the law" and labeled those who denounced violations of human rights as "enemies of the state" (Schirmer 1998, 137). It implied that enemies can be punished.

Such "enemies" were punished more than once. On April 24, 1998, Bishop Juan Jose Gerardi Conedra presented the four-volume study of human rights abuses—*Guatemala: Nunca Mas* [Never Again]—prepared over the previous three years by some 600 researchers working under church auspices. Two days after publicly holding the army responsible for 90 percent of the abuses, Gerardi was bludgeoned to death at his house.

Since 1999, some progress has been made in pursuing trials of alleged perpetrators of specific murders—those of the anthropologist Myrna Mack Chang (September 11, 1990) and Bishop Gerardi (April 26, 1998). The trials progress despite assassinations—seven lawyers were killed between October 2000 and February 2001 (AI 2002, 112)—and threats continue against witnesses, lawyers, and forensic anthropologists disinterring bodies.

However, it is not only members of (present and former) death squads who threaten the right to life in Guatemala but rural collective violence, which takes lives by setting the accused on fire. In the countryside, lynch mobs have often killed suspects of ordinary crimes—sometimes after an informal trial. There were 421 such cases between 1996 and 2001. Angelina Godoy argues such violence is a response to "social trauma"—the elimination by the army of traditional leaders in indigenous areas, the abandonment of traditional practices of conflict resolution when people were under army rule, the disruption of bonds among indigenous people during the Civil Patrol period, as well as the rise in crime after 1996, the incapacity of the Guatemalan justice system, and a popular belief in self-help (Godoy 2002). Other tensions stem from the demand by members of the Civil Defense Patrols to be paid for their services during the war (*New York Times,* August 19, 2002, A1).

Evaluations of the state of democracy and human rights in Guatemala vary, some seeing the glass one-quarter full and others seeing it three-quarters empty.

Schirmer concludes: "After decades of naked military rule, the Guatemalan military have crafted a unique Counterinsurgent Constitutional State in which State violence has been reincarnated as democracy" (Schirmer 1998, 258). Conflict (including strikes and public disorder) was conceived by the generals as a threat that justified repression for the "next twenty to twenty-five years of the transition" (Schirmer 1998, 259).

Carothers, evaluating Guatemala's democratic transition in a comparative perspective, concluded: "Guatemala's democratic transition has been slow, excruciating, and littered with casualties. Nonetheless, the country made real progress in the 1990s.... Some segments of the business elite and the security forces remain outside the new political bargain, and remain potential threats to democracy. Indigenous people, who make up more than half the population, are still largely citizens in name only.... Economic power remains extremely concentrated, limiting real political pluralism" (Carothers 1999, 315).

Whatever the level of continuing conflict within Guatemala, U.S. intervention to support a new repressive regime seems less likely to recur. President Clinton said on March 10, 1999, "that support for military forces and intelligence units which engaged in violence and widespread repression [in Guatemala] was wrong, and the United States must not repeat that mistake."

Iraq

To understand the roots of terror and genocide in Iraq, one has to go back to its origins. There has been a persistent lack of solidarity among its people, which instigated its rulers to construct a fictive identity and then justified all means to reinforce that identity. Iraq arose as an independent entity under British tutelage in 1921 after the disintegration of the Ottoman Empire (OE) and the division of land by the victorious allies after World War I, validated by mandates from the League of Nations. Iraq was patched together by the British from three provinces of the Ottoman Empire, joining the predominantly Kurdish province of Mosul with the Arab provinces of Basra and Baghdad in order to enable the latter to draw on the oil revenue from Mosul, without which they could not subsist. The French governed in Syria and Lebanon. The British sought to counter French influence in the area and installed Faisal (leader of the Bedouin Arab revolt during World War I) as monarch; they continued to rule indirectly.

On the eve of his death in 1933, King Faisal wrote: "There is still ... no Iraqi people but unimaginable masses of human beings, devoid of any patriotic idea, imbued with religious traditions and absurdities, connected by no common tie, giving ear to evil, prone to anarchy, and perpetually ready to rise against any government whatever" (Makiya 1989, 160).

Violence against minorities proved popular and was repeatedly used by armies and elites. The Iraqi Army became an independent political force in the 1930s and played a prominent role in pogroms against minorities. In that decade, the Assyrian community, which had formerly aided the British, now sought autonomy or resettlement, fearing for its future. The Iraqi Army, against the wishes of King Faisal, massacred the Assyrians, staging a pogrom that elicited much popular enthusiasm (Makiya 1989, 167–169). Although British intervention prevented the total genocide of the Assyrian Nestorian community, "hundreds and possibly thousands of Nestorians had been massacred in what became known as the Assyrian affair" (Levine 1998). The army overthrew the government in 1936.

The fate of Iraqi Jews was linked to the spread of ideologies hostile to Jews—Nazism, pan-Arabism, and antisemitism. Antisemitism grew in the late 1930s along with pan-Arabism, manifested in demonstrations and bomb-throwing incidents in August 1938; Iraqis also blamed Jews for a massive fire in 1939. In 1941, a pan-Arabist group of four generals proclaimed a state of emergency, siding with the Axis powers. This spurred pro-British Iraqi politicians to flee and British forces to invade the month after, routing the pro-Axis generals and installing a pro-British government. During the next month, June 1941, a pogrom—organized, like most pogroms, with the police siding with the rioters—that killed several hundred Iraqi Jews was instigated by "disgruntled junior officers of the Iraqi army" who thought that they could lead a counterrevolution against the British (Makiya 1989, 180, 312).

Party politics and popular participation spread in the 1940s with the convention of the Ba'ath Party in 1947, a pan-Arab socialist party begun in Syria. Yet the first popular movement was the Iraqi Communist Party (ICP), which emerged in the 1930s and later developed a mass base. After the rise of Nasser in Egypt, his nationalization of the Suez Canal provoked the invasion of Egypt by France, Great Britain, and Israel in 1956. Iraq's monarchy was overthrown by a widely popular officers' coup in 1958, followed by another coup in 1959.

In the next decade, antigovernment demonstrations on the streets were used to register popular disaffection, but changes in government were always made by military coups. A Ba'athist hit team (including the twenty-two-year-old Saddam Hussein) failed to assassinate the ruling general, Brigadier Qassem, in 1959, but a Ba'athist coup overthrew

Qassem in 1963. In 1968, a second Ba'athist coup brought Hussein to the fore as deputy chairman of the Revolutionary Command Council (RCC) in charge of internal security. He became president in 1979.

Thus, no governmental institutions emerged in the postcolonial period to represent public opinion and regulate authority. There were no nongovernmental associations except for political parties (suppressed after 1968). Power was up for grabs. The military used the streets to confirm their authority, not to take power. There was no source of legitimacy. Solidarity had hardly developed since 1933 when King Faisal said, "there is still ... no Iraqi people." This deficit reflected the absence of a historic nation in modern times, the actual diversity of the people of Iraq, and the lack of crosscutting civil institutions. In Iraq during the 1970s, Arab Muslims were divided between Sunni (about 20 percent) and Shi'a (about 50 percent), and the rest constituted Sunni Kurds (about 20 percent), Christians (3 percent), Jews (only 2 percent but estimated to be one-third of the population of Baghdad), and other minorities, mainly Turkic (Batatu 1978, cited in Chirot 1994, 296; Makiya 1989, 180).

Periodically, people joined in mobs (generally government instigated) to kill and terrorize others labeled as enemies. The disunity and potential fratricide of the populace were illustrated by the fighting in Mosul in 1959 and later Kirkuk, precipitated by Ba'athist mobs burning down left-wing bookshops and an ICP bookshop. This led to massacres instigated by ICP supporters. "For four days and four nights Kurds and Yezidis stood against Arabs; Assyrians and Aramean Christians against Arab Moslems.... It seemed as if all social cement dissolved and all political authority vanished.... The struggle between nationalists and Communists had released age-old mechanisms, investing them with an explosive force and carrying them to the point of civil war" (Batatu, cited in Makaya 1989, 237–238).

How was one to unite such disparate people? One classic strategy to produce greater cohesion and conformity is to unite against enemies (Simmel 1955). This could not work with the Kurds, who had real conflicts with the regime, but it did work among others for several decades prior to 1990. The modern history of Iraq illustrates its leaders' strategies of seeking enemies and labeling individuals and groups as enemies, a strategy reinforced under Saddam Hussein. Makiya observes that "the post-1975 secret police in Iraq invent their enemies [after real opposition had been squashed] ... suspects do not have to do anything to be victimized" (1989, 20). The choice of groups to be victimized was based both on realistic conflicts and on symbolic threats created by projecting prejudice and ideological myths on groups—that is, scapegoats.

Attacks on the Jews in 1941 and later in 1969 exemplify the latter: Jews were associated with outside enemies or ideological constructions of enemies. The pan-Arab movement (sympathetic to Nazi Germany) and the Iraqi regime in 1941 disseminated images of Jews depicted in Nazi propaganda as demonic enemies—despite the fact that German Jews and Iraqi Jews were powerless. In 1968–1969, Iraqi Jews were blamed for the failure of Iraq and other Arab states in the 1967 war, although Iraq (not a state bordering Israel) had few losses. Jews became scapegoats for Zionism, Western imperialism, and the backward state of the Arab world. After further charges of spying and the public hanging of thirteen Jews (out of seventeen alleged spies) in 1969, Iraqi Jews fled and could no longer serve the function of uniting the body politic against them.

Potential political participants in Iraq expanded in the post–World War II decades. The Iraqi political class was composed of a developing middle class in the army, civil service, and professionals as well as landowners. The political class needed a political formula or ideology to justify governing.

There were three theoretical political formulas: liberal Iraqi nationalism or binationalism with equality of non-Arabs (e.g., Kurds); communism, a universalistic creed in theory without distinction of tribe, ethnicity, or religion; and pan-Arabism or Ba'athism, which proposed a fictive unity, held together principally (after 1967) by an enemy—Israel. Liberal Iraqi nationalism scarcely existed in Iraq as a theory, party, or movement. The Iraqi Communist Party was the first modern political party in Iraq and had the largest mass following but was suppressed by the Ba'ath (Farouk-Sluglett and Sluglett 1987, 55, 63–65; Makiya 1989, 227).

From its theoretical beginning in the 1930s, Ba'ath (which first arose in Syria) expounded a totalitarian doctrine. Ba'ath was an Arab nationalist movement based on a mystical notion of the Arab nation, rejecting Western culture. A founder of Ba'ath, Michel 'Aflaq, wrote in 1944 that "the nation is not a numerical sum, but an 'Idea' [read Spirit] embodied either in the total or in part of it.... The Leader, in times of weakness of the 'Idea' and its constriction, is not one to substitute numbers for the 'Idea,' but to translate numbers into the 'Idea': he is not the gatherer, but the unifier. In other words he is the master of the singular 'Idea' from which he separates and casts aside all those who contradict it" (Makiya 1989, 195–196).

The Iraqi Ba'ath Party constitution of 1947 called for restricting political rights to those "who have been faithful to the Arab homeland" and denied the legitimacy of existing differences (Makiya 1989, 197). Ba'ath preached "an unbreachable basic moral norm [which] entails as a necessary consequence that all deviance is immediately and directly an act of treason.... This is the fundamental source of the party's coherence, and its license to power" (Makiya 1989, 198).

The use of violence against enemies began before the Ba'ath came to power. Ba'athists began to attack ICP members as early as 1961, murdering 286 on the streets (Farouk-Sluglett and Sluglett 1987, 65). Although the Iraqi Communist Party accommodated to pan-Arabism under Saddam Hussein's regime, he had virtually destroyed the ICP by 1979, by imprisoning, executing, or exiling its leaders (Makiya 1989, 233–234). Whether Saddam needed the cooperation of the ICP depended on how well he balanced temporary alliances with Kurdish leaders; ultimately he did not need them.

Although the Ba'ath Party incorporated pan-Arabism and socialism as an ideal, its identification with the Soviet Union was as a strong national state rather than as a state that professed to be socialist. The Ba'ath emphasized the struggle against imperialism and Zionism (Makiya 1989, 248–253). The Soviet Union was a ready patron of Iraq. Although torture and brutality were not new to the Ba'ath Party, which massacred, killed, and tortured when it came into power in 1963, Soviet assistance enabled the party to claim a higher degree of "professionalism" and control.

Saddam Hussein rose to become head of the Revolutionary Command Council (RCC), or security service, in 1968 and became head of state in 1979. His base has been widely attributed to reliance on family and tribal associates from Takrit. The routine reliance on force in politics in Iraq plus his personal qualities enabled him to take over initially. His characteristics were noted: "Husain's shrewdness and utter ruthlessness" (Farouk-Sluglett and Sluglett 1987, 121); "the young Saddam had made his mark inside the party as a tough and fearless assassin" (Makiya 1989, 225). Hussein's elevation in intra–Ba'ath Party struggles to the Iraqi leadership, "it is said, came through 'Aflaq's intervention ... in 1963" (Makiya 1989, 225).

In power, the Ba'ath reconstructed Iraqi society using tactics from both Nazi Germany and some communist states that transformed the family. Children and teenagers were enrolled in party youth organizations and taught to judge and spy on their parents and to be wary of foreigners. "Non-Ba'athist parents commonly put on a show of support for the regime in front of their children, or even compel them to join the youth organizations. Such conformity draws less attention and provides more security for their children" (Makiya 1989, 79).

Traditional authority structures were subverted but not in the spirit of modernity, which aims to emancipate individuals. Although universal literacy was encouraged and made compulsory, it went along with a state monopoly of the press. There was a great increase of education among women, and they entered the professions. At the same time, patriarchal and traditional authority was undermined in the new Code of Personal Status in 1978. But it did not necessarily protect the rights of women, now subject to judgments by "popular committees" in matters of separation, divorce, and child custody. Nor did it reform Islamic law of polygamy, divorce, and inheritance (Makiya 1989, 89–91).

The Ba'ath Party claimed to have 10,000 activists and half a million sympathizers in 1976, but this increased by the early 1980s to 25,000 activists and 1.5 million sympathizers (Farouk-Sluglett and Sluglett 1987, 185). The Soviet KGB advised Saddam Hussein on the reorganization of internal security, supplied surveillance and interrogation equipment, trained key Iraqi personnel, and exchanged intelligence on the basis of the Iraqi-Soviet Friendship Treaty of 1972 (Makiya 1989, 12–13).

Support for Saddam relied both on rewards and punishment, on awe and fear. Public support was produced by widespread economic dependence on government—about half of the urban workforce by 1980 were government civilian and military employees. By 1980, armed forces and party militia had grown to 677,000—one enforcer for each twenty civilians. One-fifth of the economically active Iraqi labor force had charge of some type of state violence (Makiya 1989, 38).

Government employees (as well as scholarship students) were expected to be informers. The state "had turned the people into its employees.... The party on behalf of the new polity has actually manufactured its own social base" (Makiya 1989, 44). This expansion was made possible by oil revenues to the state, which increased per capita national income in 1979 to thirty-nine times its level in 1970 (Makiya 1989, 94).

The structure of terror followed the totalitarian model of secret police and informers, expanding followers through Ba'ath Party membership and enlisting participation through demonstrations against alleged enemies. The secret police had Baghdad and the rest of the country divided into security zones; video cameras surveyed all major roads. The secret police, ironically known in code as *Jihaz Haneen* (instrument of yearning), was first based in the Ba'ath Party and guided by Saddam Hussein from the beginning (Makiya 1989, 6). Its methods included interrogation, torture, and execution. In the first five years of Hussein's rule, the regime killed "possibly a few thousand people" (mainly communists and Kurds), and unsuccessfully attempted to assassinate Kurdish leader Mulla Mustapha al-Barzani (Makiya 1989, 6).

Security was reorganized with Soviet assistance on the basis of the 1972 Iraqi-Soviet Friendship Treaty, which also included plans for operation outside Iraq, including the provision of aid by Iraqi embassy personnel to Soviet agents abroad (Makiya 1989, 12–13). "The result [of these organizational changes] was virtually absolute control by the party through its own intelligence and the formalization of a system of spying on spies" (Makiya 1989, 16). Some innovative deadly methods were also used beginning in the late 1970s, including heavy metal poisoning in soft drinks offered to suspects and relatives of escapees (Makiya 1989, 64–65).

The chief of internal security, Nadhim Kzar, was executed in 1973 in a party purge, and the bureau was disbanded after accusations that some members were involved in crimes in Baghdad. The growing conflict between party and state enabled Hussein to restructure the secret police in three branches—the *Amn* (state internal security), the *Estikhbarat* (military intelligence), and the *Mukhabarat,* or party intelligence (Makiya 1989, 12–16).

At the same time, Saddam built up the cult of personality (with pictures everywhere), reiterating his name in the media, plastering his image everywhere on the roads, and requiring rituals of obeisance in the schools. Obedience was secured by many reinforcing motives—self-interest, traditional attitudes toward authority, identification with the leader, and internalized fear.

Iraq became "the republic of fear," observed Kanan Makiya (1989)—originally writing under the pseudonym Samir al-Khalil for fear of Hussein's reprisals. Terror was internalized on several levels.

1. There was the perception that Iraqis supported Saddam, reinforced by their enthusiasm at visible popular spectacles. Watching public hangings, they could identify with the union of power and cruelty.
2. There was the knowledge that dissidents or potential dissidents were alone, a message absorbed through experiencing private

terror when relatives disappeared and were brought back to the family in a sealed box along with a death certificate saying that the victim had died in an accident. The relative had to pay the police for the privilege of accompanying the unseen corpse to a hasty interment.

3. There was the consequent belief in the regime's omnipresent oversight and feared reprisals that even prevented Iraqis in exile from going to Amnesty International in the 1970s to report what was happening in Iraq. "Nothing fragments group solidarity and self-confidence like the gnawing suspicion of having an informer in your midst" (Makiya 1989, 63).

4. Finally, there was the knowledge that one was part of the system. Members of the political elite who in other countries might rebel were deterred not only by periodic purges of the leadership but by the knowledge they too had dirty hands. Saddam regularly forced top ministers and party leaders to kill their former colleagues at his order (Broder 2000; Makiya 1989, 72).

Wars—Internal and External

Solidarity was fomented and tested by wars that Hussein waged against enemies, often of his creation, and by internal violence masked by wars. Saddam led Iraq into three wars: against the Kurds, against Iran, and against Kuwait, precipitating the 1991 Gulf War.

Iraq's ability to prosecute these wars was undermined by Saddam's repression. He appointed commanders because he appraised them as not intelligent or not ambitious enough to challenge him. Fear of his response undermined the likelihood the military and civilian experts would give him accurate information, realistic judgments, and advice he didn't want to hear (Woods et al. 2006).

In 1982, at a "low point during the Iran-Iraq War, Saddam asked his ministers for candid advice. With some temerity, the minister of health, Riyadh Ibraham, suggested that Saddam temporarily step down and resume the presidency after peace was established. Saddam had him carted away immediately. The next day, pieces of the minister's chopped up body were delivered to his wife" (Woods et al. 2006, 9).

Wars and their aftermath enabled Saddam to mask the genocide of the Kurds (1987–1988) and decimation of the Marsh Arabs (1992). These were both related to his pursuit of enemies and his attempt to create a monoethnic, monolithic dictatorship out of the disparate people of Iraq.

The most enduring demographic and political schism in Iraq is based on the Kurds. The Kurds had been involved in recurrent internal war for twenty years before the Anfal campaign of genocide (1987–1988). Although the regime was in a conflict in which both sides have had realistic motives, it was a conflict that could have been settled had Iraq adhered to its promises of 1966 and 1970.

Kurdish leader Mulla Mustafa Barzani's major victory in 1966 forced a temporary change in Iraqi government policy. The government acknowledged Kurdish rights in the declaration of June 1966, which was never implemented, leading to periodic fighting of more than eighteen months at the time the Ba'ath took over (Farouk-Sluglett and Sluglett 1987, 128). In 1970, the Ba'ath government made peace with the Kurds on the basis of an autonomy agreement. The Manifesto of March 1970 and the new constitution of July 1970 stated for the first time that "the People of Iraq is formed of two principal nationalities, the Arab nationality and the Kurdish nationality," and promised national rights, cultural rights, and autonomy in the Kurdish regions. But the regime didn't go beyond words, stalling on taking a census because it did not want to prove that a major oil field at Kirkuk was in a Kurdish-majority region. It was not just the Kurdish rebellion or their later collaboration with Iran during the Iran-Iraq War that led to their expropriation and displacement, but also the designs of the regime to exploit their resource—oil (Farouk-Sluglett and Sluglett 1987, 142–143; Saeedpour 1992).

Cooperation between the regime and the Kurds diminished, especially after disclosure of Saddam Hussein's foiled attempt to assassinate Barzani in 1971 and the deportation of 40,000–50,000 "Iranians" long resident in Iraq, including many Kurds, to Iran (Farouk-Sluglett and Sluglett 1987, 158). The latter act was seen by Barzani as part of Hussein's plan to reduce the number of Kurds in Iraq. Barzani then turned away from the regime and began working first with the United States and then with Iran. In June 1973, he proclaimed in an interview with the *Washington Post* that the Kirkuk oil fields were the inalienable property of the Kurdish people and invited the United States to assist him militarily.

The war with the Kurds broke out again in 1974. The government razed the Kurdish towns of Zakko and Quala'at Daza by napalm and bombing. Hundreds of thousands of Kurds fled their cities, some to

Iran. Deportations, summary executions, execution of surrendered Pesh Merga fighters, and public hangings followed.

The Kurdish resistance collapsed after Saddam Hussein and the Shah of Iran negotiated the Algiers Agreement in March 1975, demarcating the border. However, after the Iranian revolution of 1979 and Hussein's initiation of war with Iran, Barzani turned again to Iran. But Kurds were split politically, and Jalal Talabani's Patriotic Union of Kurdistan (PUK) sided with Baghdad.

Hussein is believed to have initiated the war against Iran, because of fear of the spread of the Islamic Revolution (triumphant in Iran in 1979) among Iraqi Shi'is and Hussein's interest in becoming the master of the Gulf region and prime mover in the Arab world (Farouk-Sluglett and Sluglett 1987, 256–257). This was an especially adventurous act because of the much greater resource base of Iran. Iran had 2.8 times the population of Iraq at the time and 3.8 times the land area. The war resulted in an inconclusive end and devastated the Iraqi people with 200,000 killed and wounded, more than 1 percent of all Iraqis (Farouk-Sluglett and Sluglett 1987, 262). In 1984, Iraq began using poison gas in the war against Iran, a fact confirmed by the United Nations in March 1986.

The Kurds saw the Iraq-Iran War as an opportunity to gain the autonomy that Ba'ath had promised but never delivered. Both Kurdish parties cooperated with Iran during the war. The gas attacks on the Kurdish town of Halabja in March 1988, in which between 3,200 and 5,000 died (Human Rights Watch 1995a, 8), drew much international attention, but few realized that it was part of a wave of forty attacks on Kurdish targets between April 1987 and August 1988.

The significance of these attacks was largely overlooked. Although all poison gas attacks in war are war crimes, because they are attacks with a banned weapon, purposeful attacks on civilians (in this case citizens of the attacking state) are more than war crimes—they are crimes against humanity if not genocide (see chapter 6 discussion). However, the Western press expressed doubts as to what had happened, which were "compounded by Iraqi denials and Turkish ambivalence about the influx of Kurdish refugees with their tales and symptoms of gassing" (Ezell 1992, 100–101).

Saddam's terror was undermined, and his rule in several instances was directly challenged in the 1990s after the unsuccessful ending of the Iraq-Iran War (1980–1988) and defeat of Iraq in the subsequent Gulf War (1991) by an international coalition led by the United States after Iraq invaded Kuwait (1990). The Iran-Iraq War led to the genocide of the Kurds (overlooked in the West at the time). The aftermath of the Gulf War led to the mass flight of Kurds to Turkey, only to return to Iraq after the allies in the Gulf War created a protected zone monitored by air. Defeat in the Gulf War also led to outright rebellions in Iraqi cities that were suppressed by government forces and to an insurgency among the Marsh Arabs of the South, which the government defeated by draining the canals, making the marshes uninhabitable (Wood 1994).

It was not until late 1991, after the Gulf War was over, that Western human rights researchers were alerted by Kanan Makiya to the trove of documents that Iraqi State Security had left in the protected Kurdish areas. These documents enabled Human Rights Watch to establish the pattern of *Anfal* (a term from the Koran meaning "the spoils"), or genocide, against the Kurds from February 23 to September 6, 1988 (Human Rights Watch 1995a). Anfal was organized by Hassan al-Majid (later known as Chemical Ali), a cousin of Saddam Hussein and secretary general of the northern branch of the Ba'ath Party. The war masked the Iraqi genocide, as the government sought to resolve the Kurdish problem by eliminating some and terrorizing the remainder who would be under government control in resettled areas.

The Anfal can be seen as the endpoint of more than twenty years of government discrimination, disempowerment, and displacement of the Kurds. These processes began in the 1970s after the agreement between the government and Kurdish group on Kurdish autonomy was not implemented and the government "Arabized" Kurdish areas around the Kirkuk and other oil regions—demographic revision by resettling Arabs and evicting Kurds. Later, Kurds were forcibly evacuated from towns along the border in the oil-rich region and detained in government "strategic" villages.

Two thousand Kurdish villages were destroyed and bombing was authorized against anyone returning to the prohibited areas (Human Rights Watch 1995a). Al-Majid authorized random bombardments and chemical weapons attacks on the prohibited areas. Men were "disappeared" and later killed in mass executions reminiscent of the German Einsatzgruppen in 1941—50,000 to 100,000 victims are estimated. Women and children were incarcerated and removed to remote prisons; most were released after a September 1988 amnesty except for those who died from malnutrition and disease.

The genocide followed the classic pattern discerned in the Holocaust by Raul Hilberg (1961) of definition, concentration, and annihilation. However, only part of the group was destroyed, and selection

was supposed to be individual based on "rigid bureaucratic norms ...
only adhered to casually in practice" (Human Rights Watch 1995a,
13). Displacement, arrests, and executions of Kurds continued after
1988. The October 1987 census allowed just two categories—Arabs
and Kurds. Minorities (such as Assyrian and Chaldean Christians)
who rejected these choices were classed as Kurds.

After the First Gulf War

Many believed that Hussein had invaded Kuwait primarily for economic reasons, needing its oil wealth to restore the Iraqi economy.
Both before and after the first Gulf War, commentators reflected on
the role of Western states in building up Iraq in the decade before
the invasion of Kuwait and the misleading assurance given by the U.S.
ambassador, who said that the United States had no stake in border
disputes with Kuwait. The U.S. secretary of defense, Donald Rumsfeld,
met twice with Saddam Hussein (first in December 1983) to assure him
of U.S. support against Iran. The United States had been providing
intelligence and other support to the Iraqi regime. Iraqi officials were
told not to take seriously official U.S. statements denouncing the use
of chemical weapons. The U.S. Senate's passage of the Prevention of
Genocide Act of 1988 led Iraqi officials to protest to representatives of
Bechtel, arousing threats from Bechtel to turn to technology suppliers
outside the United States. In April 2003, Bechtel won a $680 million
grant from the U.S. Agency of International Development for help
in the reconstruction of Iraq (see Byrne, www/gwu.edu/~nsarchiv/
NSAEBB/NSAEBB107index.htm, "Saddam Hussein: More Secret History," December 18, 2003). Where once Iraq had been just a Soviet
client state, now, with its wealth and state ambitions, it offered equal
opportunity to all exporters.

Kenneth Timmerman, special assistant on foreign affairs in the U.S.
Congress (1993), said, "Saddam was really our Frankenstein's mon-
ster. . . . In the end we had to take him down because he had become
too powerful. All this because of the greed of Western companies
and the lack of strategic awareness of Western governments. Saddam
Hussein had held out the carrot, if you wish, of multibillion dollar
contracts. Everybody wanted to get a piece of the cake. There are literally hundreds of suppliers. Hundreds of companies in West Germany,
in France, in Britain, even in the United States, in Italy, supplying
him with dual use technologies [for agriculture and weapons of mass

destruction], manufacturing equipment, entire weapons factories"
(Wood 1994, 4).

In the 1990s, after his defeat in the Gulf War, the fear and awe of
Saddam Hussein visibly diminished, resulting in uprisings, mass flight,
critical defections, and visible new cruel punishments in reprisal—and
personal and group defiance of such punishments. The public un-
masking of Saddam as strongman was seen when the commander of
a column of Iraqi tanks fleeing from Kuwait on February 28, 1991,
arrived in a central square in downtown Basra and denounced Saddam
in front of a gigantic mural of him. He aimed his guns at Saddam's
face and shot, blasting away his image. "Saddam lost his face, literally,
in a classic revolutionary moment, one that sparked the post–Gulf War
intifada [uprising]. Within hours there was a meltdown of authority
in Iraq, and Saddam Hussein was confronted with the most serious
threat ever to his power" (Makiya 1998, xix). Uprisings against the
Iraqi state in several cities resulted in local crowds taking over the
state security headquarters, killing in some cases security chiefs.
These uprisings were put down by Hussein, whose military means of
repression—tanks and helicopter gunships—were not removed by
the 1991 cease-fire.

The United States feared popular rebellion, preferring that Hussein be brought down by a coup (impossible given the structure
of his regime); it did not want to take the side of antigovernment
forces. National Security Advisor Brent Scowcroft registered the Bush
administration's dismay in an interview with ABC news reporter Peter
Jennings: "I frankly wish it hadn't happened" (Makiya 1998, xx).

Iraqi Kurds, fearing Hussein's revenge, fled to Turkey. The image
of their flight stirred Western public opinion to demand that a safe
haven for them be created. This was established under the authority
of UN Resolution 688, backed by allied flights and denial of Iraqi access to territory north of the thirty-sixth parallel.

The uprising in Kerbala produced evidence that al-Majid, executor
of the Anfal, also called for the extermination of three Marsh Arab
tribes (Wood 1994, 3). The Shi'ia-led revolt led many to seek refuge
in the marshes, which were virtually impossible to patrol. The regime
went on to make their existence impossible by a genocidal campaign
of draining the swamps in which they lived, poisoning the marsh
water, blockading marsh villages, withdrawing food, and burning
houses, so that by 1992 "marsh lakes and streams were choked with
putrefying fish in a deliberately engineered environmental disaster"
(Wood 1994, 3). Iraq told the UN that this was part of a flood control

and land reclamation campaign. Iran recorded almost 50,000 Iraqi refugees from the south in 1993.

After the first Gulf War, Hussein initiated cruel public punishments—such as cutting off ears, amputation of hands, and branding on the forehead—for petty crimes, for example, car thefts, which had increased in this period. A revolt of doctors who had been required to perform amputations and branding and the self-immolation of a victim limited the ability of the regime to implement terror.

Terror no longer deterred highly placed people, including members of Saddam's family, from defecting. Yet the defection of Saddam's son-in-law (Husayn Kamil—who subsequently returned and was killed), the attempted assassination of Saddam's oldest son, and the squashing of plots against him in the Republican Guards showed that Saddam could still foil coup attempts and reconstruct security forces to eliminate potential dissidents (Baram 1998).

Makiya concluded that Hussein, who had always "proceeded by inventing and reinventing his enemies from the entire mass of human material that was at his disposal—including members of his own family ... [had now] switched to a policy of promoting sectarianism between Shi'is and Sunnis in Iraq" (1998, xxxi). Baram viewed Hussein as shifting from primary reliance on his family to reliance on Ba'ath Party old-timers while at the same time reviving Islamic rhetoric as a means of appeal (Baram 1998, 38–41).

Saddam's victims in 1999 reflect his targeting of enemies as well as routinized terror and cruelty: assassinations and attempted assassinations of prominent Shi'i leaders, expulsion of Kurds and other non-Arabs (including Turkmen and Assyrians) from the Kirkuk regions to the Kurdish provinces, torture—including gouging of the eyes and rape of family members in front of detainees—and massive use of the death penalty (AI 1999).

After the 1991 flight of the Kurds, little attention was paid by the West to how Hussein continued to oppress and victimize Iraqis. Instead, the international frame of reference was shifted to all Iraqis as alleged victims of the international community. The domestic conditions affecting the lives of ordinary Iraqis had increasingly become the result of both internal and external pressures. UN sanctions on oil sales, intended to be temporary until Iraq complied with demands of the international community to monitor its chemical, biological, and nuclear weapons, became increasingly ineffectual in monitoring and curbing Iraq's weapons of mass destruction, because Iraq simply refused to comply with the agreements it signed. How the impact of sanctions was manipulated by Hussein's control of the economy and diversion of revenues is seldom discussed, but there is extensive evidence of Hussein's evasion and defiance of the UN sanction regime (mandated by the UN Security Council [UNSC] in 1990), which resulted in the ending of inspections in 1998 without any response from the UNSC (Leitenberg 2002).

By the fall of 2000, the ban on commercial flights had been broken. Although the UN had amended the Oil-for-Food program several times to improve the health of the Iraqi people, the regime refused to cooperate with it. The Iraqi people appeared enervated and preoccupied with maintaining their existence, bitter at the West.[2]

In 2002, U.S. president George W. Bush linked Iraq to potential terrorist attacks on the United States (such as the bombings of the World Trade Center and the Pentagon on September 11, 2001). He declared the need for the disarmament of Iraq's weapons of mass destruction, derogating the effectiveness of UN inspections; called for a regime change in Iraq; and organized war, despite the lack of backing for military intervention from the UN Security Council and world public opinion. The U.S.-led invasion in 2003, which caused the downfall of Saddam Hussein's regime, is discussed in the concluding chapter, as is the question of intervention.

The Persistence of Terror

Terror is a force that inscribes its message in the body of victims: I (or we) make the rules. It violates and humiliates men and women, individuals and families. The methods and tools of terror are learned and cross cultural boundaries. Rape is commonly used as a tool of torture, a ritual of degradation, which also serves to brutalize the perpetrators and reinforce male bonding in patriarchal societies. Chapter 6 discusses the uses of rape and sexual abuse in genocide against both women and men.

State terror emerges from the gap between the state's excess of coercive power and its lack of authority. Power or the ability to control the action of others has two poles: coercion or violence on one hand and authority on the other. Terror relies on violence and fear. Obedience to a government is motivated not only by belief in its legitimacy (authority), but also by self-interest, a generalized human tendency to obey, and calculation of the cost of disobedience. The states under study had more coercive force than authority.

In the four states of terror examined, there was an ongoing or recent conflict over the legitimacy of government and no (or very limited and discontinuous) experience of democratic self-government (suppressed in Guatemala and Argentina). Terror was used as a weapon by a military or party elite, which seized power in Argentina, Guatemala, and Iraq to repress and deter opposition.

Torture and repression were used by the colonial government in Algeria—an administration appointed in Paris, which neither the indigenous Algerians nor the pieds noir believed represented them—to combat terror by the FLN aimed at Muslims as well as settlers. The first objective of the FLN was to demonstrate their power over the indigenous population. The counterinsurgent strategy of the French authorities that justified torture understood this. Yet the conflict between French values and norms against torture and French use of terror—as well as the increasing cost of the war and the improbability of winning—was an element in delegitimizing the war in France, undermining the French government's readiness to fight to maintain the French connection.

The need for terror and patterns of support for (and opposition to) these regimes was largely based on the fact that three of the four states—Algeria, Guatemala, and Iraq—were divided societies, split by nationality or indigenous status or by class. Voice and power in most of these states before the terror depended on ethnicity and ethno-class. In Algeria, the one state in which citizenship openly depended on ethnoclass (ethnicity and religion), Muslim Algerians were legally excluded from power. The excluded in Iraq, Guatemala, and Argentina were demonized as subversives who must be eliminated. This was especially important in Argentina, where victims did not usually differ ethnically from perpetrators.

In these dictatorships and military regimes, virtually no citizens—regardless of ethnicity—had a voice, nor were they secure from terror. Although these states were based on governments of dubious legitimacy, significant sections of the population approved these regimes initially. Some groups indeed benefited from these regimes.

Churches played different roles in different countries in legitimating state terror. In Algeria and Argentina, the Roman Catholic Church largely supported or rationalized state terror. In Guatemala, some elements of the Catholic Church identified with the victims, whereas others conspired with the government.

Although terror was used against all real or perceived sources of opposition in these states, the victims of state terror were selected individually (rather than by targeting whole families, neighborhoods, or regions), as long as the victims belonged to the same group as the ruling elite. When members of excluded groups rebelled against the state in Guatemala and Iraq, the state responded with genocide in regions where these groups were concentrated geographically. These states aimed to destroy the group "in part" (as the UN Genocide Convention—see chapter 6—puts it), slaying many before installing a new regime for social control such as resettlement camps or "model villages" to enforce their rule over the remainder. Divided societies in which political power and rights depend on group identity are more likely than other societies to produce genocide and collective violence when previously subordinated groups reject their place (Fein 1977, 1993b; Kuper 1981). Terror can easily escalate to genocide under these conditions.

However, there is a difference between the contexts in which the same states used terror and genocide. Although the ruling elite might be threatened in both cases, *they only use genocide or mass killing against groups of victims excluded from the universe of obligation of their group, which are physically and culturally distinguishable and who are or might be segregated, isolated, and eliminated.*

In contrast to Algeria, Guatemala, and Iraq, Argentina was a rather racially and ethnically homogeneous society (of predominately Spanish and Italian origin) but polarized politically with few civil institutions not centrally controlled. The Argentines' inability to create a civil society and enduring democratic political order and the authoritarianism of the church and military can be related to the terrorism before 1976, episodes of which might have been constructed by the military in order to find a pretext to intervene. The terrorism was perceived by many Argentines as a justification for the military takeover in 1976. Authoritarianism was a continuing tradition in Argentina throughout the twentieth century and engendered much popular support during the tenure of Peronism, "the fascism of the working class" (Germani 1978, viii).

Argentines appeared to be divided not only about who they were and what they wanted to become but also about the means to change themselves. It was not just the violence, polarization, and inflation of the 1970s that undermined Argentina. The Argentines' lack of independent leadership on the level of civil society, the absence of a class committed to liberalism, and lack of trust in the efficacy of nonviolent change prepared the way for their readiness to accept the "Dirty War" that began in 1973, preceding the terror after the military coup of 1976.

In the states surveyed, doctrines and ideologies were invented to depict a better future, which justified terror and demonized the designated victims. These dogmas spelled out ends and enemies. Some doctrines stressed apparently positive ends, as in Algeria, where French administrators reiterated their historic "civilizing mission" (based on the taken-for-granted notion of their superiority) and the myth of one nation—"Algérie française"—which implied the need to protect Algerians from FLN terror. But other Frenchmen and -women with similar ends maintained that torture was unacceptable. Ordinary French soldiers often did not subscribe to the ideology of the civilizing mission and just regarded the Muslims with racist contempt. FLN ideology justified collective punishment and massacre of the French as both a reprisal and a means of liberation.

In Argentina, the junta promised a Process for National Reorganization, which aimed "to eradicate subversion and to promote economic development ... [to enable Argentina to] 'join the Western, Christian concert of nations'" (Feitlowitz 1998, 22–23). No group except "subversives" was denigrated. Classifying all dissenters and opposition—whether priest or peasant—as subversive was also common in Guatemala. Only after some from the Mayan community joined the insurgents did Indians come to be seen as the collective enemy, a perception drawing on traditional fears. In Iraq, the principles of Ba'athism—"Unity, Freedom, and Socialism" for the Arab nation—led to excluding non-Arabs (e.g., Kurds) and dissidents from the concept of people.

There were few great powers that were actually bystanders in any of these cases. Models and methods (as well as weapons and advisers) to destroy insurgencies came from the major powers, but they usually reinforced local traditions of cruelty and authoritarianism. Such patrons and mentors came from France (governing in Algeria and doctrinally emulated in Argentina), the United States (in Guatemala and in Argentina), and the Soviet Union (in Iraq). Great power patrons focused on historic spheres of influence (the United States in Latin and Central America) and new opportunities (Africa and the Middle East). They studied other employers of terror, including Germany in World War II, to derive new methods, such as "disappearances."

Although patrons could underwrite the costs of the military and defend these states in international arenas, their aid to terror states also drew scrutiny from the media in free states, domestic opposition in Western democracies, and international criticism. Americans protested disappearances and U.S. aid to Argentina and Guatemala. The French protested the moral and other costs of holding on to Algeria. As has been noted, the U.S. role in Algeria was very different from its role in Latin America, forcing France to negotiate with radical adversaries. The United States believed that the Algerian War and France's unrealistic stance compromised its influence in Africa and Asia.

State terror in Algeria and Argentina ended in less than ten years but continued for more than thirty years in Guatemala and Iraq. Foreign support helped but does not wholly account for the duration of these regimes. Let us consider other explanations for why societies support dictators for shorter and longer periods of time.

1. *Perhaps people in such states truly believed in their leaders, whose image was enhanced by a cult of personality.* Saddam Hussein did develop a cult of personality in Iraq, but there is no evidence that awe alone (rather than fear of his reprisals) compelled obedience.

2. *Such states provide order and enhance the standard of living of their people.* This is sometimes true in the short run. Crude compulsion was not generally needed in Argentina and Iraq, where it appears that the majority of the population supported the government initially, perhaps not least because of the rise in their economic fortunes. Argentines enjoyed the years of "sweet money," with luxury goods secured by large loans on easy terms from the International Monetary Fund and U.S. banks (Feitlowitz 1998, 154–155). Iraqis saw their incomes and educational opportunities multiply, as Hussein nationalized and exploited oil revenues for social development.

   Workers and peasants had different perspectives than did the urban middle classes. Terror undermined class bargaining, as union and peasant organizers were slain in Argentina and Guatemala. Class-based organizations were especially targeted in Guatemala where there was widespread opposition to the policies supported by the military and oligarchy.

3. *Choices are limited under dictatorship, and a majority or part of the population is complicit with it.* This explanation is often true but for different reasons. Citizens might be complicit because they believe in the state, because they fear the state, or because they work for the state.

Terror states present many new opportunities for collaboration. Agents, informants, and denouncers were systematically employed by the state in Iraq on a grand scale. Complicity can be motivated by belief and self-interest but also can be seen as a rational response to a forced choice. Terror presents people with a problem: They can either be part of the apparatus sharing power and do its bidding or be its victim (Walter 1964). Many prefer the former.How did the bystanders who were not collaborators reconcile themselves to the disappearance of their fellow citizens? Was their support for the regime based on the exclusion of "subversives" from their universe of obligation? It was not that simple, because the "subversives" were often neighbors, family, and friends. Two mechanisms have been noted. Argentines in retrospect often say that they did not see anything, but contradictory evidence presents itself consistently in anecdotes. When people in their circle became victims, bystanders suppressed sight and insight.

Another way to distance the victims is to blame them. Disappearances might be explained away as the fault of the disappeared. A former Argentine political prisoner whom I met recalled what his aunt said when first hearing of his disappearance, "Por algo sera"—it must be for something; he must have done something. Thus, the bystanders were complicit in denial, perhaps to maintain their belief in a just world, to maintain their innocence, or to suppress fears that might arise if they acknowledged that their neighbors and relatives were being abducted, tortured, and killed.

In Guatemala, slain bodies disfigured by torture were repeatedly left along roads in the countryside, but few people interviewed peasants, who fled in large numbers. Visibility was diminished in the cities by government order, including control of the media, which did not report rural deaths. Some urban Guatemalans say that they did not know about the terror.

There are many variations on knowing, not knowing, and denial. As Stanley Cohen puts it, there is often "passive support" for repressive governments and "passive opposition" (or inner emigration) (Cohen 2001, 147). "Geras [*The Contract of Mutual Indifference,* 1998] nicely captures the nuances of not knowing, even about mass murder. 'There are the people who affect not to know, or who do not care anyway, who are indifferent; or who are afraid for themselves or for others, or who feel powerless; or who are weighed down, distracted or just occupied (as most of us) in pursuing the aims of their own lives'" (Cohen 2001, 146).

Because of this and because of the terror itself, citizens are not likely to challenge successful terror states openly. The exceptions (as in Guatemala and Algeria) occur when the state is at war with a majority of the population and the rebels are organized along military and paramilitary lines. However, the level of brutality was checked in both cases not by the rebels but by external pressure on the regimes to negotiate peace. The opposition of the United States to military leaders in Argentina and Guatemala and international support for Algerian independence were among the factors pressing the leaders of Argentina, Guatemala, and France in Algeria to give in or get out.

Terror ended in these states by the government stepping down, except in Iraq (discussed in chapter 9). In Algeria, France negotiated its retreat, agreeing to complete Algerian independence. In Argentina, the junta, responding to public uproar after its defeat in the Falklands War, stepped down. In Guatemala, the regime agreed to a protracted internationally brokered truce between the government and the guerrillas for a transition to democracy, which the regime expected to be able to control.

Lost and unwinnable wars were critical in destabilizing dictatorships in these states. Terror states are more likely than other states to invade their neighbors and trigger wars between states: for example, Argentina in the Falkland Islands and Iraq in Iran and Kuwait. But military defeat alone is not always enough to bring down a regime.

Military defeat in two wars did undermine authority and activate opposition in Iraq after the first Gulf War, but the response of Saddam Hussein was to repress revolts brutally and institute a reign of public cruelty. The absence of sufficient and timely international support for the opposition in Iraq allowed Saddam to put down a popular rebellion and continue in power until the U.S.-led intervention in 1993.

Unless governments are persuaded to step down or are disabled, it is unlikely that a terror state that completely controls the means of violence can be replaced. Issues about intervention are discussed in the last chapter.

Notes

1. Although accusations of genocide in Guatemala were made in the 1980s by some (McClintock 1985, 256–259), estimates of the identity and number of victims by human rights organizations were absent or vague. An exception is anthropologist Ricardo Falla, "We Charge Genocide" (Jonas et al. 1984, 112–119), who traced the pattern of massacre of Mayans and evidence of intent in terms of the criteria of the UN Genocide Convention in a 196-page brief. The evidence in the CIIDH report showed a pattern of

group targeting and massacres of indigenous peoples, leading the CEH to call the killings in the Mayan highlands from 1980 to 1982 genocide. The victims include the Maya-Canjobal, Maya-Ixil, Maya-Quiche, and Maya-Achi. CIIDH statisticians estimated that from 1981 to 1983 almost half the indigenous people were killed in three of six regions whereas less than 10 percent (in most cases much less than 10 percent) of nonindigenous people were killed in these regions in those years (figure 4 in memorandum, "Estimation of killing rates, by ethnic group and region," from H. Spirer to H. Fein, July 17, 1999).

2. Despite the Oil-for-Food program, begun in 1996, the reported rise in infant mortality—which Richard Garfield (1998) estimated to have resulted in 96,736 to 216,669 excess deaths between 1990 and 1997—has been attributed by many to the sanctions per se, whereas others attribute them to the Iraqi government's response as well, including the UN secretary-general, Kofi Annan, who observed that Iraqis are "often victims both of their own government and of the measures taken against it." The only way to end that, he added, "is for Iraq to comply with council [UN Security Council] decisions" (Crossette, *New York Times,* March 25, 2000, A3). It has also been estimated that Iraq has sold $32 billion worth of oil since 1996 under the Oil-for-Food program, spent $1 billion for medical supplies and more than $6 billion for food, and exported medical supplies and food in this period (Leitenberg 2002).

6
States of Genocide, Genocidal Massacres, and Ethnic Cleansing

The main thesis ... is that the sovereign territorial state claims, as an integral part of its sovereignty, the right to commit genocide, or engage in genocidal massacres, against people under its rule, and that the United Nations, for all practical purposes, defends this right.
—Leo Kuper, *Genocide: Its Political Use in the Twentieth Century,*
1981, 161

A strongly worded report issued today [December 16, 1999] by an international panel of experts holds both the United Nations and leading member countries, primarily the United States, responsible for failing to prevent or end the genocide in Rwanda in 1994, which cost hundreds of thousands of lives. The report, commissioned by Secretary General Kofi Annan, who was then head of the peacekeeping department, spares no one, naming those in the highest reaches of the United Nations who were running the operation in Rwanda, including Mr. Annan and his predecessor, Secretary General Boutros Boutros-Ghali.... Today Mr. Annan called the report "thorough and objective." "On behalf of the United Nations, I acknowledge this failure and express my deep remorse," he said.
—*New York Times,* December 17, 1999, 1

Genocide in the twentieth century has belied the hopes aroused by the 1946 international trials of Nazi war criminals at Nuremburg—never again would mass murder of people as an act of policy unroll undeterred and unpunished. This chapter examines such acts and related causes of mass death: genocidal massacres and deadly ethnic riots or pogroms (which may be precursors to genocide), and "ethnic cleansing." It will focus especially on the genocide of the Rwandan Tutsis in 1994, a genocide that destroyed the overwhelming majority of the people targeted—as did the genocides of the Armenians and Jews during World Wars I and II, respectively—and the ongoing genocide (in 2007) in Darfur, Sudan, a genocide viewed by some observers as Rwanda in slow motion.

Many people have only become aware recently that war was not the greatest killer of civilians in the twentieth century. State killings of civilians exceed the toll of victims of war in the twentieth century— R. J. Rummel estimated 169 million dead from what he calls "democide"—and claimed four times the number of citizens killed in war during the twentieth century to 1990 (Rummel 1994).

Frank Chalk (see figure 6.1) shows the overlap of acts denoted as genocide, crimes against humanity, and war crimes in international law. David Scheffer (2004) proposed that those are best classed as "mass atrocity crimes" for prevention.

Genocides and politicides—state killing of people in groups targeted because of organized political opposition (Harff and Gurr 1988)—caused an estimated 2.6 times the number of lives lost in the aftermath of natural disasters between 1967 and 1986 (Fein 1993a). The use of genocide spread in Africa, Asia, and Latin and Central America since 1945, and it reappeared in Europe. Table 6.1 (later discussed) illustrates the range and toll of twentieth-century genocides that elicited indictments by national or international tribunals and commissions or by human rights organizations based on the UN Genocide Convention—including pre-1948 cases meeting these criteria. It is not a comprehensive list of allegations and cases of genocide (see table 6.1 notes and later discussion).

What Is Genocide?

To some, genocide is a discredited charge, because the term is so often used as rhetoric and hyperbole in political attacks—for example, against discrimination or against integration, and against drug use or against methadone programs (Fein 1993a, 4–5). However, genocide has a clear definition in international law, which impels us to go beyond the hyperbole. The concept and term *genocide* was created by Raphael Lemkin, in response to crimes similar to those he described

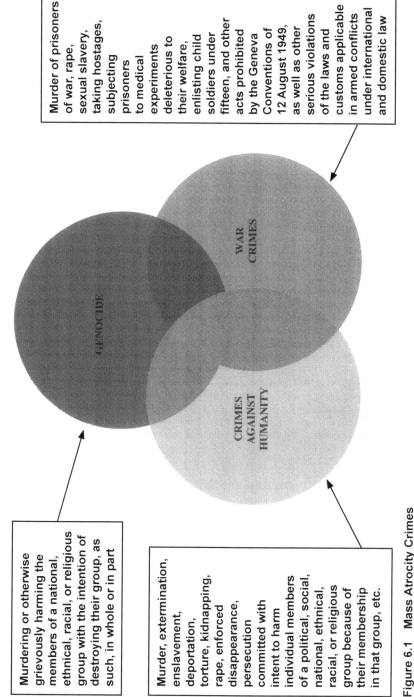

Murder of prisoners of war, rape, sexual slavery, taking hostages, subjecting prisoners to medical experiments deleterious to their welfare, enlisting child soldiers under fifteen, and other acts prohibited by the Geneva Conventions of 12 August 1949, as well as other serious violations of the laws and customs applicable in armed conflicts under international and domestic law

WAR CRIMES

GENOCIDE

CRIMES AGAINST HUMANITY

Murdering or otherwise grievously harming the members of a national, ethnical, racial, or religious group with the intention of destroying their group, as such, in whole or in part

Murder, extermination, enslavement, deportation, torture, kidnapping, rape, enforced disappearance, persecution committed with intent to harm individual members of a political, social, national, ethnical, racial, or religious group because of their membership in that group, etc.

Figure 6.1 Mass Atrocity Crimes
Source: Frank Chalk after the concepts of former U.S. war crimes ambassador David Scheffer

Table 6.1 Genocides from 1915 to 2006 Leading to Indictments and Findings by Governments, Intergovernmental Organizations, and Human Rights Nongovernmental Organizations—Tribunals, Commissions, and Investigations

Date(s)	Perpetrator	Victims	No.	% of Victims	Source
1. 1915	Ottoman Empire	Armenians	1.2 mil.	66%	*, ##, **
2. 1933	Soviet Union	Ukrainians	≥3.1 mil.	≥10%	*
3. 1941–1945	Germany et al.	Jews	5.5–6 mil.	67%	#
4. 1941–1945	Germany et al.	Russian POWs	3.3 mil.	58%	
5. 1941–1945	Germany et al.	Roma	0.5–1.5 mil.	INA	
6. 1941–1945	Croatia	Serbs	265,000–340,000	13–21%	##
7. 1959	China/Tibet	Buddhists	INA	INA	**
8. 1968–1973	Paraguay	Ache	900	43–53%	**
9. 1971	Pakistan	Bengalis	1.5 mil.	2%	**
10. 1972	Burundi	Hutus	100,000	5%	**
11. 1975–1979	Kampuchea	Khmer and ethnic minorities	≥1,671,000	≥21%	**, ##
12. 1981–1983	Guatemala/ Indians	Ixil and Rabinal regions	24,000	42%	*
13. 1983–2005	Sudan	southerners and Nubians (to 1998)	1.9 mil.	38%	**
14. 1987–1988	Iraq	Kurds	100,000	8%	**
15. 1980–1989	Afghanistan	Afghans	1.4 mil.	9%	###
16. 1992–1995	Bosnia-Herzegovina	Non-Serbs	>10,000	INA	*
17. 1994	Rwanda	Tutsis	507,000	70%	*, #, ##
18. 2003–	Sudan in Darfur	African tribes	>400,000	INA	*, **

Notes:

% represents the percent of the total victim group.

? indicates uncertainty that victimization ended at that date or that estimate and percent of victims dead can be made at this time.

INA—information not available.

Key to type of source allegation and documentation:

*	documentation by governmental commission
**	documentation by international human rights organization
#	indictments by international tribunal
##	indictments by national court
###	charge or documentation by UN body

Often there is more than one source for each case, and official sources are supplemented by secondary scholarly sources. Source references to each line are in chapter notes. Inclusion of a country/perpetrator and victim in this table is based on the state and reliability of documentation of evidence gleaned from national and international tribunals and commissions and independent nongovernmental human rights organizations and estimates of genocide. Some indictments or charges by governments not credited by independent human rights organizations excluded from this table are: Ethiopia (1983–1984), Equatorial Guinea (1968–1979), Nigeria/Biafra (1967–1969), and Romania (1989).

Sources:

1. Viscount James Bryce, *The Treatment of Armenians in the Ottoman Empire 1915–1916,* ed. Arnold Toynbee (London: HSMO, 1916)—an official UK White Paper. For postwar trials and evidence, see Vahakn N. Dadrian, "The Armenian Genocide in Official Turkish Records," *Journal of Political and Military Sociology,"* vol. 22, no. 1 (Summer 1994); and Gary J. Bass, *Stay the Hand of Vengeance* (Princeton, NJ: Princeton University Press, 2000), ch. 4. See resolutions affirming genocide of European Parliament (July 18, 1987), Russian Duma (April 14, 1995), Belgian Senate (March 26, 1998), French National Assembly (May 29, 1998), and other states at www.armenian-genocide.org/affirmintro.htm. An independent study by the International Center for Transitional Justice (ICTJ) that was requested by the Turkish Armenian Reconciliation Commission concluded in 2003 that the 1915 massacres meet the internationally accepted definition of genocide, but Armenians cannot use this finding to lay "legal, financial or territorial claim" against Turkey because the UNGC does not provide for retroactive application. It concludes that four elements of genocide were present, for "at least some of the perpetrators of the Events knew that the consequences of their actions would be the destruction, in whole or in part, of the Armenians of eastern Anatolia, as such, or acted purposively towards this goal, and, therefore, possessed the requisite genocidal intent ... the Events, viewed collectively, can thus be said to include all the elements of the crime of genocide as defined in the Convention, and legal scholars as well as historians, politicians, journalists and other people would be justified in continuing to so describe them" (ICTJ, "The Applicability of the United Nations Convention on the Prevention and Punishment of the Crime of Genocide to Events Which Occurred during the Early Twentieth Century" (New York: ICTJ, 1993).

2. Commission on the Ukraine Famine, *Report to Congress: Investigation of the Ukraine Famine 1932–33* (Washington, DC: United States Government Printing Office, 1988); see also *International Commission of Inquiry into the 1932–33 Famine in Ukraine, The Final Report 1990* (Stockholm: Stockholm Institute of Public and International Law, no. 109, 1990).

3. International Criminal Tribunal at Nuremburg, 1946. For estimates of Jewish victims, see Helen Fein, "Reviewing the Toll: Jewish Dead, Losses and Victims of the Holocaust," *Shoah* (Spring 1981): 20–26.

4. Jurgen Foster, "The German Army and the Ideological War against the Soviet Union," in *The Policies of Genocide: Jews and Soviet Prisoners of War in Nazi Germany,* ed. Gerhard Hirschfeld (London: Allen & Unwin, 1986), 15–29.

5. Ian Hancock says: "There are not accurate figures either [for the number killed or] for the prewar Romani population in Europe." The latest (1997) figure from the U.S. Holocaust Memorial Museum Research Institute in Washington puts the number of Romani lives lost by 1945 at "between a half and one-and-a-half million." In "Roma: Genocide of Roma in the Holocaust," *Encyclopedia of Genocide,* vol. 2, ed. Israel Charny (Santa Barbara, CA: ABC-Clio, 1999), 507.

6. The genocide in Croatia was presented in the indictment of Cardinal Stepinac in postwar Yugoslavia discussed (with other evidence) in Helen Fein, *Accounting for Genocide: National Responses and Jewish Victimization during the Holocaust* (New York: Free Press, 1979), 102–105, 374–376. My estimate of Serb victims therein has changed because of more recent evidence based on the 1964 census of Yugoslavia presented by Srdjan Bogosavljevic, "The Second World War—Victims in Yugoslavia" [translated], *Republika* (Belgrade), June 11–15, 1995, xi–xvi.

7. International Commission of Jurists, *Tibet and the Chinese People's Republic* (Geneva: ICJ, 1960).

8. International League for Human Rights; see Richard Arens, *Genocide in Paraguay* (Philadelphia, PA: Temple University Press, 1976).

9. International Commission of Jurists, *The Events in East Pakistan, 1971* (Geneva: ICJ, 1972). The ICJ considered that this was a prima facie case that genocide was committed by the Pakistani authorities against the Hindu population of East Pakistan, and there might be a case made for genocide against Bengalis, given the pattern of indiscriminate killings on occasion, but it did not make any numeric estimates of victims of genocide and did not believe later Bengali killings of Biharis and non-Bengalis

(believed to be collaborators) in Bangladesh constituted genocide (ICJ 1972, 56–57). Because of the wide range of estimates and lack of access to authoritative primary sources on victimization, I have used the median estimate of numbers killed in East Pakistan by the Pakistani authorities as calculated by R. J. Rummel, *Death by Government* (Rutgers, NJ: Rutgers University Press, 1994), ch. 8, from secondary sources.

10. René Lemarchand and David Martin, *Selective Genocide in Burundi* (London: Minority Rights Group, 1974); M. Bowen, G. Freeman, and Kay Miller, *Passing By: The United States and Genocide in Burundi* (New York: Carnegie Endowment for International Peace, 1973); and René Lemarchand, *Burundi: Ethnic Conflict and Genocide* (Washington, DC: Woodrow Wilson Center Press/Cambridge University Press, 1994), 26–28, 96–105.

11. This estimate is based on sample studies of surviving Cambodians cited in Ben Kiernan, *The Pol Pot Regime* (New Haven, CT: Yale University Press, 1996). Hurst Hannum and David Hawk, *The Case against the Standing Committee of Kampuchea* (New York: Cambodian Documentation Commission, 1986) cited higher estimates from various sources in the 1980s. Craig Etcheson offered new estimates, based on exhumations of mass graves and new demographic analyses, in *After the Killing Fields* (New York: Praeger, 2005), 119. He concluded that approximately 1.1 million Cambodians were victims of execution and a similar number died from "other causes, primarily starvation, disease, and exhaustion"—what I call "genocide by attrition"—with the most likely number 2.2 million, or a range of "excess mortality between 2.0 and 2.5 million, between 29 and 31 percent of the total population." There were trials of the Khmer Rouge leaders under the People's Revolutionary Tribunal in 1979 during the time of the Vietnamese-dominated government of Cambodia. There was criticism of the tribunal by lawyers who believed it did not meet international standards. In July 2006, a joint national and international Khmer Rouge Tribunal was slated to begin.

12. The Guatemalan Commission for Historical Clarification (CEH) determined genocide had occurred in Guatemala (for report, see http://hrdata.aaas.org/ciidh). I am grateful to Prof. Herbert F. Spirer of the Columbia University Center for the Study of Human Rights, statistical analyst for CEH, for the estimate of victims and population. Also see Patrick Ball, Paul Kobrak, and Herbert F. Spirer, *State Violence in Guatemala, 1960–1996: A Quantitative Reflection* (Washington, DC: American Association for the Advancement of Science, 1999).

13. United States Committee for Refugees; see J. Milton Burr, *A Working Document II: Quantifying Genocide in the Southern Sudan 1983–1998* (Washington, DC: USCR, December 1998).

14. Human Rights Watch/Middle East Watch, *Iraq's Crime of Genocide: The Anfal Campaign against the Kurds* (New Haven, CT: Yale University Press, 1995).

15. *Report of the Independent Counsel on International Human Rights on the Human Rights Situation in Afghanistan,* 42 UN GAOR C. 3 (Agenda Item 12), UN Doc. A/C.3/42/8 (1987), edited and reprinted in W. M. Reisman and C. H. Norchi, "Genocide and the Soviet Occupation of Afghanistan," *Institute for the Study of Genocide Newsletter,* no. 4 (1988), p. 7; and Marek Sliwinski, "The Decimation of a People," *Orbis* 39 (1989): 33.

16. The International Criminal Tribunal for the Former Yugoslavia Indictment against Slobodan Milosevic, Case No. It-01-51-01, enumeration from Schedules A & B. The ICTY exhibits should not be regarded as a comprehensive estimate of victims, but documentation of exemplary cases at hand. Besides these, there were an estimated 20,000 cases of genocidal rape in Yugoslavia, more than 200,000 deaths, and more than 250,000 people who fled Bosnia-Herzegovina in this period.

17. Indictments by Rwanda, International Criminal Tribunal on Rwanda, and documentation by Human Rights Watch (HRW) and International Federation of Human Rights (IFHR); for estimate, see Alison Des Forges, *Leave None to Tell the Story: Genocide in Rwanda* (New York: Human Rights Watch, 1999), 15–16.

18. Eric Markusen and Samuel Totten, "Investigating Allegations of Genocide in Darfur: The U.S. Atrocities Documentation Team and the UN Commission of Inquiry," in Joyce Apsel, ed., *Darfur: Genocide before Our Eyes* (New York: Institute for the Study of Genocide, 2005); also Reeves, Fowler, and Leaning, in Apsel; www.sudanreeves.org.

before World War II as the crime "of barbarity," including the massacre of the Armenians in 1915. Lemkin first devised the term *genocide* to explain Nazi crimes in occupied Europe. It was later specified by the United Nations and incorporated into the UN Convention on the Prevention and Punishment of the Crime of Genocide (hereafter UNGC) (Kuper 1981, 11–39; Lemkin 1944; Power 2002, 21–22).

The UNGC transformed genocide into an international crime whether committed in times of peace or war. Yet from 1946 (the International Military Tribunal at Nuremberg) until the creation of the International Criminal Tribunal on War Crimes in the Former Yugoslavia (1993), the international community had not attempted to punish genocide despite the numbers committed in this period. Although disagreement exists among genocide scholars about the best generic definition of genocide, the definition in international law is that of the UNGC (Article II):

> In the present Convention, genocide means any of the following acts *committed with intent to destroy, in whole or in part, a national, ethnical, racial or religious group, as such* [my italics]:
>
> (a) Killing members of the group;
> (b) Causing serious bodily or mental harm to members of the group;
> (c) Deliberately inflicting on the group conditions of life calculated to bring about its physical destruction in whole or in part;
> (d) Imposing measures intended to prevent births within the group;
> (e) Forcibly transferring children of the group to another group.

The legal definition has been criticized for its omission of political groups and social classes—a dangerous loophole (Drost 1959, vol. 2, 122–123; Feierstein 2006; Kuper 1981, 19–38; Van Schaack 1999; Whitaker 1985). Leblanc (1988, 292–294) points out many reasons why the inclusion of political groups would have been unwise: difficulty in identifying what is a political group, their instability, potential misuses of genocide labeling, and the right of the state to protect itself against groups who themselves might use violence and terror against the state.

Many scholars prefer a generic definition that embraces all groups, including political groups and social classes. Some have proposed a broader definition (Chalk and Jonassohn 1990; Charny 1999, vol. 1, 4–9), and others have differentiated politicide from genocide (Harff and Gurr 2001) or constructed a more embracing category, *democide,* to encompass all state killings of civilians (Rummel 1994).

My generic definition, which parallels the terms of the UNGC, focuses on collectivities—persisting identity groups that include, but are not limited to, ethnic, religious, racial, and national groups. It assumes (with much historical validation) that the intent of the UNGC was to protect nonviolent collectivities, real groups that are the source of identity and exist apart from the invention of the state perpetrators, whose members are persecuted for who they are, not what they have done. Its terms encompass the more specific prescribed acts (see UNGC article 2 subparts in brackets) of the UNGC. "Genocide is sustained purposeful action by a perpetrator to physically destroy a collectivity directly [see UNGC, Art. 2, a-c] or indirectly, through interdiction of the biological and social reproduction of group members [UNGC, Art. 2, d-e], sustained regardless of the surrender or lack of threat offered by the victim" (Fein 1993a).

For practical purposes, when discussing contemporary genocides, I employ the UNGC definition, because I believe that it is useful to maintain a common universe of discourse among genocide scholars, international lawyers, and human rights monitors; to discriminate between victims of genocide and other violations of life integrity; and to recognize related violations in international law, such as war crimes and crimes against humanity (see figure 6.1 and Gutman and Rieff [1999]).

All political victims of state terror are not victims of genocide with intent to destroy a real group "in whole or in part." Some are not members of a real group, and others are alleged to belong to fictive groups, categories created by the arbitrary labeling of dictators—for example, "wreckers," "enemies of the state," "subversives," and the like.

States of terror are prone to become states of genocide, especially when they face opposition from certain identifiable minority groups (see discussion of genocide of Kurds in Iraq and Mayan Indians in Guatemala in chapter 5), but not all the victims in such states are victims of genocide, and not all victims of genocide have challenged the state.

Definitions, Cases, and Accountability

Table 6.1 lists cases of genocide from 1915 to 2005 *documented* by trials and commissions (national and international) and international human rights groups. Exclusion of other cases does not imply that a mass killing reported by another source did not occur. For this table, official sources are supplemented by secondary scholarly sources. Inclusion of a country/perpetrator and victim in this table is based on the state and reliability of documentation of evidence gleaned from national and international tribunals and commissions and independent nongovernmental human rights organizations and estimates of genocide. Some indictments or charges against governments not credited by independent human rights organizations that have been excluded from this table are: Ethiopia (1983–1984), Equatorial Guinea (1968–1979), Nigeria/Biafra (1967–1969), and Romania (1989).

Including cases recognized by other scholars but avoiding duplication of cases cited (Ezell 1989 in Fein 1993a; Harff and Gurr 2001; Kuper 1981; Rummel 1994), I estimate that there have been more than three times as many alleged cases of genocide and political killing in the twentieth century as cases documented by judicial standards listed in table 6.1 (58:18). Looking at the cases documented (counting multiple perpetrators in one case), in only about one out of four cases was anyone tried and punished—or is now serving time (omitting judgments in absentia)—for genocide and crimes against humanity: In the Ottoman Empire, post–World War II Germany, Yugoslavia and Bosnia-Herzegovina, and Rwanda. If all the alleged perpetrators are taken into account, the probability of trial and punishment is only one out of about twelve alleged cases. Genocide is almost the perfect crime from the calculus of the potential *génocidaires* (French term for "perpetrators of genocide"). In the overwhelming majority of cases, state killers got away with mass murder. In virtually all massacres in which *génocidaires* aim to annihilate all the members of a group ("with intent to destroy in whole") and succeed in killing a majority, the victims belong to a "national, ethnical, racial or religious group" (UNGC II), which the *génocidaires* aim to eliminate "as such."

"Causing serious bodily or mental harm to members of the group" and "deliberately inflicting on the group conditions of life calculated to bring about its physical destruction in whole or in part" can include imposing disease-producing conditions and starvation in communities, camps, and ghettos; slave labor; torture; and poisoning air and water. This is "genocide by attrition," which I have documented in Sudan, in the Warsaw Ghetto (1941–1943), and in Democratic Kampuchea (1975–1979) (Fein 1997).

Chapter 6

Detection of Genocide in the Making

In order to identify genocides, one needs not only a clear definition but criteria indicating what to look for on the ground. For this reason, the following paradigm (box 6.1) cites necessary conditions and questions to distinguish genocide from war crimes and genocidal massacres.

In tracing the toll of genocides historically, we often rely on estimates of death, the easiest act to identify and tally. It is easy to forget

---

Box 6.1 Paradigm to Detect Genocide (with Indicator Questions)

1. There was a sustained attack or continuity of attacks by the perpetrator to physically destroy group members.
   a. Did a series of actions or a single action of the perpetrator leading to the death of members of group X occur?
   b. What tactics were used to maximize the number of victims? Such tactics include roundups, isolation, and concentration of victims and orders to report.
   c. What means besides direct killing were used to destroy the victims or to interdict the biological and social reproduction of the group? Actions might include poisoning air or water, imposed starvation or disease, sexual torture and rape, forcible prevention of birth, and involuntary transfer of children.
   d. What was the duration, sequence of actions, and number of victims? Trace the time span, repetition of similar or related actions, and the number of victims.

2. The perpetrator was a collective or organized actor or commander of organized actors. Genocide is distinguished from homicide empirically by the fact it is never an act of a single individual.
   a. Were the perpetrators joined as an armed force, paramilitary force, or informal band?
   b. Was there a continuity of leadership or membership of perpetrators or similar bases of recruitment for such forces?
   c. Were these forces authorized or organized by the state or a counter-authority?
   d. To whom were those forces responsible—an agent of the state, army, party, or counterauthority?
   e. Were they organized and garbed to display or to deny government responsibility?

3. Victims were selected because they were members of a collectivity.
   a. Were victims selected irrespective of any charge against them individually?

---

that *génocidaires* aim not just at immediate destruction, but at severing generational bonds (see UNGC II b–e above), which means that they must plan what to do with women and children. The immediate killing of all group members—men, women, and children—is rare. *Génocidaires* might choose to prevent reproduction within the group or to appropriate the progeny in order to destroy the group in the long run. Rape, forced marriage and sexual slavery, enforced pregnancy, forced adoption and conversion of children, and forced abortion

---

Box 6.1

b. Were they chosen on the basis of a state administrative designation of their group identity, their own criteria of identity, or by physical, linguistic, or other signs or stigmata of identity?

c. Were they chosen on the basis of status within the collectivity, e.g., priests, religious leaders, or educated class?

d. What was the basis of the collectivity, e.g., religion, race, ethnicity, language, tribe, or other bond?

e. Were victims preselected before killing? Evidence of preselection includes their prior legal definition; stripping of citizenship, civil rights, state posts, licenses, state pensions and benefits, and legal group recognition; segregation and marking; rounding up and ghettoization or concentration.

4. The victims were defenseless or were killed regardless of whether they surrendered or resisted.

a. Is part of the victims' group armed and organized to physically resist the perpetrators' group?

b. Is their level of armament sufficient, and is their stated intent to wage war against the perpetrators? Or is it to defend themselves from being seized?

c. Is there evidence—if the victims were armed—that they were killed after surrender and that unarmed members of the group were systematically killed?

5. The destruction of group members was undertaken with intent to kill, and murder was sanctioned by the perpetrator.

a. Can deaths of group members be explained as accidental outcomes?

b. Is there evidence of repetition of destruction by design or as a foreseeable outcome?

c. Is there direct evidence of orders or authorization for the destruction of the victims?

d. At what level did the authorization occur?

e. Is there prima facie evidence that the pattern of acts and personnel involved show that authorities had to plan, organize, or overlook a pattern of destruction?

f. Is there any negative evidence of sanctions against agents responsible for such acts?

are means to these ends. Rape is not just a means of torture, causing serious bodily and mental harm to women. Rape also threatens the future of the group by often impeding the future marriage of unmarried women, who are shamed by the stigma, and threatens the classification of the child as a member of the mother's group (rather than that of the rapist).

Why Do Genocides Occur?

Many scholars have differentiated four causes or types of genocide, which are summarized in table 6.2. In examining cases, mixed motives are often found. Typology can be a useful guide to the range of rationales and motives, but these types are best observed as variables—causes with different effects in different cases. Many of the genocides listed in table 6.1 can be viewed as retributive—murderous responses by a regime that were preceded by threats to the regime by the victims' group. However, it is important to note that in several cases in which the state accused the victims' group, they were not the source of the threat. In other cases, the state provoked the threat.

Genocide has appeared on all continents since 1945, but in recent decades it has been more prevalent among newer states than among older ones. Reviewing genocide in Asia, Africa, and the Middle East after 1945 (Fein 1993b), I found the use of genocide during conflicts within the state between 1968 and 1988 was three times that of 1948 to 1968.

Table 6.2 Typologies of Genocide, 1990–2003

Chalk and Jonassohn (1990)	Fein* (1990/1993c)	Fein (2003)
1. To eliminate a real or potential threat	retributive	I. power-driven a. retributive
2. To spread terror among real or potential enemies	despotic	b. preemptive
3. To acquire economic wealth	developmental	II. developmental
4. To implement a belief, a theory, or an ideology	ideological	III. ideological

Source: * Table 1 (Fein 1990/1993c, 28–29) was based on the work of Dadrian (1975), Kuper (1981), Fein (1984), Smith (1987), and Chalk and Jonassohn (1990) and also included Harff and Gurr (1987, 1988); complete citations are in Fein 1990/1993a. My present correction is intended to make the typology more consistent logically, focusing on motive or function in all cases.

States of terror can become states of genocide when rulers detect members of a distinctive ethnic group challenging the state, as in Guatemala and Iraq (chapter 5). When a majority becomes the dominant power, genocidal massacres can occur during the transition, as in Algeria (chapter 4). In the post–World War II era, genocide was often a response by dominant or powerful ethnoclasses (i.e., groups having a monopoly of power because of their ethnic identity) to rebellions by the disempowered—suppressed ethnoclasses. Unfree, authoritarian, and one-party communist states (in ascending order) were most apt to use genocide. *Génocidaires* were often two-time users. Genocide and genocidal massacres occurred so often in conflicts in these areas, they could be considered normal (Fein 1993b; Kuper 1981).

There is general agreement that genocides are most likely to occur during government upheaval or transitions of power (Fein 1993b; Harff 2003; Krain 1997; Melson 1992). States involved in wars—between states and within the state—have been most apt to use genocide (Fein 1993b). Although in some cases genocide triggered war, in most cases, war was a cover for genocide. There are several reasons for this: Wars justify aggression, and victims of genocide might be viewed as enemies or related to enemies outside state borders. Some genocides and wars can be linked to movements spurred by resentment over past lost wars: the Young Turk movement in the Ottoman Empire and the Nazi Party in Germany. In virtually all cases, war masks the crime of genocide—a premeditated and rational crime.

No single precondition or trigger causes genocide, but rather a series of assumptions, preconditions, events, and opportunities do. Although opposition and paramilitary groups can perpetrate genocides, in most instances in modern times the *génocidaires* either have been the state or have seized the state. Assuming that the state is the authority, one can discern the following preconditions for genocide:

1. The exclusion of the victims from the universe of obligation of the dominant group. They are decreed to be outside the law and can be killed with impunity. They are considered disposable minorities, groups that can be eliminated with another group taking their place, property, and habitat. (Sometimes the loot or takeover is also an incentive.)
2. A crisis or opportunity occurs that is viewed as caused by or impeded by the victim. Crises may be the result of war, social upheaval (such as revolution), the transfer of power (e.g., decolonization), or the breakdown of empires and multinational

states. Opportunities often are related to internal expansion—population movement to the interior, settlement and economic development—which especially threatens indigenous people who are viewed as being in the way of development.

3. The state is governed or taken over by a dictatorial elite relying on violence without any checks on their action or restrictions of rule by law as occur in democratic states.

4. More powerful states, bystanders, or patrons or allies either aid the *génocidaires* or fail to check them. Often, the *génocidaires* have tested in advance the likelihood that they will be stopped.

The twentieth century has seen (see table 6.1) three instances of almost total genocide of citizens by their own states during international and interstate wars: the genocides of the Armenians in the Ottoman Empire (1915–1919), the Jews and the Gypsies (Roma)—in occupied and German-allied Europe as well as in Germany (1941–1945)—and the Rwandan Tutsis by Rwanda (1994).

The history of twentieth-century genocide and mass killing earlier in the century in Africa is less well-known. Developed states were directly responsible or implicated in these twentieth-century crimes, which were understood earlier by the public as crimes against humanity.

Germany was directly responsible in genocides in German southwest Africa and the Holocaust and indirectly implicated in the Ottoman Empire. Belgium was directly implicated in the Belgian Congo (Hochschild 1998), and indirectly involved in Rwanda, because of its previous governance and policies. France was directly implicated in Rwanda (to be later discussed). Edward Kissi observes that "as scholars situate the Holocaust in its wider historical and social contexts, they cannot afford to ignore the aspects of Nazi racial ideology and some key elements of German genocidal mentality that can be traced to German imperialist thought and colonial policy in Africa" (2002, 1–2). European racism was transferred from Africa to Europe with the propagation of racial antisemitism and recast in Rwanda, racializing differences among Africans.

The Ottoman, Nazi, and Rwandan genocides stand out from the colonial genocides preceding them and most other genocides in table 6.1 because of the ideology and the totality of their aim and accomplishment, destroying the great majority of the group targeted. The architects of genocide drew upon a formula for rule or national myth based on one nation, one people, excluding a distinct group. Such formulas (restricting the state to one group) have been variously called exclusive nationalism, organic nationalism, tribalism, messianism, and national socialism. However, as René Lemarchand (2002) points out, in the case of Rwanda, the state was confronted by a real threat from invading Tutsis (the Tutsi diaspora in Uganda)—not the Tutsi citizens killed by the *génocidaires*. In contrast, it is fantastic to believe that the Jews were a threat to Nazi Germany and dishonestly contrived to accuse the Armenians in the Ottoman Empire of "provoking" the state—a later justification denying and excusing the Armenian genocide (Melson 1992). Thus, the annihilation of the Rwandan Tutsis had elements of retributive and ideological genocide.

There is abundant documentation of the genocides of Armenians and Jews and excellent comparisons between them (Fein 1979; Melson 1992; Midlarsky 2005 also consider comparison to the Rwandan genocide).

Destruction of the Rwandan Tutsis in 1994

In April 1994, the West avoided recognition and intervention to stop a genocide in Africa that was both foretold and observable at the time. This genocide was staged after a military advance by Tutsi exiles from Uganda, organized by the Rwandan Patriotic Front (RPF), whose army, the Rwandan Patriotic Army (RPA), had fought since 1990 "to go home on its own terms" (Des Forges 1999, 48). After it succeeded in occupying part of the country, the RPF and the government of Rwanda were urged to negotiate by donor nations (including France), surrounding African nations, and the Organization of African Unity (OAU). According to the terms of the Arusha accords of 1993, Rwanda was supposed to participate in a new power-sharing arrangement that divided the government, creating a new army (cut by half), involving the government of Rwanda, the Rwandan political parties, and the RPF. The donors, the United Nations, and the OAU pressed Rwanda to consent to this agreement, which would bring in 500,000 refugees, increasing the population of the most densely settled country in Africa (257 persons per square kilometer) by 7.4 percent.

The aims of the *génocidaires*, their identity, and that of the victims were not usually understood outside Rwanda. Much of the Western press and public were ignorant about Rwanda and misinterpreted what was going on; they did not know who the Hutus and Tutsis were. Hutus (the majority group) and Tutsis (the largest minority) are best understood as ethnic groups, or descendants of past ethnoclasses from different origins with different occupations and social ranks. However, they had lived together for centuries, developed a common culture, spoke the same language, intermarried, worshipped together, and had many overlapping bonds.

> The word "Tutsi," which apparently first described the status of an individual—a person rich in cattle—became the term that referred to the elite group as a whole and the word "Hutu"—meaning originally a subordinate or follower of a more powerful person—came to refer to the mass of the ordinary people. The identification of Tutsi pastoralists as power holders and of Hutu cultivators as subjects was becoming general when Europeans first arrived in Rwanda at the turn of the [twentieth] century, but it was not yet completely fixed throughout the country. (Des Forges 1999, 32–33)

The Europeans who colonized Africa in the nineteenth century drew on contemporary fashionable racial theories to justify what they were doing there and to classify the people they encountered. They decided, following John Hanning Speke (the explorer of the Nile), who noted characteristic somatic differences between Hutus and Tutsis, that the Tutsis were a superior race of non-Negroid origin—better looking, brighter, and destined to rule (Prunier 1995, 5–9). Thus, the Tutsis were idealized by German rulers and (after World War I) by Belgian rulers as a superior racial group. Both Tutsis and Hutus seem to have internalized this myth, leading to much later resentment among Hutus. Burundi and Rwanda were carved out of the same colonial territory—first German, then Belgian—making events in one resonate in the other.

The Belgians fixed the status of Rwandans with individual ethnic identity cards and co-opted the Tutsi to serve as administrators and soldiers, giving them better educational opportunities and higher rank. These ethnic identity cards were maintained after independence. In the 1990s, foreign assistance staff urged replacing these with nondiscriminatory identity cards, but this was not done (Des Forges 1999, 17). These cards were among the means used to identify Tutsis during the genocide as scores of years of intermarriage had blurred the visible physical distinctions between Hutus and Tutsis.

As independence loomed around 1960, the Belgians switched sides and espoused a Hutu-led party, which developed a "Rwandese ideology" that identified the majority Hutu as *the people*. Tutsis were a minority of the population (14 percent is commonly cited). A 1961 report by the United Nations (which had previously called for group reconciliation) concluded that "the developments of these last eighteen months have brought about the racial dictatorship of the one party.... An oppressive system has been replaced by another one.... It is quite possible that some day we will witness violent reactions on the part of the Tutsi" (Prunier 1995, 53).

The invasion by some Tutsi exiles in 1963 provoked not only government-instigated slaughter of an estimated 10,000 Tutsis but also the execution of all surviving Tutsi politicians in Rwanda (Prunier 1995, 53–56). The new Hutu leaders began replacing Tutsi chiefs with Hutu chiefs and encouraged reprisal attacks (in response to incursions by Tutsi guerrillas), which led to the flight of 336,000 official Tutsi refugees to neighboring countries (Prunier 1995, 61–62).

The ranking of groups had been inverted, with Hutus the ruling class and Tutsis as the ruled, but real power resided in a small faction or regional clique of Hutus. However, under the Second Republic of President Habyarimana, the government recognized Tutsis as an ethnic group in Rwanda (rather than an alien people with no rights) and promoted an "affirmative action" program to improve the chances of Hutus for education and advancement. The great majority of students in Rwandan universities in the late 1960s were Tutsis (Mandami 2001, 134–139). Tutsis were subject to quotas in public employment and schools and were virtually excluded from the government and the army.

The crisis in 1990 was instigated by both the invasion of the Rwandan Patriotic Front and internal problems of the Rwandan state and society. Political forces in Uganda periodically tried to expel the Rwandans from Uganda during the 1980s, leading the Rwandan exiles to organize the RPF and mobilize for the "Right of Return." Within Rwanda, President Habyarimana, who had ruled as a military dictator for eighteen years, responded to domestic critics (influenced by the international turn toward democratization) and announced that there would be multiparty competition in new elections in 1991.

Rwandan problems stemmed from the decline in international commodity prices, a drop in their own food production, increases in military spending, and an expanding population, which the government was unwilling to try to check; in fact it banned contraception. These pressures led to greater competition among elites for the foreign aid they needed to maintain the lifestyle to which they had become accustomed. Among the less privileged, there was general hopelessness, especially among young men who could not foresee ever getting the land or income that would allow them to marry. This group was later easily recruited by the planners of the genocide. Yet the World Bank and other aid donors (who contributed 70 percent of public investment between 1982 and 1987) believed Rwanda to be a model developing country and overlooked the evidence of institutionalized inequality and group discrimination (Uvin 1998, 4–46).

Government-organized collective violence was part of the repertoire of the Rwandan state, disguising orders to kill as obligations for compulsory collective labor. Rwandan government officials organized anti-Tutsi massacres in more than a dozen communities from 1990 to 1993 in response to RPF victories, rumors, and false allegations of a local Tutsi uprising and the Arusha agreement itself (Des Forges 1999, 87–95; Prunier 1995, 136–137, 162). The Arusha agreement proved unacceptable to radicals within Rwandan parties. One may ask: Why did the *génocidaires* target the Tutsi who were Rwandan citizens rather than just defending Rwanda against the RPA?

The *génocidaires* held Tutsis collectively responsible for RPA incursions and killings and magnified fears among Hutus by accusing the Tutsi of attempting to exterminate the Hutu as a race, invoking memories of earlier colonial myths of Tutsi racial superiority and of Nazi attempts to create a "pure" race (Des Forges 1999, 80). They drew on the growing fears generated by Hutu refugees who fled from areas that the RPF had conquered, in response to the assassination of the Hutu president of Burundi in 1993 by the Tutsi-dominated army, and previous genocides and ethnic massacres in Burundi directed against Hutus (Des Forges 1999; Lemarchand 2002; Mandami 2001; Prunier 1995). Hutus could readily recall the genocide of educated Hutus in Burundi in 1972 and massacres of Hutus since then. These fears were elaborated in accusations by advocates of Hutu Power that there was a Tutsi master plan to destroy the Hutu people.

The Hutu Power ideology of the *génocidaires* depicted the Tutsis as aliens. It stemmed from both earlier European racism and the French revolutionary tradition (adapted by labeling the Hutu majority as *the people* and the Tutsi minority as counterrevolutionaries). It also drew on knowledge of Nazism. Leon Mugesera, a prominent propagandist, charged that the Tutsi were attempting to create a kingdom for themselves "on the model of the Aryan race" (Des Forges 1999, 80).

Hutu extremists formed a youth movement with its own paramilitary and founded a new hate media to reach the masses—radio is the principal means of communication in Rwanda. Radio Télévision Libre des Mille Collines (RTLMC) broadcast injunctions to kill all Tutsis and specific Hutus who opposed the Hutu Power movement.

RTLMC depicted Tutsis as an alien demonic people and nonpeople: grasshoppers or cockroaches to be squashed. The Tutsis were accused of preparing to exterminate the Hutus. They played to and magnified real fears. Both the situation in Burundi in 1993 and their memories compounded Rwandan Hutus' hatred and existential fear of the Tutsis. The examples of Burundi also taught them that the international community would not step in to respond to massacres or genocide—that is, the Hutu Power movement could get away with murder, as had the army and *génocidaires* in Burundi in 1972 and 1993.

The trigger for the 1994 genocide in Rwanda (which had been planned months in advance) was the death of Rwandan president Habyarimana, who flew back with the president of Burundi from a meeting with African heads of state on April 6, 1994. Both were killed in an airplane crash, responsibility for which has never been established. The *génocidaires* in Rwanda attributed this act to the RPF and erected roadblocks in hours. They took over the government (after assassinating the legitimate successors to the president) and coordinated the army, militia, and youth movement brigades and the local burgomasters. The *génocidaires* demanded and elicited mass participation to identify and kill local Tutsis (with peasants using simple weapons and farm tools) and to rape Tutsi women.

The Hutu Power propaganda before the genocide depicted Tutsi women as desirable, predatory, powerful, and contemptuous of Hutu men. The *génocidaires* (sometimes with comments expressing their revenge and satisfaction at the humiliation of Tutsi women) not only practiced mass rape of Tutsi women but rape unto death with torture, mutilation, display of body parts, and sexual slavery (Human Rights Watch/Africa 1996; Landesman 2002). Systematic gang rapes, torture, and mutilation were committed by the Interhamwe (voluntary militia), government military, and the presidential guards.

From reported pregnancies, we can estimate there were at least 250,000 cases of rape, according to the UN Special Rapporteur on Rwanda, René Degni-Segut (Human Rights Watch/Africa 1996, 24). The purposeful use of rape during those days in Rwanda was recognized in the precedent-setting Akayesu decision (September 2, 1998) of the International Criminal Tribunal on Rwanda. The decision held that systematic rape in those circumstances was an act of genocide, and sexual slavery was judged a crime against humanity.

During 1994, the bodies in open fields, churchyards, and rivers attracted notice from observers. The pace of killing rivaled that of the Holocaust—over 500,000 persons slain in 99 days—but the killing was open, not concealed, as in the Holocaust. Des Forges observes that there was nothing inevitable about the way the genocide unrolled; it depended on co-opting the local authorities to mobilize people to do the dirty work of killing, often labeled "collective labor," which they were accustomed to and obligated to perform. Many, rich and poor, joined in enthusiastically and others reluctantly, drawing their own lines. "The genocide was not a killing machine that rolled inexorably forward but rather a campaign to which participants were recruited over time by the use of threat and incentives." The participants and potential participants looked to the international community—what would the outsiders do to deter the *génocidaires*? (Des Forges 1999, 6, 26–27, 596).

The victims begged Westerners in Rwanda, such as the soldiers of the UN Assistance Mission in Rwanda (UNAMIR), to protect them. But in most cases they were ordered not to do so by the UN. The international community rejected opportunities to intervene in the genocide before June 1994, when France introduced troops, Operation Turquoise, whose purpose has been disputed: to save lives, prevent an RPF victory, to enable the *génocidaires* to escape? (Des Forges 1999, 668–691; Prunier 1995, 281–311). With their goal completed and fearing retribution, the *génocidaires* fled the country as the RPF advanced. Systematic killings by RPF forces of between 25,000 and 30,000 unarmed Rwandans from April to June 1994 instigated the UN High Commissioner for Refugees to dispatch an investigatory team headed by Robert Gersony. His report was subsequently suppressed and denied by UN officials: "the 'Gersony Report' *does not exist*" (Des Forges 1999, 726–731).

The questions repeatedly raised since then involve the ability and lack of will of the international community to anticipate and stop the genocide (Dallaire 2003; Des Forges 1999; Dextehe 1994; Fein 2000a; Power 2002; Prunier 1995). There were many indications that the government could organize collective violence against Tutsis from 1990 to 1993 because it had done so repeatedly. Local massacres stopped when the International Commission on Human Rights came to Rwanda in January 1993 to investigate and commenced when they went away, indicating government direction—the ability to turn violence on and off. During the six months preceding the genocide, there were multiple warnings reaching embassies, missions, and aid groups (Des Forges

1999, 141–172). France, which supplied the Rwandan Army and was in charge of counterinsurgency, was most responsible for Rwandan official use of deadly force. Donor countries played a large role in Rwanda, as foreign aid constituted 22 percent of the government's budget in 1991 (Prunier 1995, 79).

The most specific warning conveyed to the United Nations was that of Gen. Romeo Dallaire, commander of the UNAMIR force, who cabled UN headquarters on January 11, 1994, to tell them that a key informant involved in the plot had told him that the *génocidaires* had plans to murder 800,000 Tutsis (the whole group) and thousands of Hutus who might oppose the plot. The planners were compiling lists, training their militia to kill, and stockpiling arms. They planned to massacre Belgian troops (part of UNAMIR) to provoke Belgium and the UN to withdraw. In January 1994, General Dallaire asked the UN for permission to raid weapons caches and help the informant to escape with his family from Rwanda. The fax reached the former undersecretary-general for peacekeeping operations (now UN secretary-general) Kofi Annan, who refused, saying that it was not within the peacekeeping mandate. Dallaire's repeated requests elicited no effective response. The *génocidaires* enacted this scenario in April 1994, and it worked just as they expected. The UN secretary-general refused General Dallaire's request, after the killing started in April, to provide him with new rules of engagement to protect innocent civilians (Dallaire 2003).

The UN Security Council (UNSC) not only failed to respond, its members never questioned the legitimacy of the representative of Rwanda (then on the UNSC), or the responsibility of his government for the killing. France, the United States, and the UNSC were at fault for not authorizing or even considering intervention and fudging the question by refusing to label the ongoing massacre as genocide. Other frameworks to avoid calling the genocide a genocide implied bilateral or no responsibility: tribal killings, ethnic conflict, chaos, and a failed state. "Rwanda became the first application of President Clinton's admonition in an address to the United Nations on September 27, 1993, that the UN must learn 'when to say no'" (Leitenberg 1994, 37).

U.S. opposition to intervention in Africa is believed to have stemmed from its perceived humiliation in Somalia in 1991, the causes of which were never properly analyzed. The administration reinforced its defense by denial. While hundreds of thousands were being killed, the U.S. Department of State representative refused to say the g-word in response to reporters' questions but replied that there were "acts of genocide" (Power 2002, 358–364).

Des Forges stresses the impact of international response on the actions of Rwandans:

> International censure, timid and tardy though it was, prompted Rwandan authorities to restrict and hide killings. If instead of delaying and temporizing, international leaders had immediately and unambiguously called the genocide by its awful name, they would have shattered the masquerade of legitimacy created by the interim government and forced Rwandans to confront the evil they were doing.
>
> Once Rwandans were faced with the consequences for themselves as individuals and for their nation of being declared international outlaws, they would have made choices in a different context. Perhaps those completely committed to exterminating Tutsi would have continued that course. But they had been few at the start and they would have found it more difficult to recruit others—or to retain their loyalty—once it was clear that the interim government could not succeed in the international arena. (1999, 26)

The refusal of the United Nations to intervene to support disarming of the *génocidaires* in January 1994, Belgium's pull-out of its UNAMIR forces once they were attacked, the refusal of the United States to help fund an expanded peacekeeping operation in April or May, the refusal of the UN Security Council to recognize the situation as genocide, and France's aid and active support in hiding the *génocidaires* have prompted widespread shame and embarrassment in the West. This reaction led to self-investigations in Belgium, France, and the United Nations and by Western aid organizations. Such sentiments seem to have prompted President Clinton's declaration of regrets in Kigali in 1998, which characteristically avoided taking personal responsibility.

Rwanda and Remembrance of Genocides Past

The genocide in Rwanda was similar in many respects to the major genocides of the twentieth century occurring during wars—that of the Armenians under the Ottoman Empire during World War I and that of the Jews and the Roma during the Holocaust of World War II. Genocide was instigated and masked by wars enabling the *génocidaires* to depict their victims as an enemy intent on destroying them, increasing the fears of the people they represented and deterring domestic opposition. The *génocidaires* blamed the victims as a collectivity for all acts against the state by members of their ethnic group, and especially for the wars in which they were involved.

The threat to the state in Rwanda of the RPF invasion was represented by the Rwandan state and propaganda machine as a security dilemma: If we don't kill them first, they will kill us. Because of Rwanda's demographic similarity to Burundi and the past massacres of Hutu in Burundi, this seemed credible to many. "By mid-1993, propagandists were asserting, 'We know that they have attacked us with the intention of massacring and exterminating 4.5 million Hutu and especially those who have gone to school'" (Des Forges 1999, 78). Ultimately, the Rwandan Tutsis became victims of the RPF strategy.

The *génocidaires* in Rwanda, as in the Holocaust, also demonized their victims as subhuman but all-powerful—cockroaches (Inyenzi) and aliens and enemies who had infiltrated the economy, dominated the professions, and undermined Hutus by their sexual aggression, for example, intermarriage and sexual liaisons between Hutu men and Tutsi women. This reminds us of Nazi charges against the Jews as being subhuman—bacilli, lice, vermin—and members of another race who undermined Germany (Fein 1979, ch. 1).

The *génocidaires* achieved a monopoly of power by coups d'état in the Ottoman Empire and in Rwanda and by constitutional means in Nazi Germany. There were no longer any constitutional or political checks to their power. Last, no outside power checked the *génocidaires*. Their foreign patrons and allies did not intervene to deter them. Nor did the international community seek to deter genocide.

What the international community did instead was to warn the *génocidaires* of postwar prosecution in 1915, 1942, and 1994. International trials were held at Nuremburg (1946) and at the International Criminal Tribunal for War Crimes (ICTWC) in the Former Yugoslavia/ Rwanda after 1994. The Nuremburg Tribunal held Nazi war criminals guilty of crimes against humanity; the UNGC did not become international law until 1948. The ICTWC Rwanda in June 2006 indicted the director of RTLMC for incitement to genocide.

The lack of international trials after the Armenian genocide has enabled Turkey to continue denying state responsibility for it. However, trials were held in 1919 under an Ottoman Court, which found the instigators of the deportation and massacre of the Armenians guilty, but these were eventually aborted because of political threats against Britain at the time (Bass 2000, ch. 4).

Although postwar judgment can neither prevent nor redress genocide, the failure to judge makes it more likely that the causes and effects of the genocide are never addressed and the *génocidaires* are granted a reprieve in the court of public opinion. The failure to learn from previous genocide and persecution might also preface genocide. Ironically, where the West and the international community interceded before the Nazi and Rwandan genocides, it was to make peace, negotiating agreements that did not work: Munich in 1938 and Arusha in 1993. Thus, peacemaking and conflict resolution can at times undermine the perception of genocidal plans and inhibit the intervention needed to stop genocide (see discussion in chapter 9).

After Rwanda: Genocide in Darfur and International Tolerance

Darfur, the western region of Sudan, is the home of the Fur tribe and others of Arab and African descent. Dar Fur, "which literally means land of the Fur," was only incorporated in the Sudanese state in 1916 (Fowler 2005, 19). Although the inhabitants of Darfur are predominantly Muslim, as is the Government of Sudan (GOS), the region has been marginalized under both the earlier British colonial rulers and the GOS and deprived of resources and investment in education and health (Flint and de Waal 2005; Fowler 2005; Prunier 2005, 25–53).

The elite who dominated the GOS viewed it as part of the Arab world. This vision and their attempt to impose Islamic law were prime factors behind the Sudanese civil war. The GOS was involved for most of the decades since independence in 1954 with war against southern Sudan, the people of which are predominantly African and Christian (discussed in chapter 2). The Machakos process (from the Kenyan town at which negotiations were held) resulted in a preliminary peace accord between Sudan and the Sudan People's Liberation Army (SPLA) in 2002 and a final agreement in January 2005.

But the Darfuris, who contributed their manpower disproportionately to the GOS during the civil war, got nothing at the negotiating table. Disputes about land use between African tribes and Arab tribes along with Libyan influence exacerbated conflict and polarization between "Africans" and "Arabs" in Darfur:

> "Arabism" spread through the region in the 1970s and 1980s (along with a lot of weapons) because of the efforts of Libyan strongman Muammar Gaddafi to create an Arab belt across the Sahel region of North Africa, a supremacist ideology that was reinforced by the Arab-centric view of the Khartoum-based elite. In reaction, leaders of non-Arab

ethnic groups increasingly tended to adopt from the discourse of the North-South conflict the language of "African" identity, both for the political advantages it might entail and as a defensive response to the growth of Arab supremacism. This Arab-African distinction includes a substantial racial component. The perception, impossible to justify in any objective sense in Darfur, is that the "Africans" are darker skinned than the Arabs....

Even as the factors cited above were changing perceptions of identity, climactic changes were steadily reducing the availability of the region's most important resource, land, as the desert moved south at the rate of about five kilometers per year. The increased distinction between "Arab" and "African" identity was overlaid onto differing lifestyles. Some of Darfur's Arab tribes are nomadic, moving their herds season-ally along a North-South axis; the non-Arab tribes tend to be more sedentary and farm the land. As land became scarcer, the potential for conflict eclipsed the possibility of symbiosis. A drought in the 1980s first brought the situation to a head and led to a round of open fighting, which was eventually ended by negotiations among tribal leaders. But the connection between polarized ethnic/racial identity and resource competition did not disappear. Refugees interviewed by the author in Chad in May 2004 and July 2005 overwhelmingly alleged that the goal of the violence was to take land away from the "black skins," an effort that many traced back to the mid-1980s. (Refugees universally distinguished themselves, with their "black skin," from the Arabs who they say have "red skin.") They reported that the Arabs who attacked their villages would call them "Nuba" or slave, terms that they said were directed at them because of their skin color. (Fowler 2005, 22–23)

Rebel groups, drawing recruits from non-Arab groups in Darfur, attacked police stations and military installations in early 2003 with unexpected success and few losses. The GOS responded by mobiliz-ing Arab tribal militias operating on horseback, the "janjaweed," who killed and raped villagers from African tribes, taking their land (Flint and de Waal 2005, 17–117; Fowler 2005, 23; United Nations 2005). "As a communiqué ... from Musa Hilal's [leader of janjaweed] said, citing orders from the president of the Republic [GOS]: 'You are informed that directives have been issued ... to change the demography of Darfur and empty it of African tribes' through burning, looting and killing 'of intellectuals and youths who may join the rebels in fight-ing'" (Flint and de Waal 2005, 106). Alex de Waal observed in 2004 that the GOS response "is not the genocidal campaign of a govern-ment at the height of its ideological hubris, as the 1992 jihad against the Nuba Mountains was.... This is the routine cruelty of a security cabal, its humanity withered by years in power; it is genocide by force of habit" (de Waal 2004).

Eliminating the African (by their and others' identifications) peoples of Darfur by direct violence—killing and raping—and by driving them from their villages into camps, destroying their livelihoods, and producing death by famine and disease (Leaning 2005) fit four clauses of UNGC, Article 2: (a), (b), (c), and (d).

The United States recognized this as a genocide in September 9, 2004 (Secretary of State Colin Powell's testimony to the U.S. Senate Foreign Relations Committee) on the basis of findings from systematic interviews by the U.S. Atrocities Documentation Team among Darfuri refugees in Chad in July–August 2004 (Markusen and Totten 2005). The UN Security Council appointed its own Committee of Inquiry, which visited Sudan and countries in the region in November 2004 and January 2005. Its conclusion agreed in large part with that of the U.S. team—it documented crimes against humanity or war crimes and acts prohibited under the UNGC, but said that it could not confirm genocidal intent by the GOS but indicated individuals, including government officials, "may entertain a genocidal intent" (Markusen and Totten 2005; United Nations 2005). On the basis of this report, the UN secretary-general, Kofi Annan, handed over a sealed list of names of fifty-one people to the International Criminal Court in April 2005.

The UNSC supported the placement of 7,000 troops from the African Union in Darfur, an ineffectual number—the best experienced military observers, such as General Dallaire, say that a minimum of 20,000 are needed—with an ineffectual mandate: to monitor the peace (which does not exist) rather than to intervene against the *génocidaires* to protect the people.

Although the UNSC in February 2006 voted to plan to deploy an expanded force, and again voted in August 2006, it has been persistently blocked by GOS noncooperation. A truce was signed between the GOS and the largest rebel group on May 5, 2006.

The failure of the international community to press the GOS has been attributed to political and ideological divisions within the UNSC and fears of the United States and European Union of sending in North American and European troops. Russia and China depend on the GOS for oil and oppose sanctions against other governments for repressing their minorities, fearing the use of sanctions against them (such as happened in Chechnya). The United States, although impelled to act by a strong domestic constituency (observed in rallies, social movements, popular television series incorporating Darfur themes) to "save Darfur," has cooperated with the GOS to secure intelligence about terrorism, undermining its own sanctions against the GOS. Further, the United States is alleged not to have surplus troops and/or to fear a backlash in Islamic countries against U.S. troops because of the war in Iraq. NATO and the European Union have said little about their rationale for stalling.

The genocide continues. It is anticipated that the rainy season in North Africa from June to September will create great problems in getting humanitarian aid to the camps, even if the GOS were cooperative, which it is not.

Related State and Collective Violence

Many state and collective killings of people based on group identity—pogroms, communal massacres, deadly ethnic riots—with state tolerance or instigation are of briefer duration than genocide. Genocide scholars have labeled these "genocidal massacres" (Fein 1993, 18–19, 86–88; Kuper 1981, 10, 32, 60). Horowitz, studying the "deadly ethnic riot" transnationally, observes similarities between these and genocides (2001). Such a riot has "a protogenocidal quality about it; it is an augury of extermination." Episodes historically labeled pogroms, in which state officials participate, "may shade into genocide," and other episodes could be both riots and genocide (Horowitz 2001, 8, 20, 465). Like genocides, such riots are more common in times of crisis, transition, and transfer of authority.

Riots are usually facilitated by official support, Horowitz observes (2001, 8). "Slaughter among neighbors," Human Rights Watch also pointed out, often is fomented by the state for its own political ends (Human Rights Watch 1995b). Like genocide, the deadly ethnic riot uses violence and rituals of degradation to humiliate the victims, but riots are restricted to direct assault and don't employ the indirect methods included in the definition of genocide, says Horowitz (2001, 431, 23). However, Horowitz notes but does not observe upon the frequent use of rape in genocidal massacres and frequently in genocide. Mass rape was employed in the genocidal massacre in Gujarat in 2002 directed against Muslims (Nussbaum 2003). India and the government of Gujarat were complicit in this massacre ("We Have No Orders to Save You," hrw.org/reports/2004/india1). The riot is commonly viewed by the aggressor as a means of retribution for observed injuries in order to "teach them a lesson" (Horowitz 2001,

535); similarly, most genocides appear to be retributive. But in most cases of massacres and riots, killing ceases after one episode or a few days, and there appears to have been no longer-term plan to eliminate the group. Such massacres might be clues to, if not warning signs of, future genocidal states. The deadly ethnic riot can also trigger and propel ethnic cleansing. Occasionally, the planners admit their culpability, as did the leader of the Sikh community who explained why they precipitated massacres in the Punjab during the partition of India (1948), which led to the forced flight, killing, and rape of millions. "In February 1967, however, Master Tara Singh, whom I interviewed then and who was the principal political leader of the Sikh community 20 years earlier, said ... 'We took the decision to turn the Muslims out'" (Brass 2003, 77). This enabled the Sikhs to seize lands of Muslims in the Punjab, resettling Sikhs on them.

Ethnic Cleansing and Genocide

The forced expulsion of minorities during the last decade of the twentieth century became known as "ethnic cleansing," then believed to be a translation of a Serbian term describing their policy of terrorizing Muslim inhabitants of Bosnia-Herzegovina and forcing them to flee. "The UN Commission of Experts, in a January 1993 report to the Security Council, defined 'ethnic cleansing' as 'rendering an area ethnically homogeneous by using force or intimidation to remove persons of given groups from the area'" (Cohen 1999).

However, the practice and term (or translated equivalents) date back to earlier periods in the twentieth century. It includes the expulsion of Greeks from Anatolia after the Greco-Turkish war of 1921–1922, the German expulsion of Jews, making occupied territory "*judenrein*" (preceding their genocide) and of Poles during World War II; and the postwar policies of Eastern European countries, which expelled ethnic Germans (Bell-Fialkoff 1999; Kramer 2001; Naimark 2001; Pohl 1999). It is difficult to say anything conclusive about ethnic cleansing and genocide, because the writers cited use the term *ethnic cleansing* to mean different practices. Looking backward, one can find cases in which "ethnic cleansing"—that is, forced deportation and expulsion—was (1) an alternative to genocide, (2) a step toward genocide, and (3) the means of genocide.

If we must use the concept—and it seems to persist—we should both discriminate ethnic cleansing from genocide conceptually and evaluate each case under the terms of the UNGC. I propose that ethnic cleansing requires either a protected reservation within a state or a free exit for the victims to escape violence; genocide precludes both protection and exit.

Two massive deportations and expulsions related to World War II are often labeled as ethnic cleansing: the relocation of about two million citizens of fifteen ethnic and national groups within the Soviet Union between 1937 and 1948 and the expulsion of about 14.6 million ethnic Germans from Eastern Europe after World War II (Moeller 2001; Pohl 1999; Werth 1999, 216–234). Commentators differ about whether ethnic cleansing can and should be accepted by the international community and whether it works to prevent future conflict by separating peoples. Separation is hardly ever total, and conflict often reemerges among divided peoples in cases where minorities confront a majority; for example, the Roman Catholics and Protestants in Northern Ireland, Muslims and Hindus in India, and Israeli Jews and Israeli Arabs and Palestinians in Israel and the occupied territories.

Three interrelated contexts recur in cases of ethnic cleansing cited: war (and wartime fears of disloyalty), division of land and transfer of power, and postwar retribution for disloyalty. Expulsions recurred in the second half of the twentieth century—sometimes reciprocal expulsions by two governments representing groups in conflict—including cases in Armenia and Azerbaijan, Burundi and Rwanda, Israel and Muslim states (adjacent and in North Africa), and the states of the Federal Republic of Yugoslavia (FRY). African states, for example Algeria and Zaire, expelled Europeans and persons cooperating with them after independence. Asian states expelling minorities include Burma, Cambodia, and Vietnam. This list is not comprehensive. It might, however, enable us to anticipate situations that call for prevention.

The aftermath of the Balkan wars dissolving the former FRY, ended by the Dayton Agreement in 1995, did not end ethnic cleansing. The Dayton Agreement provided no redress for the Albanian Muslim citizens of Kosovo (later known as Kosovars), a province of Serbia, in which conflict between ethnic Serbs and Albanians festered in the 1990s as the FRY instituted discrimination against the Albanians of Kosovar in order to restore the domination of Serbs who had become a numerical minority there. The conflict had been waged nonviolently by the Albanians for nearly a decade, until the breakdown of neighboring Albania, releasing a ready supply of arms, enabled an armed militant organization, the Kosovo Liberation Army (KLA), to arise.

The KLA attacked Serbian forces, who responded with collective kill-ings of Albanian kin and villagers in Kosovo in some instances. In the spring of 1999, representatives of the Federal Republic of Yugoslavia expelled more than 850,000 ethnic Albanians from Kosovo during the intervention against the FRY by the North Atlantic Treaty Orga-nization (NATO). The success of NATO enabled the latter to return, and the Kosovars (ethnic Albanians) forced thousands of Serbs out of Kosovo or impelled them to flee. The permanent status of Kosovo has not yet (2006) been settled.

Sometimes genocidal massacres and ethnic cleansing are bilateral or trilateral. Best known among the latter are the massacres, loot-ing, and rape that led to the forced flight of millions of members of religious minorities in India and Pakistan at the time of partition (1948). Paul Brass (2003) showed that the massacres in the Punjab (the province where they began) were not spontaneous acts of crowds but were instigated.

Prevention and Punishment of Genocide and Ethnic Cleansing

The best way to prevent genocide would be to prevent the conditions that are likely to precipitate it or to deter the potential *génocidaires*. For example, in the case of the former Yugoslavia, it would have meant that Europe and the United States should have prevented its breakup, which led to the consequent civil war in Bosnia-Herzegovina in which paramilitary aided by the Yugoslav Army engaged in massacres and ethnic cleansing. In Rwanda, the international community could have held Rwanda responsible for pre-1994 ethnic massacres and withdrawn foreign economic and military aid to impel Rwanda to suppress hate radio and to arrest the plotters of the genocide—which the United Nations force could have done if given the mandate by the UN. Table 6.3 lists the many warning signs at different levels that make preventive diplomacy and sanctions against genocide possible and shows ways to check *génocidaires*.

The world community still prefers to promise postwar retribu-tion—as it did during World War I, World War II, and in Bosnia and Rwanda—rather than to recognize and label genocide and intervene to stop genocide. The failure to prevent or stop genocide usually implies a failure to detect the warning signs, to label genocide. Inter-vention is discussed in chapter 9.

Many people have noted that the UNGC had two aims. Although we are on the road to punish genocide, through the establishment of

Table 6.3 Processes Leading toward Genocide and Ways to Check Them

Past Generation	Present Generation	Precipitating Events
STATE DECLINE, REGIME CHANGE OR DECLINE	Nondemocratic weak state; transfer of power/breakdown	WAR STATE CONSOLIDATION forces of violence
DESPOTISM	Gross violation of human rights (GVHR) HRNGO monitoring; cut or withhold aid; strengthen civil society	ESCALATION GVHR
HISTORY OF GENOCIDE OR POGROMS OR DEADLY RIOTS AND COMMUNAL VIOLENCE	Ethnic hierarchy: political exclusion, discrimination, severe inequality Advise depolarizing structures; international divestment; sanctions	ETHNIC/CLASS MOBILIZATION Assist nonviolent challengers REBELLION or challenge stirring fears
ISOLATION OF INDIGENOUS PEOPLE	Conflict over land use; economic development in indigenous areas Require human rights and environmental impact reports; withhold aid; lobby multinationals; develop competing uses to protect indigenous peoples	
EXCLUSION OF THE OTHER FROM UNIVERSE OF OBLIGATION	Ideology: growth of movements, exclusive nationalism, communist or fascist parties Monitor local media; label and denounce negative messages; aid local opposition; assist refugees; diplomatic warnings Lack of external control Ban military sales and transfers; international and regional sanctions	JUSTIFICATION ANNIHILATION OF VICTIM Block hate media; information intervention to warn victims and arouse noncooperation ANTICIPATION OF IMMUNITY International threats and intervention

an International Criminal Court (ICC), the lack of U.S. participation in the ICC and attempts to exempt U.S. citizens from its jurisdiction by the Bush administration (2000–) can only undermine the influence of the ICC and the principles of universal jurisdiction. Despite increased awareness in the last decade of the twentieth century, little has been done to prevent genocide. Our failure to deter and stop genocide is not just a moral question but also is a political and economic failure—an economic black hole because of the immense costs tolerating genocide has generated. First, *génocidaires* are apt to murder twice if they get away with it. Second, past genocides can instigate new genocides with roles reversed. Third, there are the immense costs in rehabilitating countries after genocide and judging the *génocidaires*. Last, genocides can spread conflict to adjacent regions.

To take the last case first, we have only to look at Rwanda (further discussed in chapter 9). The United Nations and Western states, in responding to genocide in Rwanda, substituted punishment for *génocidaires* and war crimes (through the International Criminal Tribunal for War Crimes in the Former Yugoslavia/Rwanda [ICTY/ICTR]) and aid for prevention or stopping genocide in 1994. The exodus of *génocidaires* and Rwandan Hutus from Rwanda in 1994 led to new ethnic warfare within the Democratic Republic of Congo (DRC), fomented by the entry of Rwandan and other African forces there. This led to an international war, reprisal massacres against the Hutus, and about 3.3 million "excess deaths" (estimated by the International Rescue Committee) from the collapse of institutions, leading to malnutrition and untreated diseases from the lack of medical care as well as direct killing.

Past genocides also foment sensitivity to present threats, which can lead the children of former victims to become *génocidaires*, as in Bosnia-Herzegovina, where Serb leaders often played upon the threat of a repetition of Croatian genocide of Serbs, recalling World War II in which leaders of the Muslims in Croatia supported Croatia (Fein 1998, 6).

Similarly, the genocide of Hutus in Burundi in 1972 and killing of a Hutu president of Burundi in 1993 increased the sense of threat of Hutus in Rwanda in 1994, lending credibility to the Hutu Power ideology, which alleged that Tutsis were prepared to kill all Hutus. This leads the *génocidaires* to present their campaign to kill as a forced choice: They will kill us unless we kill them first.

The international community is implicated in tolerating or deterring ethnic cleansing as well as genocide. Ethnic cleansing presents strategic choices for perpetrators and other states. Perpetrators must calculate whether another nation-state can take in their citizens belonging to groups they want to eliminate. Ethnic cleansing that does not turn into genocide requires a free exit; genocide precludes exit. For bystanders—other states, intergovernmental organizations, and human rights monitors—the question is: Are we are observing "just" ethnic cleansing or a step in a genocidal process? Are deportees observable? Are their life and health protected? Are neighboring countries willing to take in the expellees? Does this protect their lives? Does it increase the probability that expulsion or cleansing will become more widespread by the perpetrator or a model for other states? What is different about the international community (including the United Nations) after Bosnia and Rwanda (1995 on) is the sense of shame. Although Leo Kuper observed with sadness in 1981 that the United Nations defended the rights of states to commit genocide and genocidal massacres, UN Secretary-General Kofi Annan admitted in 1999 his personal and institutional responsibility for the failure to prevent or stop genocide in Rwanda (see quotes introducing this chapter). Later, he spoke out repeatedly against using sovereignty as a justification for states' invasion of the fundamental human rights of their citizens.

Scholars and activists have shown the possibility of prediction and warning and proposed ways to stop genocide (Fein 2000a; Harff and Gurr 1994; Riemer 2000; Schmeidl and Adelman 1997). Although democratic states are not *génocidaires,* they have been enablers of genocide in the twentieth century. What is most alarming about the U.S. inaction in the twentieth century, Samantha Power says, is not the failure to intervene.

> Indeed, on occasion the United States directly or indirectly aided those committing genocide. It orchestrated the vote in the UN Credentials Committee to favor the Khmer Rouge. It sided with and supplied U.S. agricultural and manufacturing credits to Iraq while Saddam Hussein was attempting to wipe out the country's Kurds. Along with its European allies, it maintained an arms embargo against the Bosnian Muslims even after it was clear that the arms ban prevented the Muslims from defending themselves. It used its clout on the UN Security Council to mandate the withdrawal of UN peacekeepers from Rwanda and block efforts to redeploy there. To the people of Bosnia and Rwanda, the United States and its Security Council allies held out the promise of protection—a promise that they were not prepared to keep. (2002, 304)

The United States has also been held indirectly responsible for failing to check genocide in Pakistan, Paraguay, and Guatemala (see table

6.1) and genocidal massacres in Indonesia as well as failing to deter or check the destruction of European Jews during the Holocaust (Fein 1979, 166–182).

In many cases, responsibility for intervention is divided, and the question is, which state will act. In such situations, there is less incentive for individual states to act and less onus on avoiding taking responsibility. The terrorist attacks of September 11, 2001, and after might either fortify empathy in the West with foreign victims of genocide and massacres against civilians (attacks that could be seen as genocidal massacres, crimes against humanity, or hate crimes) or diminish concern for others.

The flaccid international response to genocide in Darfur illustrates the elements that diminish the international capacity to respond. Chapter 9 considers what might be done and what problems persist. So far the expressions of remorse from high officials over their failure to deter or stop genocide in Rwanda have been empty, cost-free sentiments, not incentives to act.

7
No Brave New World:
Democracy and Human Rights

I have sought to show what a democratic people is in our days.... To those who make to themselves an ideal democracy, a brilliant vision which they think it is easy to realize, I undertake to show that they have arrayed their future in false colors.... To those for whom the word "democracy" is synonymous with disturbance, anarchy, spoliation, and murder, I have attempted to show that the government of democracy may be reconciled with respect for property, with deference for rights, with safety to freedom, with reverence to religion. (xvi–xvii)

The more I advanced in the study of American society, the more I perceived that the equality of conditions is the fundamental fact from which all others seem to be derived. (3)

The very essence of democratic government consists in the absolute sovereignty of the majority; for there is nothing in democratic States which is capable of resisting it. (156) ... I have already spoken of the natural defects of democratic institutions, and they all of them increase in the exact ratio of the power of the majority. (158) ... When I see that the right and the means of absolute command are conferred on a people or upon an aristocracy or a democracy, a monarchy or a republic, I recognize the germ of tyranny. (162)

The same interests, the same fears, the same passions which deter democratic nations from revolutions, deter them from war.... War is nevertheless an occurrence to which all nations are subject, democratic nations as well as others. (446)

—Alexis de Tocqueville, *Democracy in America* (1946 [1835–1840])

Many of the same questions that instigated Alexis de Tocqueville 170 years ago to study America *in order to study democracy* still preoccupy us: Does democracy lead to tyranny? What are its effects on minorities? How can one counter its oppression? Is democracy possible without equality? Does it deter states from war?

Tocqueville "was deeply struck—and appalled—by the position of the Negro in the United States," but believed that their emancipation would only lead to greater racial prejudice among whites and not result in their equality unless it was followed by complete assimilation (Nisbet 1966, 193–195). His stress on equality should alert us to consider this in contemporary societies.

Post–Grand Ideologies: Is Democracy the Answer?

Democracy is valued today by many theorists not just as a way of life but as a path to international peace, because of a general finding that democracies do not fight each other, although Miriam Elman found many exceptions to the democratic peace thesis. She attributed these to domestic politics, among other causes (Elman 1997, 473–506).

Many thoughtful people also esteem democracy highly because it takes fewer lives than dictatorships, which were major killers in the twentieth century (see ch. 6). By the end of the twentieth century, history recorded the defeat of fascism and communism, competing totalitarian systems that had killed millions. Many hoped that this defeat marked a new beginning.

These changes seemed to mark a continuing opening toward freedom. In the 1980s, there was the collapse of the national security states of Latin America (identified with or supported by the United States). After 1989, the breakdown of the Soviet empire led to the disintegration of the Soviet Union, its satellites, and independent communist states in Eastern Europe as well as the delegitimation of communism. In 1994, the last racial state—the Union of South Africa—dismantled apartheid by a negotiated agreement and instituted democracy—one person, one vote.

Many of the successor states in Eastern Europe also installed democratic governments. The democratic model was also emulated by some formerly military-ruled and authoritarian states in other regions from 1989 to 1992; Huntington called this the "third wave" of democratization (1991). The only competing model was Islamic authoritarianism—based on one interpretation of Islamic law. Although religious extremist movements arose among other religions in other states, the dominant model for mixed and plural societies was liberal democracy.

The impact of democratization on basic human rights, such as life integrity, was not considered, in part owing to the premature spirit of triumphalism rampant in the West, best exemplified in Francis Fukuyama's heralded "end of history" (1992). Because civil liberties and the rule of law are integral foundations of Western democracy, it was commonly taken for granted that democracy implied respect for human rights. Contemporary forms of slavery were simply ignored. Free people in free states are prerequisites for liberal democracy. Liberal democracy appears to be the best way to prevent and to redress major causes of violation of human rights—dictatorship and state repression. Its basic design provides for political participation and establishes rules for determining who governs, but there are many structural variations: parliamentary and presidential systems, two-party and multiparty systems, single-slate and proportional representation voting, unicameral and bicameral legislatures, and unitary or federated states.

Freedom, Slavery, and Liberal Democracy

In a time in which free markets and free labor are shibboleths, norms taken for granted in Western societies (despite violations of their laws) and espoused by democratization advocates, it is hard for many people to believe that slavery still exists. Modern slavery, which was scarcely researched by social scientists in the contemporary world until recently, is believed to entrap 27 million people worldwide, principally through bonded labor (Bales 2005, 17) in less-developed states (see chapters 2 and 3 herein). The incompatibility of slavery and repressive labor—such as serfdom, bonded labor, and latifundia—with democracy is a long-term finding. Looking at the historical development of democracy and dictatorship comparatively, Barrington Moore (1966) concluded that "repressive labor control" in Germany and Japan was among the critical factors leading such developed nations to despotism rather than democracy. Both Germany and Japan became stable democracies only after losing World War II and being governed by occupiers.

The issue of freedom from slavery and free labor has unfortunately been neglected in the contemporary discussion of democracy, which tends to assume that all members of a nation-state or community are citizens. Slavery, an extreme form of parasitic exploitation, is an institution incompatible with respect for life integrity and liberal democracy. For all these reasons, states with slavery are not expected to be free states. Nor are slave states expected to respect other dimensions of life integrity, for slavery is a violation of life integrity that abrogates most other basic rights (see chapter 1, table 1.1, rights 2–6). Scholars generally agree that liberal democracy includes not only free competitive elections but also civil and political liberties: freedom of speech, press, organization, and religion (O'Donnell 1999, 18). Most liberal democratic states today are predominantly secular states, although historic national churches are supported in some countries in which people enjoy full religious freedom (e.g., the United Kingdom, Denmark, Norway). Islamic states, such as Afghanistan (under the Taliban), Sudan, Libya, Saudi Arabia, and Iran, reject the separation of church and state and religious freedom or tolerance. Although not all predominantly Muslim states are Islamic states, few are liberal democratic states. In Islamic states in which religious authority is the primary source of legitimacy, bans and persecution or harassment of non-Muslims (and sects seen as deviants from Islam—Baha'is and Ahmedis) are the rule. There are many reasons for expecting life integrity violations (see table 1.1) to diminish or disappear in liberal democracies, including the following:

1. Democracy is inclusive in its assumptions, in contrast to totalitarian, authoritarian, and Islamic states, whose ideology assumes some groups or classes have no right to exist or participate in the state.
2. Because democracy depends on bargaining, accommodation, and coalition building, the need to repress—demonstrated by torture, political imprisonment, banning parties, and censorship—should diminish. Practical politics would require that opponents be co-opted or dominated by legitimate means rather than repressed.
3. Last, violations of life integrity should disappear or diminish because their authorization and organization would be deterred or easily exposed. The means of repression and annihilation that are intrinsic violations—torture, murder, and genocide—would be illegal. The organizations that might use these tactics would be subject to democratic oversight and checked by an independent judiciary, and misuses would be exposed by a free press.

Yet, there are other reasons and experiences to suggest that democratic institutions are not always sufficient to protect human rights against gross violations of life integrity, that is, torture, extrajudicial execution and "disappearance," massacre, and mass killing. First, problems stem especially from the relationships between majority and minorities, such as the following:

1. It has been assumed that the will to violate would be checked by the presence of a democratic electorate. But the majority might want to persecute or eliminate a minority or feel no obligation to protect them.

2. Local majorities might impose their particular cultural norms on the state—Islamic law, or shari'a, is a recent case in several countries—norms that are seen by minorities as diminishing their freedom.

3. In federal states, local majorities might impose regimes depriving minorities of civil rights and liberties. For example, in the United States, African-Americans were segregated and many were deprived of voting rights for a century after emancipation (Cell 1982, 82–102; Fredrickson 1981, 239).

4. In its zeal to protect itself and to punish crimes, the majority might sanction violations (deprivation of liberty and torture) and inflict collective punishment when the victims are outside their universe of obligation—that is, noncitizens and citizens belonging to excluded ethnoclasses or deviants considered not worthy of protection (Fein 1977, 17–19). Sometimes this is directed against criminals. Crowds and majorities in some countries kill and lynch (or tolerate police killings) of suspected (and actual) criminals and delinquents—a practice known today as "social cleansing" in Latin America (see discussion of Guatemala in chapter 5). In other places, upper classes or castes use violence against minorities and subordinated and degraded strata, such as the "Scheduled Castes" in India, *dalits,* or untouchables. When people in such groups reject their place, as many have done in India, sanctioned lynch mobs representing the majority at times torture or execute those who are viewed as defying social expectations and inflict reprisals against arbitrarily chosen members of the group (see chapter 2). In addition, problems are sometimes created or magnified by the state itself or by the process of democratization or the incapacity of the state.

5. Collective violence might be state initiated or sanctioned, as regimes magnify or suppress divisions for their own ends. This problem is especially evident in states divided by ethnic conflict

in cases where minorities rebel, usually groups who have not achieved a response from peaceful protest (Gurr 1993, 318–320), but state manipulation is not restricted to such cases. Violence might be fomented or tolerated by the state against minorities who do not rebel, including foreign workers, dissident religious groups, and scapegoat minorities, in order to channel social tensions and antigovernment dissent (Human Rights Watch 1995b). State policies might trigger collective violence (sometimes covertly), and collective violence or riots might provide the state with a rationale not to protect the victims.

6. The structure of democratic government might make majority rule itself a threat. In societies where citizens are deeply divided by ethnicity, tribe, or race, and political parties are divided along these lines (representing one group), electoral victory in a "Westminster-type" electoral system—winner take all—could exclude a major group from participation and increase conflict that destabilizes democracy. Systems of multigroup parties, proportional representation, and intergroup consensus have been devised to prevent this (Horowitz 1985). Democratization, the process in which previously authoritarian governments are expected to transform their practices and institutions to democratic ones, is particularly problematic because of the increase in conflict, the lack of law and personal security, and the rise of social demands.

7. Democratization and premature elections, as in Rwanda and Yugoslavia (1991–1992), can actually spur deadly competition and violence (Chau 2003; Snyder 2000). Democratization in Rwanda promoted the organization of genocide by enabling radical racist elements of the majority Hutu to mobilize, to radicalize public opinion through radio, and to deter implementation of the Arusha Accords (Klinghoffer 1999; Prunier 1995, 127–158; see also chapter 6). In the former Yugoslavia, the German and European Union policy of rewarding majorities in its federated states who voted for independence with recognition is believed to have instigated the wars, genocide, or "ethnic cleansing" begun in 1991 in Croatia and Bosnia.

8. For many citizens of newly democratized states, security needs take precedence over rights because of the frequent absence of the rule of law in such states. New democracies have several problems to overcome: inheritance of authoritarian structures (in police, prison, and judiciary) that negate respect for individual

rights and often the sheer inability of the state to exert control in large areas within its territory. O'Donnell calls these "brown areas" (1999)—urban slums or rural hinterlands ruled by gangs, drug lords, private armies, and mafias.

9. Last, there is the increase in dissent to be expected among people in new democracies whose basic needs are not being met—as is the case in many of the poorer states in the world. The expansion of democracy opens the way for greater class and group self-organization and unrest. This unrest challenges elites who fear being overthrown (or overtaxed or overwhelmed). Ruling elites might then be incited to repress dissent and opposition.

Comparing Countries during and after the Cold War: 1987 and 1997

To discover whether changes between 1987 and 1997 promoted respect for life integrity as well as freedom, for each nation-state, I analyzed the level of violations of *one dimension of life integrity* (Dimension 1) in 1987 (Fein 1995) and 1997. The levels or ranks of violation are shown in box 7.1. Table 7.1 lists the other variables in the study, their level, and sources.

Box 7.1 Dimension I of Life Integrity: Levels and Signs of Violation

Level 5
mass indiscriminate killing and massacres

Level 4 (calculated deaths)
pattern of killing selected individuals in summary or extrajudicial executions, open or covert (i.e., "disappearances")

Level 3 (pattern of bad and routine violations)
prevalent torture, ill treatment of prisoners, rape and sexual abuse. psychiatric hospitalization, and coercive use of drugs for social control without sanctions

Level 2 (some violations)
pattern of political imprisonment/incidents of torture and ill treatment reported without sanctions

Level 1 (few violations)
incidents of torture or ill treatment with sanctions against perpetrators

Level 0 (no violations reported)

Table 7.1 Variables and Measures Indexed for This Chapter

Concept	Measure/Level/Author	Year(s) of Data	Source(s)
Life Integrity Violation Dimension I	Ordinal ranking based on Fein's Life Integrity Violation Analysis coding form	1987, 1997	Human rights reports: Amnesty International, Human Rights Watch, U.S. Department of State
Freedom	Ordinal ranking based on Freedom House scale: Free, Partly Free, Not Free	1987, 1997	Freedom House
Slavery	Ordinal ranking	1990–2000	Bales 2002
Religion	Majority religion: Muslim, Christian, etc.—interval level data (percent population in religion) coded by Fein as dummy variable, 1/0	1990–2000	*World Christian Encyclopedia* 2001
Economic Development	Gini index, 0-1 (World Bank interval)	1990–1997	World Bank 1997
Inequality within Country	Income classes of gross national product per capita; ordinal	1990–1997	World Bank 1997
Internal Conflict	Level of internal armed conflict; ordinal (Fein coding)	1997	PIOOM (Leiden University) unpublished data; Wallensteen and Sollenberg 1998
Ethnic Discrimination	Gurr's Political Discrimination Index; ordinal (Fein recoding)	1997	Minorities at Risk project (T. Gurr), see Web site

Democracy and Human Rights Violations

Most researchers have found a positive relation between democracy and abstention from human rights violations, for example, Davenport (1998); Henderson (1991); Milner, Poe, and LeBlang (1999); and Poe and Tate (1994). David Cingranelli and David Richards, in a sample of seventy-nine countries from 1981 to 1996, found that torture, disappearances, and extrajudicial killings continued at about the same rate after the Cold War as before, but political imprisonment declined; they concluded that this improvement is related to democratization (1999). Steven Poe, Neal Tate, and Linda Keith, in a global cross-national longitudinal study of countries between 1976 and 1993, confirmed their earlier findings that past levels of repression, democracy, population size, economic development, and international and civil wars have a substantial impact on "personal integrity abuse," as do military regimes and past British colonial influence; the latter leads countries to be less abusive (1999).

Critics of the expectation that political democracy will necessarily lead to respect for life integrity include Sonia Cardenas (1998) and Zehra Arat (1998). I compared the similarities and differences among *the same* 140 countries surveyed both in 1987 and 1997 and among *all countries* assessed in 1987 (145) with all 183 countries assessed in 1997 on Dimension 1 of life integrity—the sample in both years was limited to countries with populations greater than 100,000. The selection of countries in 1987 was based on countries cited in the 1987 Amnesty International (AI) Report. For 1997, coders evaluated the annual country reports of AI, Human Rights Watch (HRW), and the U.S. Department of State (USDOS), providing evaluations of many more countries and a more representative range. Little difference was found between these sources in 1997.

In presenting these findings, states are sometimes divided between "respecters/not gross violators" (Respecters/NGV) of life integrity (levels 0, 1, and 2) and "gross violators of life integrity" (levels 3, 4, and 5) for ease of discrimination.

Respecters/NGV include states that regularly observe life integrity rights (levels 0 and 1) and states that are sometimes violators but not gross violators—that is, states that usually adhere to international human rights norms, although some incidents of violations (such as torture) occurred without sanctions or political imprisonment (level 2). Human rights monitors' reports have cited incidents of problematic practices in such NGV states, but coders judged these reported practices as not routine.

Gross violators are states that are *bad violators*—states that routinely use torture (level 3) but no routine violation beyond that—and *terrible violators*—states also using calculated executions and mass killing (levels 4 and 5).

My previous research (Fein 1995, 1988) showed that these were like steps on an escalator: That is, states at levels 5 and 4 using massacre and calculated execution have almost always practiced (or still practice) routine use of torture (level 3). Gross violators can readily escalate from level 3 to levels 4 and 5 and can also deescalate. Massacres often create an afterlife of terror and inhibition of protest, enabling regimes to diminish their level of violation, for example, China after Tiananmen Square.

State Violations of Life Integrity

Among all states for which there are indices of slavery (2002) and life integrity (1997), among states with slavery above the lowest level (indicating it was just a deviant and criminal activity there), the great majority of states were gross violators of life integrity in 1997, confirming expectations.

1. Comparing both all states and the same states in 1987 and 1997, we find that the majority of states were gross violators in 1987 and in 1997; there was no improvement. The majority of states outside Europe were gross violators of life integrity in 1997. Looking at the same countries in 1987 and 1997 by region, the greatest percent increase of gross violators was in Africa. But there was a substantial increase in the percent of states using or tolerating calculated—"extrajudicial"—execution (level 4)—these almost doubled between 1987 and 1997, going from 10 percent to 18 percent.

2. The majority of states outside Europe were gross violators of life integrity in 1997. Looking at the same countries in 1987 and 1997 by region, the greatest percent increase of gross violators was in Africa.

3. The dissolution of three formerly communist states since 1987—the Soviet Union, the Federal Republic of Yugoslavia, and Czechoslovakia—had a varied impact on the successor states' respect for life integrity, related to the degree of freedom achieved, leadership, conflicts, and the conditions of disunion.

4. Viewing all countries, free states in 1997 (as in 1987) were much more likely than other states to respect life integrity. An overwhelming majority (85 percent) of them were respecters.

   The great majority of unfree states (80 percent) and partly free states (71 percent) surveyed in 1997 were gross violators. In 1997 there was not "more murder in the middle" in partly free states than in unfree states—as expected and found in 1987

(Fein 1995)—but there were more patterns of murder in both partly free and unfree states than in free states.

5. The impact of changes in freedom on life integrity violations is ambiguous. However, among states moving toward more freedom between 1987 and 1997, states showing more respect for life integrity in 1997 than in 1987 were twice as likely to move into the ranks of free states than were states that did not diminish violations. Rather than freedom being the motor for respect for life integrity, it appears that an increase in respect for life integrity is more likely to be the motor that leads the state to become fully free. States that showed this pattern and in which it persisted are Namibia, Chile, South Korea, Panama, Poland, and Benin.

6. The context most clearly related to states' life integrity violations was armed threats to the state, that is, low- and high-intensity conflict. The higher the intensity of armed conflict within states, the more states practiced calculated execution and mass killing. Most nongovernmental actors in states practicing mass killing or extrajudicial execution also used mass killing and extrajudicial executions. Free states were much less likely to experience high-intensity conflict than partly free and unfree states.

One cannot infer from such a snapshot in time how much state violations of life integrity precipitated armed threats and how much armed threats provoked or justified state violations. Although proportionately far fewer free states than other states experienced such conflict (and in these cases it was low-intensity conflict), when they did experience such conflict, one in three free states became terrible violators.

7. Both economic development (indexed by gross national product [GNP] per capita) and the level of freedom were related to respect for life integrity in 1997. Richer states were more likely to be free states, and free states were more likely to respect life integrity than other states. They were also less likely to be involved in violent internal conflict.

Although middle- and lower-income states were less likely to be free than high-income states, the great majority of free states among the former also generally respected life integrity. Among low-income and middle-income states, free states were from two to six times more likely to respect life integrity than partly free and unfree states in the same income class.

8. High inequality sharply reduces respect for life integrity. In 1997, low- and middle-income states with high inequality were more than twice as likely (62 percent:27 percent) to be terrible violators than such states with low inequality.

9. Among the 112 countries for which an index of discrimination was found, the higher the ethnic discrimination, the greater was the likelihood of states being terrible violators in 1997. Half the states with high discrimination were terrible violators as compared with 25 percent of states with lower levels of discrimination.

10. Countries with high discrimination in 1997 were almost twice as likely to be involved in high-intensity conflict than countries with less discrimination (27 percent:15 percent). Similarly, in 1987 the states with high discrimination were found to be 2.3 times more likely to be involved in war than states with lower levels of discrimination.

11. States that were gross violators of life integrity often employed or tolerated other violations of life integrity and gender and group punishments: slavery and forced labor, government officials' use of rape, group punishments, and failure to protect against collective violence. The overwhelming majority of states using these practices were unfree or partly free.

Underlying Causes of State Violations

How Slavery and Some Religious Traditions Undermine Freedom

Exploring how contemporary slavery is maintained (see chapters 2 and 3) led me to bring religion into the inquiry. Previously, it was observed that majority non-Christian states—Muslim and Hindu-Buddhist are the largest categories among them—were more likely to be high on slavery than majority Christian states. Chapter 2 also shows how both Islam and Hinduism support slavery, caste, and bonded labor, practices that make millions of people unfree in Southeast Asia and Africa, areas influenced by these traditions.

The continuation of slavery in Islamic states of North Africa could in part be explained by the expansion of Islam and the lack of an Islamic-sanctioned emancipation movement there, which perpetuated racial contempt for the enslaved.

Examining how the dominant religion and respect for life integrity are related, I found that in 1997, non-Muslim states were almost twice as likely to be rights respecters or not gross violators as Muslim majority states (54 percent:28 percent).

Can differences between Muslim and other states on life integrity be explained by disparities in economic development? Or does the likelihood of Muslim states not being free states better explain the greater proportion of gross violators of life integrity among them? As has been noted, predominantly Muslim states are less likely to be democracies than other states. To put it simply, is it the economic or the freedom gap that explains these differences best?

There is little relationship between whether or not states are predominantly Muslim and economic development as measured herein. Nor was there any evidence that rich Muslim states respected life integrity more than poor Muslim states did. Muslim states in 1997 and 2006 were much less likely to be free states than were non-Muslim states. In 1997, only 1 of 44 Muslim states—Mali—was classed by Freedom House as free compared with almost half (49 percent) of the 139 non-Muslim states studied herein. In 2006, 3 states (6.5 percent of all Muslim states) were ranked by Freedom House as free as compared with 58 percent of the other 146 states.

The absence of freedom best explains Muslim states' lack of respect for life integrity. The aspects of contemporary Islamic civilization, states, and societies that account for this lack of freedom is a subject of much debate today. Some answers are: religiously ordained authoritarianism, which joins religious and political authority; differences of values; the delegitimation of dissent and pluralism within Islam; and the sanctification of patriarchal attitudes excluding women from full participation. Many Muslim and other scholars (and activists) counter Samuel Huntington's thesis of a "clash of civilizations" between Islam and the West (Huntington 1993) and view the ongoing cultural conflict as a struggle within Islam, between politicized Islamic extremists and other Muslims seeking both to go back to the sources and to redefine Muslim norms. These activists include outspoken Muslim women, likely to be in exile in the West, and students of Islam such as Noah Feldman, who views Islamic values as compatible with democracy (2003).

Authoritarianism, whatever the source, diminishes respect for life integrity and discourages free thought, discovery, and innovation, which can stimulate economic growth. The exclusion of women not only denies civil and political rights to half the population but also denies society the benefits of their participation.

The related question of the condition and future of twenty-two Arab (predominantly Muslim) countries was the focus of the *Arab Human*

Development Report 2002, put together by prominent Arab policymakers and Arab intellectuals for and by the UN Human Development Programme (2002). The report stresses at the outset that the lack of freedom and "participatory governance," gender inequality, led to the deficit of "intellectual capital development," "bridled minds, [and] shackled potential" (UNDP AHDR, 2002, 2–3).

Gender Discrimination Underlies Some Violations of Life Integrity

Neither the concept of life integrity nor the original method used in my 1987 study (Fein 1995) of countries focused on gender discrimination as an explanatory or independent variable. After the end of racial apartheid in South Africa, restrictions on the movement of women had effectively created "gender apartheid" in Afghanistan under the Taliban regime—bans on public movement outside the house, denial of passports, bans or segregation on use of public transport, prohibition of driving by women, denial of access to medical and other public facilities, and dress codes. Many of these bans violated rights of life integrity: the freedom to own one's own body and labor and the right to free movement without discrimination. Such violations occur in less severe degree in some other Islamic countries, although gender discrimination, however sanctioned by Islam, is not restricted to Islamic countries.

Life integrity violations of women as women in the family and community, excepting rape by state authorities, which was classed as a form of torture, were not scaled in my earlier studies, because data were not available. Reliable comparable data are still not available. Extrajudicial executions of women, through "honor killings" of alleged adulterers and "dowry killings" (household murders by kin), which are not prosecuted, and domestic and collective violence against women (as a punishment) are frequently reported among gross violators in Southeast Asia and the Middle East—in Muslim, Hindu, and mixed societies. Virtually all states in which extrajudicial killings of women are reported were classed as gross violators without taking these into account; it seems unlikely that indices of violations of the life integrity of females would change the ranking of countries.

How Freedom and Development Relate to Respect for Life Integrity

Only among states already enjoying full freedom did most states set limits barring gross violations of life integrity. Liberal democracy achieved in the most appropriate form (especially important in divided societies) is the best answer among systems that we know for protecting citizens against gross violations of life integrity and ensuring their participation in social and political life.

After the end of the Cold War and dissolution of the USSR, there was a movement away from command economies and toward open markets. But there is no evidence that open markets are a sufficient condition for democracy and respect for human rights, given the variety of capitalist states that have sponsored slavery, terror, and genocide.

In the late twentieth and early twenty-first centuries, virtually all developed states were capitalist or mixed economies. Looking at the effect (or concomitant impact) of development (usually capitalist or social democratic development) on democracy and respect for life integrity in 1997 raises the question: Why at this time were richer states much more likely to be free and democratic and to protect basic rights than poorer states? Why was respect for life integrity and freedom positively related to development (as indexed by wealth alone—i.e., GNP per capita) in the late twentieth century?

The significant exception is the Arab states, where there was virtually no relationship among wealth, freedom scores, and women's empowerment in 1998; Arab countries had lower freedom scores (as scaled by the UN Development Programme [UNDP]) in 1998–1999 than any other region in the world (UNDP AHDR 2002, 27–29).

The UNDP concludes that "the level of economic development has no significant effect on the rate of change to democracy ... [but] democratic regimes are much more likely to survive in high-income countries" (Przeworski et al. 2000, 136–137; UNDP AHDR 2002, 56).

Renske Dorenspleet (2003) found that economic development could not explain transitions to democracy after 1989. She observed that the probability of a state becoming democratic varied over time and that it had declined in the last decade of the twentieth century. Theorists differ over why people in more developed countries were likely to demand freedom and sustain democracy. Robert Barro noted that "this seems to be the case in which the analysis works better in practice than in theory" (1999, S160).

Democracy is not an inevitable outcome in richer states (Islamic oil producers are the most notable contemporary exception), nor is authoritarianism inevitable in poorer states; there are less-developed states that have not only sustained democracy (Hadenius 1992) but also might have become more developed in this process (see also chapter 8 herein). In this study, although free states were a minority among the lowest-income states, most free states in such brackets were respecters of life integrity. There were low- and lower-middle income states (with a GNP of under $3,035 per capita) that were generally respecters of life integrity in 1997 and in 2006 on all continents. These states' achievements deserve more study.

What is often forgotten is that the link between development and democracy is a historically contingent one.

Poverty and Power Reexamined: How Resources and Opportunities Make Gross Violations More Likely

Rather than explain why richer countries are more likely than poorer countries to be free and to respect life integrity, it is useful to reverse the question: Why are poorer countries more likely not to be free or to be only partly free and to be gross violators? It is not poverty qua poverty that leads to conflict and violation of life integrity but the struggle for riches and power that leads to tyranny and anarchy, "failed states," and internal war, producing life integrity violations that reinforce poverty and undermine development.

Democracy and authoritarianism are different strategies to ensure stable government chosen by leaders in view of the other models and opportunities and their costs at the time. There have been different paths of development leading to dictatorship and democracy, and the same states have followed different paths at different times. Not only imperial Germany and Japan, but also at least two highly economically developed states—South Africa before 1994 and Iraq between 1979 and 2003—were not democracies.

Neither should readers forget that in the decade between 1975 and 1985, several upper-middle-income Latin American states with initial U.S. patronage (McClintock 1992) did use terror—torturing, disappearing, and murdering their citizens—but such states later rejected the "national security state," or the dictators resigned in the end (see discussion of Argentina in chapter 4).

However, in 2006 as in 1997, the great majority of wealthy, or high-development, states were free states. Not only centuries of history but also contingencies, models, and opportunities help to explain why virtually all developed states at the end of the twentieth century chose the liberal democratic model and why the model, when fully implemented, largely succeeded in safeguarding life integrity rights. The first contingency determining this outcome in the second half of the twentieth century was the fact that the Allies won World War II, imposed democratic and demilitarized regimes on the conquered Axis states, and extended the idea of self-determination to delegitimate colonialism over the next twenty-five years, giving rise to scores of new states in Africa and Asia.

But, one might ask, how is it that the formerly Axis states have sustained democracies and most of the new states of Africa and Asia have not? Again, to reverse the usual question, one might ask: Why don't wealthy and free states usually practice gross violations of life integrity? There are two kinds of answers: (1) it wouldn't be tolerated, and (2) they don't need it. The first answer observes that citizens of free states are both more tolerant of differences and intolerant of abuses; they rely on institutions intended to prevent and punish gross violations. The second explanation is that free and wealthy states do not need to rely on coercion and repression.

Rich and poor states have similar problems at the outset. However, command and coercion are more likely to be the "mode of domination" than economic incentives, "purchase" (McCamant 1991), or persuasion in poorer states, for several reasons. First, poor states often have less physical control and command of their land than richer states. The most terrible state violators in 1997 were unsuccessful in claiming a monopoly of force over their territory; challengers had captured parts of the country. Because of such challenges, many states leased their claimed monopoly of violence to paramilitaries to further the state's objective. But the state often did not or would not control these paramilitaries for whom slaughter, rape, and looting sometimes became ends in themselves as well as tactics to secure power.

Second, such states were not effective in sustaining and improving the lives of their peoples. They had meager means to persuade them to obey or to purchase their loyalty. There was less wealth to distribute and few material incentives to reward and control the majority, except for the selected few whose loyalty could always be purchased by despots. Wealthy predatory rulers of poor (but potentially rich) countries include President Mobutu, who ruled Zaire (now Democratic Republic of Congo [DRC]) for thirty-two years until 1997, and undermined the future of the DRC.

Third, there is more material stake among contenders in controlling the state in low- and middle-income societies than in high-income societies, because more means of enrichment outside the state are available in rich states. Contenders often are moved to control the state in poorer countries because most opportunities for wealth—rents, licenses, contracts, bribery, and so on—depend on the state.

Thus, exchange does not work as a mode of domination in these cases. Conflict usually becomes more acute with fewer resources to share. Low- and middle-income states are most threatened by inter-group conflict, which challenges the legitimacy of the state. State legitimacy is often low at the outset when one group or ethnoclass dominates government and the army, when there is a lack of cross-cutting associations, common symbols, and leaders appealing across groups. Such states are also challenged by resource wars instigated by contenders claiming highly profitable (and portable) resources—for example, diamonds—and who aim to take over the state to enrich themselves. These have often been labeled as "failed states" (Rotberg 2004). Although the state fails, the struggle for existence and wealth continues. It was usually greed, rather than grievances, that was the primary motive for civil wars between 1960 and 1999 (Collier and Hoeffler 2001). In Africa especially, predators have conquered and occupied the state in several areas to loot the land of precious re-sources—gold, diamonds, minerals (Bates 2001; Berkeley 2001)—and slain, tortured, and maimed citizens.

Frequently, in the developing world, the military are the best-endowed sector of government and society, generously aided by for-eign patrons, and ready to use their power without check (Tilly 1990). Yet, in many countries of Africa, the military is too weak to control the state's territory (Herbst 2001), inciting challengers to rebel.

The competition for wealth and power depends not only on forces within the state, but also on foreign trading partners and patrons. Until the 1990s, foreign patrons often reinforced gross violations of human rights. During the almost half-century-long Cold War, both the United States and the USSR backed proxies with economic and military aid and encouraged or ignored gross violations of human rights, sponsoring repressive elites. But international contingencies and models have changed. The West was seen to have won the Cold War, and its standards—free markets and liberal democracy—became the economic and political gold standard. Many power holders ac-cepted free markets but did not adhere to the restraints and norms that underlie civil liberties, the rule of law, and respect for life integrity.

How Group Competition, Discrimination, and Exclusion Make Gross Violations More Likely

Despite political changes, conflicts among groups and classes persist, and ethnic conflicts within states appear to have increased or become more visible (Cingranelli and Richards 1999; Diamond and Plattner 1993; Snyder 2000). In 1993, Ted Gurr observed: "Minority peoples also [since the end of the Cold War] have become the principal victims of gross human rights violations" (Gurr 1993, 314). However, he later reported that at the end of the twentieth century both political discrimination against minorities and the number of ethnic wars had declined. A new international regime of emergent rulers pressed groups to negotiate settlements and share power (Gurr 2002).

In the 1990s, the post–Cold War Western drive for democratization led to internal strife, as contending ethnic entrepreneurs mobilized ethnic groups and appealed to intergroup hostility, as has been discussed. Gross violators, including free and partly free states—for example, India, Israel, Turkey, and the Philippines—often struggled with minorities demanding self-expression or self-rule (autonomy or separation) in reaction to state policies denying them recognition. Virtually all states using mass killing in 1997 had high minority discrimination or concentrations of insurgent minorities in particular regions; Colombia is the singular exception. Victims of gross violations included sizable ethnic and tribal groups, social groups distinguished by color (Haiti), minorities based on caste (India), dissident religious groups, and the Roma in Europe, a people who have been traditionally held in contempt.

Since the end of the Cold War, the social problems of the Roma have been exacerbated by the dismantling of the command economy in Eastern Europe and adoption of the free market, increasing unemployment and social discrimination. The harassment of the Roma is a case where the majority of citizens in free states—Bulgaria, the Czech Republic, Hungary, and Romania—appear to concur in the violation of the victims.

The violations and violence against the Roma illustrate the fact that not all gross violations of life integrity stem from purposeful state repression of threats against the state. There are also threats to personal security or norms that seem to incite many citizens to tolerate state violations and to take the law into their own hands. The popular demand for order in states with rising crime often leads to police and vigilante executions of alleged criminals and social deviants—homosexuals, drug addicts, street children—known as "social cleansing." Security, whether national security or security on the street, is a value that easily becomes a justification for violations.

After 9/11

We might expect greater violations among free states that are liberal democracies and were previous respecters of life integrity that experienced attacks and terror during 9/11/01 and after (or appre-hended threats of these)—the United States, the United Kingdom, Spain, and Canada—than before. After this date, the United States and its allies were involved in interventions in Afghanistan and Iraq and the United States maintained a detention camp in Guantánamo Bay, Cuba. These have all led to violations and alleged war crimes, which have been widely criticized (further discussed in chapter 9). There were no comparable conditions in 1997.

To check this, I assessed violations reported from Amnesty Interna-tional about these states in 2005 and about a small systematic sample of other free states that were respecters or not gross violators in 1997 (AI 2006). Not only did the level of respect decline in the states ex-periencing or apprehending terror attacks, it also declined in other free states sampled. In some cases of the latter, this could be attrib-uted to ethnic discrimination or racism or reaction to riots involving the Muslim population in Europe, and to attempts to deport illegal refugees. The increase could also be related to expanded concerns of AI, which now recognizes violence against women and ethnic minori-ties among its concerns. Based on my preliminary assessment, one cannot conclude that there has been a greater decline in respect in states affected by terrorism than in other free states, although both the United States and the United Kingdom would probably now be classed as bad violators.

What is most interesting is how the motives for and targets of violation illustrate the concerns about democracy and the types of discrimination and violence sanctioned by democratic countries, for example (all citations from AI 2006):

In Latvia, "the Latvian government's definition of a minority in practice excluded most members of the Russian speaking community ... the Prime Minister stated on television [in banning a Gay Pride march] that he could not 'accept that a parade of sexual minorities takes place ... next to the Dom Cathedral.... Latvia is a state based on Christian values. We cannot advertise things which are not acceptable to the majority of our society."

In the Czech Republic, "Roma continued to suffer discrimination in employment, housing and education. They also suffered frequent violent attacks by racist individuals.... In May the European Court of Human Rights in Strasbourg decided to admit a complaint filed by 18 schoolchildren of Romani origin against the Czech Republic.... The applicants claimed that their 'placement in special schools' for men-tally disabled children on the basis of their ethnic origin constituted racial discrimination and contravened international human rights principles."

In Belgium, "Racist attacks directed against ethnic, religious and other minorities continued to be reported." Victims cited included gays, Jews, and Muslims.

In 2002, the Simon Wiesenthal Center reported "a total of 1,000 antisemitic attacks in France over the past two years," including destruction of a synagogue, firebombing, stoning of schoolchildren—and similar crimes throughout Europe. The center said: "Most attacks were met with indifference or silence of local authorities," who attributed them to Arabs and Muslims in France, but French federal authorities took a firm stand against hate crimes (Response 2002, 2–3).

Implications for Policy

Although there is no single mechanical path (e.g., increasing wealth) that leads to freedom and respect for life integrity, it might help people to wrest human rights if policymakers made it known how freedom makes a difference for poor as well as rich peoples. In this study, although free states were a minority among the lowest-income states, most free states in such brackets were respecters of life integrity. In chapter 8, I also show that citizens of states that respect life integrity in some of the poorer areas observed actually live better and longer than citizens in states that are gross violators.

During the 1990s, democratization became a U.S. goal—although such support was not restricted to the United States—and the United States spent $719.4 million on this in 1998 (Carothers 1999, 54). Although the liberal democratic model was virtually the only model for emulation—except for Islamic authoritarianism—the great majority of partly free states (of which almost two-thirds were considered electoral democracies by Freedom House) in 1997 were still gross violators of life integrity. Such states were in many cases only superficial facsimiles of democracy, that is, "illiberal democracies" (Zakaria 1997). According to Thomas Carothers (2002), the Western paradigm for democratization just doesn't work in many states.

Carothers reported that challenges to democratization programs came not only from resistance to change at the top (impelled by reliance on cronies, patronage, and corruption) but also from the lack of support among the majority, who do not see their lives improved by the changes democratization programs impart: elections, political parties, nongovernmental organizations, and media that are principally based on a detached urban elite (1999, ch. 5).

He also observed that the assumptions of the "transition paradigm" are wrong—most states in the middle are not going anywhere. These assumptions, for example, "that the establishment of regular genuine elections will not only give new governments democratic legitimacy but foster a longer term deepening of democratic participation and accountability," and the formulaic recipes for democratization or "checklists," miss the point that in some systems, promoters of democracy should be "helping to encourage the growth of alternative centers of power" and work for socioeconomic reform (Carothers 2002, 19–20).

The earlier widely held conventional wisdom that states in the middle are moving toward freedom or "mature democracy" is not necessarily so. Many states that started toward democratization in the early 1990s have regressed. Democracy is not a one-way street on which a car must go to the end once it enters, turning on free elections to enter. Partly free states that are not life integrity respecters appear to be stuck, and the consequences of getting stuck are stark.

To promote successful democratization, these findings suggest that democratization advocates need to put more emphasis on preventing gross violations of life integrity and need to counteract the social forces that support them. As noted previously, "Rather than freedom being the motor for respect for life integrity, it appears that an increase in respect for life integrity is more likely to be the motor that leads the state to become fully free." This strategy is applicable to Muslim and non-Muslim states. Prodemocracy governments and human rights NGOs in developed countries can encourage and assist women's groups and human rights NGOs in partly free states, recognizing that these people can best appreciate, argue, and reinterpret the particularity of their traditions in mobilizing for human rights.

Carothers's proposals could be complemented by promoting institutional changes to protect life integrity (institutions to curb abuse of power and install the rule of law in police stations, courts, and jails) and by foreign donors' requirements that governments receiving aid demonstrate that they have stopped using torture, extrajudicial execution, disappearances, and massacre, that is, aid conditionality. Such requirements must include that states stop tolerating these practices by surrogate forces—paramilitaries and death squads that are sometimes disguised state agents—and punish or eliminate them from security services. Such conditionality has been in U.S. law since 1971 but is seldom implemented because of loopholes in the law and the policy of successive U.S. administrations that justify aiding certain states that are gross violators of human rights on the basis of U.S. security.

An often-overlooked fundamental precondition for democracy is the inclusion of all the people in the social contract. Besides guaranteeing this in constitutions and laws, inclusion could be reinforced by helping NGOs and movements to create more respect for groups held in contempt—women, lower classes and castes, minorities, pariah peoples, foreign workers, homosexuals, and marginalized groups. Democratization will not create respect for life integrity unless it directly addresses the causes of disrespect—such as exclusion, discrimination, and severe inequality.

Democratic leaders need to create democratic followers and a political culture to appreciate and support human rights: to include women as part of the polity, to protect unpopular minorities from the majority, and to respect the rule of law in addressing crime.

How much progress has been made in the last decade to resolve these problems is questionable. Democracy is not a panacea or instant solution but a process with dilemmas to be resolved. Liberal democracy does not promise utopia but may protect us from dystopias.

8
Human Rights, Freedom, and Development

Development can be seen, it is argued here, as a process of expanding the real freedoms that people enjoy. Focusing on human freedoms contrasts with narrower views of development, such as identifying development with the growth of gross national product, or with the rise in personal incomes, or with industrialization....

Freedom is central to the process of development for two distinct reasons:

1. *The evaluative reasons*: assessment of progress has to be done primarily in terms of whether the freedoms that people have are enhanced;
2. *The effectiveness reason*: achievement of development is thoroughly dependent on the free agency of people
    —Amartya Sen, *Development as Freedom,* 1999

That all peoples desire to live long lives and live well is not only taken for granted in the modern world but enshrined as a universal right in the UN International Covenant on Economic, Social and Cultural Rights (UNICESCR) of 1966, which recognizes "the right of everyone to an adequate standard of living," "the highest attainable standard of physical health," and education, among other rights. This chapter presents evidence demonstrating that states that respect life integrity enable their citizens to live better and longer than citizens of other states in the same region that are gross violators of life integrity.

States' obligations to fulfill economic rights of their citizens are not categorical in international law. Unlike the terms of the UN International Covenant on Civil and Political Rights (UNICCPR), also issued in 1966, which obligated states signing it to establish civil and political rights without delay, the states signing the UNICESCR were expected to "take steps ... to the maximum of [their] available resources, with a view to achieving progressively the full realization of the rights recognized in the present Covenant by all appropriate means, including particularly the adoption of legislative measures." That is, the UNICESCR recognized that fulfillment of these rights depends in part on resources and development.

Paths to development have been disputed. Historical evidence shows that different courses to development can lead to dictatorship as well as democracy (Moore 1966) and that some highly economically developed countries have been authoritarian at different times. After World War II, a prominent school of thought in the social sciences held that economic development led to (and was a requirement for) democracy (Lipset 1963) but Lipset in 1994 voiced a more nuanced position. Empirical evidence demands many qualifications to this thesis (discussed in chapter 7). Ideologues and theorists on the left and on the right held that development in the poorer states depended on authoritarianism because they believed that only authoritarian governments—communist or capitalist—could extract surplus labor and increase economic performance, assuming that coercion worked.

By the 1980s, the assumptions of both sides were challenged. Donnelly concluded: "Over the past three decades there has been a growing awareness that this 'conventional' wisdom was and remains tragically misguided. Particular sacrifices of human rights may contribute to development, but the categorical tradeoffs are almost always unnecessary and often positively harmful" (Donnelly 1989, 165–166; Donnelly 2003, 198).

An empirical analysis of countries around the world between 1980 and 1995 "provide[s] no direct evidence of tradeoffs. Rather, these simple analyses indicated a tendency for these human rights to be achieved together.... The tradeoffs argument concerning development and other freedoms is merely a pretext used by regimes to counter the ever-increasing call for governments to live up to international political and security rights standards" (Milner, Poe, and Leblang 1999, 437–438). Further, when the records of all countries are examined, there is no evidence that authoritarian countries show greater economic growth, just anecdotal stories about particular countries (Kurzman 1993; Sen 1999, 15; UNDP 2002, 56–57).

Such comparisons are often based on assuming that gross national product (GNP) per capita and change in GNP per capita are an adequate measure of development and economic improvement. "Human development" is an alternate concept of development advanced by the UN Development Programme (UNDP), building on Amartya Sen's conception cited. This stresses expanding people's choices and enhancing human capabilities. In order to have other choices, there are three "capabilities" needed by people at all levels of development: (1) to lead healthy and long lives, (2) to attain knowledge, and (3) to have the means for a decent standard of living. The concept is measured by indices reflecting the UNDP's multidimensional goal: (1) indices of health (enabling one to develop physically and mentally) and (2) education (enabling one to participate in one's community) as well as (3) wealth. The Human Development Index used later in this chapter is the best-known index of this goal measuring the performance of countries.

The UNDP stresses both the need for good governance to enhance human development and that respect for human rights leads to economic dividends. "Around the world, discussions on development are placing more emphasis on institutions and governance.... Good governance is valuable in its own right. But it can also advance human development for three reasons. First, enjoying political freedom and participating in the decisions that shape one's life are fundamental human rights; they are part of human development in their own right.... Second, democracy helps protect people from economic and political catastrophes such as famines and descent into chaos.... Third, democratic governance can trigger a virtuous cycle of development—as political freedom empowers people to press for policies that expand social and economic opportunities, and as open debates help communities shape their priorities" (UNDP *Human Development Report 2002*, 3).

Sen showed:

1. the low relationship between survival rates and GNP per capita;
2. how inequality—whether based on race, gender, or group—diminishes survival rates;
3. that no democracy has experienced famine in the twentieth century; and

4. the low relationship between food production and hunger.

This chapter amplifies and amends this line of reasoning, focusing first on how well states respect life integrity (rather than freedom and democracy) while observing the high relationship between respect for life integrity and states that are fully free, using Freedom House's ranking (described in chapter 7).

Much evidence supports the corollary thesis that citizens of authoritarian states and states that are gross violators of life integrity are more likely to be uprooted and suffer displacement and hunger.

Displacement and Famine

Refugees are the displaced in the international community, fleeing or pushed out from their states and seeking asylum. Between 1987 and 1996, the number of refugees increased from 13,300,000 people to 17,600,000 in 1992, declining to 14,500,000 on December 31, 1996 (USCR 1997), and 12 million in 2006. (I use 1997 data here as a base point because I last studied violations of life integrity in 1997 and I am comparing countries based on conditions then.) Besides these, there were about 20,185,000 people who were internally displaced, meaning that more than 32 million people were uprooted.

Where did these people come from and why did they leave their homes? They most often fled from states with gross violations of life integrity—massacre, torture, extrajudicial executions—war crimes and crimes against humanity that create terror (Dedring 1992; Fein 1990; Schmeidl 1995). Such conditions lead to fear and insecurity, which instigates economic (and sometimes environmental) decline because farmers cannot till their fields, producing a decline in the food supply and disrupting markets. The ongoing effects of genocide by attrition—and direct execution—in Darfur (see chapter 6) illustrate this.

A pilot study of fifty states in 1987—selected because they had perpetrated genocide or ethnic massacres in the past or were engaged in strife—and refugees during that year showed that fifteen of them were among the top twenty refugee-generating states in the world (Fein 1990, 16, 17, 28). "Thus, refugee ratios [to the population] appear to reflect past genocides and mass killing which push people to flee as well as contemporary mass killing and internal war" (Fein 1990, 28).

Similarly, in 1997—a year with almost 14.5 million refugees in the world—I found (by recalculating refugee statistics by life integrity violation analyses) that 81 percent of the forty-three states producing more than 10,000 refugees were gross violators of life integrity—table not shown herein. Besides refugees and asylum seekers, there were 18.7–19.7 million internally displaced people, of whom 94 percent were in countries that were gross violators of life integrity (USCR 1997, table 4). The others were usually from states that split or were partitioned.

Not only do people's chances of being uprooted depend on whether the state respects life integrity, people's chances of being victims of famine usually depend on political regimes. The most glaring examples are the human-made famines of communist states: the Soviet Union, 1931–1932 (Werth 1999, 108–168); China, 1958–1961 (Becker 1998); and Democratic Kampuchea, 1975–1979 (Kiernan 1996). North Korea (1994–1999) appears also to be a case of famine stemming not only from the withdrawal of Soviet aid but also from government strategy (using resources for a military buildup), discrimination, and denial (Natsios 1999, 2002). "Since 1995 an estimated 2 million people—a staggering 10% of the population—have died of famine in the Democratic People's Republic of Korea" (UNDP Human Development Report 2002, 3). In all these cases there was state complicity in allowing the famine victims to die because the state rejected or did not seek food aid.

How did states founded on a political formula of representing "workers and peasants" kill workers and peasants? What is common in all these cases is that the communist dictatorships relied heavily on coercion and untested agricultural theories, rejecting the practices and advice of both peasants and experts and inhibiting criticism, which was viewed as suspect and subversive. Because there was no freedom of speech, such governments could not learn from experience; they labeled criticism as treason. Thus, such dictatorships produced policies that led to mass death, regardless of whether there was an intention to harm the victims.

One may ask: Is the corollary of famine resulting from dictatorship that no famine should emerge in a democracy? Sen concludes that is so. "No famine has ever taken place in the history of the world in a functioning democracy—be it economically rich (as in contemporary Western Europe or North America) or relatively poor (as in postindependence India, or Botswana, or Zimbabwe). Famines have tended to occur in colonial territories governed by rulers from elsewhere ... or in one-party states ... or in military dictatorships" (Sen 1999, 16).

However, one of Sen's examples of a functioning democracy, Zimbabwe, had become a virtual one-party dictatorship by 2002, when gross violations of life integrity and electoral manipulation by the ruling ZANU-PF party served to reelect President Robert Mugabe. Physicians for Human Rights, Denmark, charged that there was not only "mutilating torture" but "political manipulation of hunger in some areas to exclude those labeled as 'MDC [opposition Movement for Democratic Change] supporters' from all routes of gaining maize, the staple food. In rural areas, access to food is controlled by government mechanisms such as 'food for work,' and through regulation of all maize sales through the parastatal Grain Marketing Board. Food distributed by international donors is also in some districts proving to be subject to political manipulation by ANU-PF" (BBC, November 7, 2003; PHR-Denmark, 2002). By July 2006, inflation was greater than 1,000 percent, threatening life for all citizens of Zimbabwe (Reuters. co.za, July 10, 2006).

Similarly, there was abundant evidence in the 1980s and 1990s that authoritarian states that violated life integrity were more likely to produce famine, to use "food as a weapon"—in Ethiopia, Sudan (Clay 1988), Guatemala (Schirmer 1998), and "at least 32 countries" in 1994 (Messer 1996). But even in times of peace, people's ability to obtain food does not depend on the gross supply but on entitlements, especially on exchange conditions—wages and prices. So states that avoid famine do not necessarily avoid malnutrition. Sen points out that despite India's greater self-sufficiency in food production compared with sub-Saharan Africa, undernourishment is much higher in India than in sub-Saharan Africa (1999, 102–103).

Clearly, democracy was not enough to protect against undernourishment and hunger. Increasing reports of pockets of starvation in drought-ridden areas in India in 2002–2003 and chronic malnutrition were negatively related in India in part because of the disrespect for untouchables justified by caste (discussed in chapter 2). Appropriate policies for distribution of food were linked to patterns of power and entitlement. Although India was "awash in grain with the government sitting on a surplus of 50 million tons," 350 million of its billion people were estimated to go to bed hungry every night. Competing political and economic priorities of the government and international organizations prevented many people from getting enough food.

India's huge food stocks reflect the power of the farm lobby. It has pressed the government to buy grain at even higher prices, making bread and other staples more and more expensive. To help the hungry, the government has a national network of ration shops, but they have been undermined by widespread corruption and distribution bottlenecks. What's more, the government, under pressure from the World Bank and other institutions, has reduced its once generous food subsidies.

On a visit to New Delhi in early January [2003], Mr. Sen participated in a recent forum to publicize the recent starvation deaths and to promote a new "right to food" movement. While such events show how democracies can provide opportunities for "public agitation" to redress injustices, Mr. Sen said, they also highlight how poorly India has done in meeting basic social needs. "We must distinguish between the role of democracy in preventing famine and the comparative ineffectiveness of democracy in preventing regular undernourishment," he observed. (Massing, March 1, 2003)

Caste, race, gender, and class bias is important in explaining not only how long and how well people live but who lives. Sen's discovery of 100 million–plus "missing women" in North Africa and Asia was inferred from the expected number of females who would exist if the sex ratio that is normal in Europe and North America prevailed in North Africa and Asia (Sen 1999, 104–107). This discrepancy has been explained by patriarchal forms of social organization, which increase the incentives for families to produce males as well as traditional values depreciating women. Prenatal sex selection is facilitated by amniocentesis; apparatus for sex selection is advertised on the Internet in India (according to the BBC on November 27, 2001). Despite the fact that this is illegal in India, modern technology is used to promote premodern values. "A recent survey in India found 10,000 cases of female infanticide a year, and a study of a clinic in Bombay found that 7,999 of 8,000 aborted fetuses were female" (UNDP *Human Development Report 2002*, 23). In China, there are also state limitations on family size, which unintentionally promote sex selection and possibly infanticide.

Such forces influence how many females will be aborted, how many killed at birth, how well females will be nourished, and how long and whether girls will be educated. Later, these forces lead to women's lack of control over their lives and bodies. This underdevelopment of half the population diminishes their contribution to political and economic development (Sen 1999, 104–107).

Patriarchy, underdevelopment, and exclusion of women from civil life (discussed in chapter 5) are often related to violence against women. Besides physical violence—domestic violence and life integrity violations (distinctions discussed in chapter 1)—there are in many countries restrictions on enjoyment of civil and political rights and differences in political and economic participation. These traditions not only scar the lives of women but also disable families and societies from securing basic needs.

Does State Respect for Life Integrity Enable People to Live Better?

Although people around the world can observe from media representations that people in rich states generally live better and longer than do people in poor and "underdeveloped" states, this distinction does not necessarily apply to all groups in rich states, Sen observes, noting the impact of race in the United States. "For example, in the United States, African Americans as a group have no higher—indeed have a lower—chance of reaching advanced ages than do people born in the immensely poorer economies of China or the Indian state of Kerala (or in Sri Lanka, Jamaica or Costa Rica).... Bangladeshi men have a better chance of living to ages beyond forty years than African American men from the Harlem district of the prosperous city of New York" (Sen 1999, 21–23).

To what extent this difference can best be attributed to inequities in health care, socioeconomic inequality, the effects of violence, AIDS, cultural practices (e.g., smoking and eating patterns), or all of these together is an ongoing research question. Physicians for Human Rights (PHR), which developed "An Action Plan to End Racial and Ethnic Disparities ... in the United States," attributed these both to "negative ... stereotyping and bias ... [and] the inequities of a system that leaves more than 40 million Americans without health insurance" (PHR 2003, 1–2). Disparities among Americans contribute to the fact that the United States ranked lower in 2005 on the Human Development Index than six other states with per capita income lower than that of the United States (UNDP 2005, table 1, 219).

Studying Differences among Less-Developed Countries

My hypothesis was that in less-developed (usually poorer) regions, a positive record of states' respect for life integrity made it more likely that their citizens would live better and longer than those in states that were gross violators. To explore this question, I compared sets of states in two regions—West Africa (including southwest Africa) and the Caribbean and Central America, regions in which the gross national product per capita for countries selected in 1997 was less than $5,000, which were classed by the World Bank as low-income and low-middle-income states. Comparisons were within regions in order to take account of the differences among regions in historical development (state autonomy or colonialism), resources, weather, environmental problems, and disease prevalence. These regions were selected not only because of their state of economic development and their differences from each other, but also because there were a variety of states at different levels of respect for life integrity in both regions.

My expectation was that states in these regions that respect life integrity would be more likely to act so that their citizens would enjoy better health and be more likely to survive and live well. States herein are viewed not just as organizations ruling from above or sole actors, but as social systems that are apt to rely on different kinds of social relations, based on patterns of reciprocity (cooperation among civic equals and nonviolent means of solving conflicts) or patterns of repression (authoritarianism, hierarchy, exploitation, and forced choices; discussed in chapter 7).

The following theoretical sketch proposes an explanation of why one might expect better outcomes in states that generally respect life integrity than in states that are gross violators of life integrity.

What Respecters Do

1. Since such states cannot rely on coercion to get people to obey and to work, they must generate belief that their authority is legitimate and depend largely on the market to recruit free labor. This generates more incentives to invest in human capital (i.e., education, health services, sanitation) and greater participation.

2. Respect for life integrity and freedom provides the conditions that enhance social cohesion. This enables civil society to develop and new forms of economic organization to emerge that are more productive and elevate the quality of life. States in which people cooperate regularly are more apt to develop *social capital* (Putnam 1993), which generates new institutions, resources, and fiscal capital:

    "Social capital here refers to features of social organization, such as trust, norms and networks, that can improve the efficiency of society by facilitating coordinated actions.... Spontaneous cooperation is facilitated by social capital." (167) ... Trust is an essential component of social capital. As Kenneth Arrow has observed, "Virtually every commercial transaction has within itself an element of trust, certainly any transaction conducted over a period of time. It can be plausibly argued that much of the economic backwardness in the world can be explained by a lack of mutual confidence" (Putnam 1993, 170).

3. States in which people enjoy life integrity rights and civil liberties are more likely to generate political processes (through free trade unions and political parties) that lead toward social and economic entitlements for more people, eliminating gender, race, and ethnic discrimination, correcting marketplace inequities, and improving health. Although there is much variation among highly developed countries, examples can be seen in the nineteenth- and twentieth-century history of Western Europe and the United States, in which the expansion of the electorate and establishment of labor or socialist parties were among the major causes spurring the state to pass pension, insurance, and labor legislation.

4. Such political processes also lead to what the UNDP calls a "virtuous cycle" of development.

Democratic governance can trigger a virtuous cycle of development—as political freedom empowers people to press for policies that expand social and economic opportunities, and as open debates help communities shape their priorities. From Indonesia to Mexico to Poland, moves toward democratization and political opening have helped produce this kind of virtuous cycle, with a free press and civil society activism giving people new ways to participate in policy decisions and debates (UNDP *Human Development Report 2002*, 3).

What Respecters Do Not Do That Gross Violators Are Likely to Do

1. Gross violators inhibit and repress the free flow of information and criticism, which can prevent or check poor and uninformed state policies that lead to famine and environmental disasters.

2. Gross violators repress nongovernmental organizations, free trade unions, and political parties that could mobilize for better economic and social conditions.

3. Gross violators often generate internal war, which leads to their people being uprooted (by internal displacement and refugee flows), devastation, and diminished agricultural production,

undermining the present and future standard of living; they are likely to spend more on the military and control apparatus and less on social and economic development.

4. States involved in internal war cannot produce stability to attract domestic or foreign investment, which might open up greater opportunities and better health and welfare conditions if the opportunity to form free labor unions is present.

It is expected that citizens of state respecters are more likely to live longer and better than citizens of gross violator countries. They are also more likely to enjoy greater gender equality than citizens of gross violators.[1]

Table 8.1 shows background characteristics of countries in both groups. Tables 8.2 and 8.3 show the differences between respecters and gross violators in each region on indices of health and well-being, which include the Human Development Index, Gender-Related Development Index, Poverty Index, the percent underweight below age five, and mortality rates to age one, age five, and age forty. Notes on sources (mostly from United Nations and World Bank estimates) follow the tables.

Differences between and among Comparison Groups

Table 8.1 shows that state respecters were more likely to have been former British colonies than states that were gross violators. This finding is consistent with previous studies that have shown that ex–British colonies are more likely to be democratic and to show better human rights performance (Poe, Tate, and Keith, 1999) than colonies of other former colonial powers—France, Portugal, and Belgium. The distinction is truer of the Caribbean than of sub-Saharan Africa. Six of the seven Commonwealth states in the Caribbean in the larger study surveyed (described in chapter 7) in 1997—except Jamaica—were rights respecters. Three states that were independent throughout the twentieth century but were under heavy influence and occasional occupation by the United States—Cuba, the Dominican Republic, and Haiti—were gross violators.

One might ask whether the better performance of many ex–British colonies in some areas is owing to the transmission of liberal political values and investment in education (Brown 2001), native administration during the colonial period and/or recent policies of the Commonwealth that stress human rights (Anyaoku 2000), or policies that

Table 8.1 Background and Contemporary Characteristics of States Compared in Africa and Central America/Caribbean

States Classed by LIVA Ranks 1987	Avg. Annual % Growth Rates 1975–2003	2003 GDP per Capita $USD	State Income Rank per Capita 1987–1997	Past Colony	Status of Freedom		
					1987	1997	2006
AFRICA							
A. Generally Respect Rights							
Botswana	5.1	8,714	2-2##	UK	F	F	F
Cape Verde	3.0	5,214	2-2	PO	F	F	F
Mauritius	4.6	11,287	2-3	UK	F	F	F
B. Gross Violators							
Burkina Faso	1.2	1,174	1-1	FR	NF	PF	PF
Nigeria	−0.5	1,050	1-1	UK	PF	NF	PF
Senegal	INA	1,648	1-1	FR	PF	PF	F
Togo	−0.8	1,696	1-1	FR	NF	NF	NF
CARIBBEAN & CENTRAL AMERICA							
A. Generally Respect Rights							
Belize	3.1	6,950	2-2	UK	F	F	F
Costa Rica	1.3	9,606	2-2	ind.	F	F	F
St. Vincent	3.4	6,123	2-2	UK	F	F	F
Trinidad & Tobago	INA	10,766	3-3	UK	F	F	F
B. Gross Violators							
Dominican Republic	2.0	6,823	2-2	ind.	F	PF	F
Guatemala	0.2	4,148e	2-2	ind.	PF	PF	PF
Haiti	−2.3	1,742e	1-1	ind.	PF	PF	NF
Honduras	0.1	2,665	1-1	ind.	F	PF	F

Sources and Definitions of Indices for Table 8.1

Economic Growth: % average annual rate of growth between 1975 and 2003, United Nations Human Development Programme, *Human Development Report 2003* (New York: Oxford University Press, 2003), table 14, 268–269.

Past Colony: Past colonial ruler in 1945 is from several world data books and historical encyclopedias. Key to abbreviation: FR France, PO Portugal, UK United Kingdom, ind. independent.

Freedom Index is from Freedom House, *Freedom in the World 1997–2006* (New York: Freedom House, 2006) and Raymond D. Gastil, "The Comparative Survey of Freedom 1988," *Freedom at Issue* (January–February 1988). Freedom House distinguishes among Free (F), Partly Free (PF), and Not Free (NF) states based on indices of Political Rights and Civil Liberties.

LIVA or Life Integrity Violation Analysis ranks states based on coded evaluation of human rights reports (discussed in text and in chapter 7).

means not taken because data missing for half or more of cases

INA—Information not available

e—estimate made by UNDP 2003

Table 8.2 Indices of Development and Health (2003) by States' Respect for Life Integrity (1987–1997)

	Indices of Development			Health and Mortality		
States Classed by LIVA Rank	HDI	GDI	Poverty	Underweight to Age 5	Death Rates by Ages 1 & 5, Respectively	% Dead by Age 40
AFRICA/W/SW						
A. Generally Respect Rights						
Botswana	.565	.559	48.4	13	82	112	69.1
Cape Verde	.721	.714	18.7	14	26	35	7.6
Mauritius	.791	.781	11.4	15	16	18	5.0
MEAN	.692	.685	26.2	14	41.3	55	27.2
B. Gross Violators						
Burkina Faso	.317	.311	64.2	34	107	207	38.9
Nigeria	.453	.439	38.8	29	98	198	46.0
Senegal	.458	.449	44.2	23	78	137	26.6
Togo	.512	.491	39.5	25	78	140	31
MEAN	.435	.423	46.7	27.8	90.3	170.5	35.6
CARIBBEAN & CENTRAL AMERICA						
A. Generally Respect Rights						
Belize	.753	.734	16.7	6e	33	39	10.6
Costa Rica	.838	.829	4.0	5	8	10	3.7
St. Vincent & Grenadines	.755	INA	INA	INA	23	27	6.6
Trinidad & Tobago	.801	.796	8.8	7	17	20	11.6
MEAN	.787	.786	9.8	6	20.3	24	8.1
B. Gross Violators						
Dominican Republic	.749	.739	11.8	5	29	35	14.1
Guatemala	.663	.649	22.9	23	35	47	15.9
Haiti	.475	INA	38.0	17	76	118	34.4
Honduras	.667	INA	16.9	17	32	41	15.8
MEAN	.639	–	22.4	15.5	43	60.3	20.1

favor Commonwealth members economically—but this study cannot answer these questions.

States that are respecters in these two regions are also smaller states in terms of population than gross violators (data not shown). This finding, too, is consistent with previous studies that show increases in population size increase the likelihood of repression (Poe, Tate, and Keith 1999). Also, two of the four respecters in both the Caribbean (St. Vincent, Trinidad and Tobago) and West Africa (Cape Verde

Table 8.3 Mean Differences on Indices of Development and Health by States' Respect for Life Integrity in Two Regions

	Indices of Development				Health and Mortality		
Regions/ Comparison Groups	HDI	GDI	Poverty	Underweight to Age 5	Death Rates by Ages 1 & 5, Respectively		% Dead by Age 40
AFRICA/W/SW							
1. Generally Respect Rights	.692	.685	26.2	14	41.3	55	27.2
2. Gross Violators	.435	.423	46.7	27.8	90.3	170.5	35.6
3. Difference 1 minus 2	.257	.262	−20.5	−13.8	−49.0	−225.5	−8.4
4. Ratios							
1/2	1.6	1.62	.56	.50	.46	32	.76
2/1	.63	.62	1.8	2.0	2.2	3.1	1.3
CARIBBEAN & CENTRAL AMERICA							
1. Generally Respect Rights	.787	.786	9.8	6	20.3	24.0	8.1
2. Gross Violators	.639	–	22.4	15.5	43	60.3	20.1
3. Difference 1 minus 2	.148	–	−12.6	−9.5	−22.7	−36.3	−12
4. Ratios							
1/2	1.23	–	−.44	.38	.47	40	.40
2/1	.8	–	2.3	2.6	2.1	2.5	2.5

Sources and Definitions of Indices for Tables 8.2 and 8.3

Indices of development and health in 1997 are taken from the United Nations Human Development Programme, *Human Development Report 2003* (New York: Oxford University Press, 2003), statistics for 2003: tables 2, 4, and 8. These indices and their definitions follow.

Human Development Index (HDI) ranges from 0 to 1 and is an average of indices of longevity (life expectancy at birth), knowledge (adult literacy rate and combined school enrollment ration), and adjusted real gross development product per capita, i.e., GDP per capita of a country converted into U.S. dollars on the basis of the purchasing power parity exchange rate (PPP $US).

Gender Development Index (GDI) uses the same variables as the HDI, adjusting the average achievement of each country on each index for the disparity in achievement between women and men.

Poverty Index (HPI-1): The human poverty index for developing countries concentrates on deprivations in three essential dimensions of human life already reflected in the HDI—longevity, knowledge, and a decent standard of living. For discussion of computational differences in computing the HDI, GDI, and Poverty Index, see UNDP 2003, 340–344.

Percent children under 5 underweight is an index of moderate and severe child nutrition based on the percent of children under five years of age who are two standard deviations or more below the median weight for age of the reference population. It is based on the most recent year for which data are available.

Infant mortality (per 1,000 live births)

Under 5 mortality (per 1,000 live births)

People not expected to survive to age 40 (as percent of total population)

means not taken because data missing for half or more of cases

INA—information not available

e—estimate made by UNDP

and Mauritius) are islands. However, two gross violators in the Caribbean—the Dominican Republic and Haiti—are on the same island.

Experimental and other studies have shown a greater tendency of people in sustained relationships than in short-term relationships (and in small rather than large communities) to develop mutual trust and altruism (Putnam 1993, ch. 6). Whether small states' greater respect for life integrity is a product of their greater likelihood of eliciting cooperation and compromise rather than relying on repression to govern or whether people in smaller states may be better able to observe and oppose abuses of power than people in larger states—or for some other reason or all these reasons—is not clear. Again, this finding does not mean that all small states are rights respecters; one can also note that among the four states in the study that are gross violators in Africa, Togo is relatively small.

Rights respecters in both regions were also free states in 1987 but gross violators were partly free or not free. Some gross violators that were classed by Freedom House as partly free in 1987 were classed as free in 2005: Senegal (in Africa) and the Dominican Republic and Honduras in the Caribbean.

From findings in chapter 7, I expected greater inequality and ethnic discrimination among gross violators than respecters but did not have uniform indicators on enough countries in these groups to probe this systematically. Later in this chapter I discuss the impact of inequality within Guatemala.

Table 8.1 also shows in both regions the better economic performance and growth among rights respecters compared with gross violators observed over a twenty-eight-year span (1975–2003). This occurred despite the impact of HIV and AIDS (discussed later in this chapter) and their especially dire impact on Botswana in southern Africa.

Whether freedom leads to economic development or vice versa, or whether there is another "virtuous cycle" occurring, is not clear. Earlier research on the relation between economic growth and democracy generally tended to show that the former leads to, enhances, or stabilizes the latter, or they are independent (Burkhart and Lewis-Beck 1994; Diamond 1992; Moore 1995; Pourgerami 1988, 1991). The UN Development Programme finds no linear trend across regions but that "democratic regimes are much more likely to survive in high income countries, though they are not more likely to emerge" (UNDP *World Development Report 2002*, 56).

Tables 8.2 and 8.3 confirm expectations; people in states that are respecters and not gross violators live better and longer than people in states that are gross violators of life integrity. This is shown graphically in figures 8.1–8.4. In both regions surveyed, the Human Development Index (HDI) is higher among states that are respecters than among gross violators—based on the most recent international statistics (UNDP 2005). One can read table 8.3 two ways. Looking at the Africa comparisons (line 4), the mean HDI of respecters is 1.6 times that of gross violators, or the HDI of gross violators is less than two-thirds (0.63) that of respecters. In the Caribbean/Central America comparisons, the difference is less marked. The respecters' HDI is 1.23 times that of gross violators; the gross violators' HDI is about four-fifths (0.8) that of the respecters. Similarly, the Gender Development Index (GDI), assessing gender equality, of life integrity respecters is 1.62 times higher than is that of gross violators in Africa. Differences among Caribbean and Central American states on the GDI cannot be compared, because of missing data.

Clearly, the level of poverty and death rates are higher among respecters in Africa than among respecters in Central America and the Caribbean. However, comparing countries within these areas, people living in countries that generally respect rights are much more likely to see their children live. The difference becomes less substantive as people age in Africa (see the percent dead by the age of 40), which can be related to AIDS.

Differences were more marked in sub-Saharan Africa, which has greater poverty than Central America and the Caribbean. Looking at child health and mortality, the differences are even more striking and consistent. In both areas, the rights respecters have fewer children below five underweight—an accepted index of nutritional and health deficiencies. In Central America/Caribbean, the gross violator states have 2.6 times as many children under five underweight as do the respecters/NGV. In Africa, the gross violators have 2 times as many children under five underweight as do the respecter states.

Looking at the rate of infant mortality (deaths below the age of one per 1,000 births), the gross violators in the African sample have 2.2 times the rate of the respecters, and in Central America/Caribbean, the gross violators have 2.1 times the rate of the respecters. Even greater disparities are observed comparing deaths to the age of five; comparing gross violators to rights respecters, in Central America/Caribbean the gross violators have 2.5 times the death rate of the

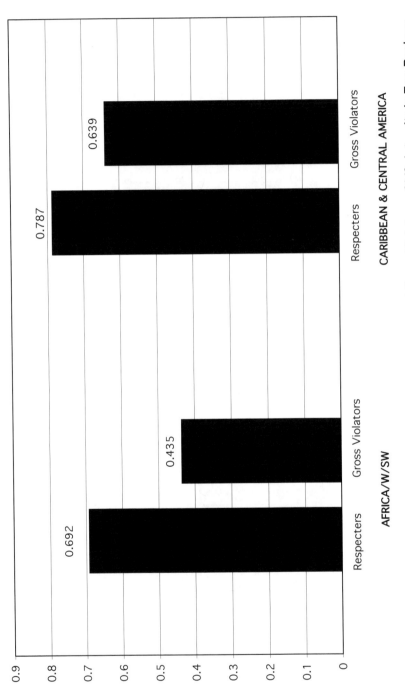

Figure 8.1 Mean Human Development Index of State Respecters and Gross Violators of Life Integrity in Two Regions, 1997

Source: See sources, Tables 8.2 and 8.3.

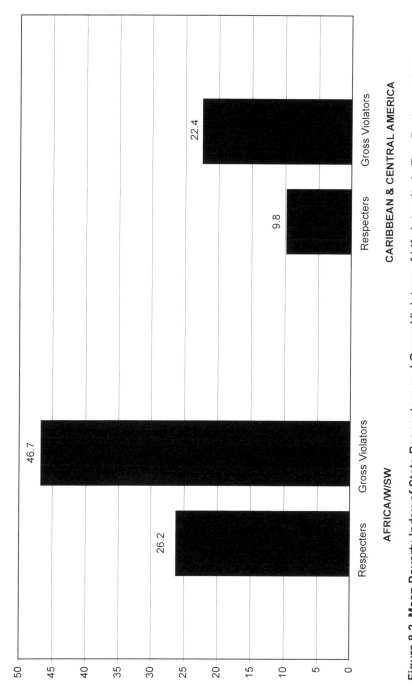

Figure 8.2 Mean Poverty Index of State Respecters and Gross Violators of Life Integrity in Two Regions, 1997

Source: See sources, Tables 8.2 and 8.3.

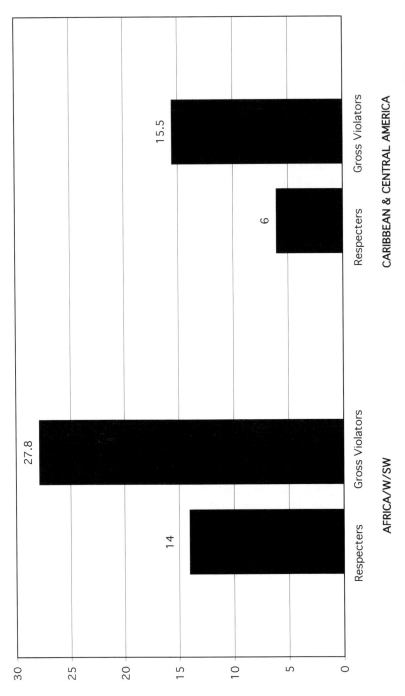

Figure 8.3 Mean Percentage of Children under 5 Underweight of State Respecters and Gross Violators of Life Integrity in Two Regions, 1997

Source: See sources, Tables 8.2 and 8.3.

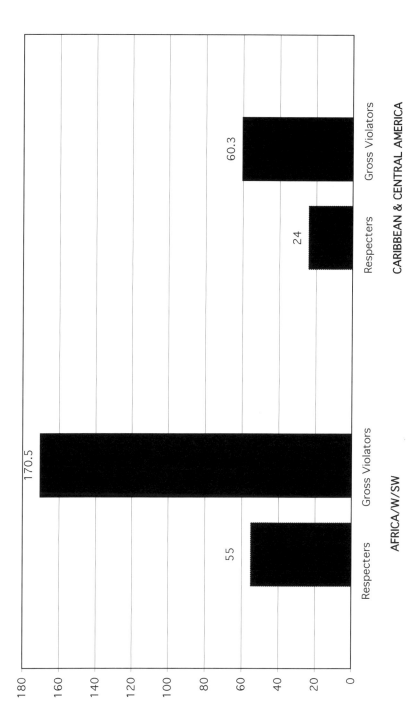

Figure 8.4 Mean Mortality Rate of Children under 5 (per 1,000 live births) of State Respecters and Gross Violators of Life Integrity in Two Regions, 1997

Source: See sources, Tables 8.2 and 8.3.

respecters, and in Africa the death rate of gross violators is 3.1 times that of respecters. The difference in probability of people surviving has more regional difference among adults. In the African sample the percent not surviving to forty among gross violators is 1.3 times as high as among respecters, and in the Central American/Caribbean sample, it is 2.5 times as high.

Effect of HIV/AIDS

The changes in longevity in comparing these findings with the same comparisons in 1997 (not shown)—the differences were greater in 1997—were largely because of the impact of HIV/AIDS. In Africa, life expectancy has declined substantively. The UNDP says that "chances of survival in sub-Saharan Africa are not much better than in 1840s England.... In Europe the greatest single demographic shock since the Black Death was experienced between 1913 and 1918, when the combined effects of the First World War and the 1918 influenza epidemic reduced life expectancy by about 16 years. Traumatic as that episode was, it pales against losses in life expectancy of 31 years in countries like Botswana" (UNDP 2005, 26, figure 1.9).

International efforts to treat and prevent AIDS have been undermined because of problems arising from the vulnerability of forced victims of sex trafficking (see chapter 3) and U.S. restrictions on modes of treatment stressing abstinence only (Burkhalter 2004). Women, whether victims of rape during war or wives at home (afraid to ask their husbands to use condoms), are particularly vulnerable because of their powerlessness (Brown 2004). Stopping the spread of AIDS is in part a question of changing sexual norms within countries. An adequate global response in which donors respect the rights of other countries to determine the most appropriate strategy is imperative.

Effect of Inequality within and between States

Inequality is particularly well documented for Guatemala, in which "rural indigenous people have an incidence of poverty almost five times the average for urban nonindigenous people" (UNDP 2005, figure 2.10, 60). The infant mortality rate (per 1,000 live births in 1998) for the poorest 20 percent of Guatemalans was 1.5 times that of the richest 20 percent—58.0 to 39.2—and the under-five mortality rate of the poorest was twice that of the richest—77.6 to 39.3. An export-led strategy of development has not produced gains for Guatemalans similar to the effects of such a strategy in Botswana and

Mauritius (Osei-Hwedie 2000). The UNDP explains why this has not improved the lives of Guatemalans:

> Over the past decade Guatemala has sustained export growth rates of more than 8 percent, with minimal progress in human development.... Since 2000 extreme poverty levels have risen ... the income share of the poorest 20 percent of the population fell from 2.7 percent to 1.7 percent ... high initial inequalities exclude people from market opportunities and limit human development. Despite being a middle-income country, Guatemala has malnutrition rates that are among the highest in the world, and one-third of its population is illiterate. Extreme inequality extends to land ownership. An estimated 2 percent of the population owns 72 percent of agricultural land, including the most fertile land.... No export growth strategy in Guatemala is likely to produce substantive benefits for human development without deep structural reforms to reduce inequalities and extend opportunity through the redistribution of land and other productive assets, increased public spending for the poor and targeted programmes aimed at breaking down the barriers facing indigenous people. Such measures will ultimately require a change in the distribution of political power in Guatemala. (UNDP 2005, 123)

This reminds us that we must observe not only national income and growth but its distribution. The share of national income going to the rich (as compared to the poor) was greater among the gross violators than among the rights observers in the Caribbean/Central American states surveyed. This was compared by deriving a ratio of the income of the richest 20 percent of the population to the income of the poorest 20 percent—table not shown (derived from UNDP 2005, table 15, 270–273). The mean ratio among the states that were gross violators was 1.8 times that of the states that were respecters in the Caribbean/Central American sample states for which data were available. For example, in Guatemala, the richest 20 percent got 24.4 times that of the poorest 20 percent, while in Costa Rica the richest 20 percent got 12.3 times that of the poorest 20 percent.

There are fewer data for our sample states in Africa. Contrary to expectations, I found greater inequality in Botswana (the only state among the respecters for which we have similar data) than among the gross violators surveyed—the richest 20 percent received 31.5 times that of the poorest 20 percent.

There are also differences in how states spend their national income (Gross Development Product, or GDP). Comparing the percent going to health expenditures in 2002 (table not shown), respecters spent more than gross violators in both regions (mean percent of respecters was 1.3 times that of gross violators in the Caribbean/Central America sample and 1.2 percent more than the violators in the African sample). Costa Rica spent appreciably more than any other state, devoting 6.1 percent of its income to health. However, among the African sample, Togo, a gross violator, spent 5.1 percent of its income on health, more than any other state in that group (data from UNDP 2005, table 20, 284–287).

Explaining Differences between Rights Respecters and Gross Violators

Although differences have been diminished by HIV/AIDS, it is evident that citizens of states that are rights respecters are apt to live better and longer and enjoy seeing their children survive.

How did the respecter states achieve their better results? Specific case studies of these countries over a longer time span are needed to answer that question. But some conjectures seem reasonable. An econometric approach suggests that the greater wealth of the respecter states itself leads to lower infant mortality, accepting the finding that "wealthier is healthier" (Pritchett and Summers 1996)—all other factors being equal. Another approach relates the better health of respecters to state policies in democracies that diminish infant mortality and invest in health protection, suggested by studies of David Bloom and David Canning (2000) and Thomas Zweifel and Patricio Navio (2000).

Zweifel and Navio, reviewing 138 states between 1950 and 1990, found that democracy, regardless of the level of development, matters. Democracies show lower infant mortality rates at all levels of development. "Fewer children die in democracies than in dictatorships" (Zweifel and Navio 2000, 98). Since it makes sense to infer that better health affects productivity and economic growth, such growth might in turn promote stability in democratic states. Bloom and Canning (2000) propose that better health leads to more income because of several factors: gains in productivity, greater investment in education, incentives to save for retirement, and more people in the workforce.

This study does not inquire into paths of development and health protection but suggests social processes stemming from respect for life integrity and freedom, which make the adoption of appropriate policies more likely. Nor does it address the impact of different economic policies and strategies (e.g., neoliberalism, sustainable development, protectionism, free markets, export strategies, import substitution) and the effects of policies of the World Bank and the International Monetary Fund.

There has been much discussion of selected case comparisons—for example (in Central America) the reasons why Guatemala has been a black hole for almost the past half-century in terms of human rights, development, and democracy. Hilde Hey (1995) compares and contrasts the path of development in Costa Rica to that of Guatemala. Guatemala emerged from a slave society in which racial contempt underlay the decades of repression and gross violation of human rights (also discussed in chapters 5 and 7 herein). Costa Rica, its neighbor, emerged from an ethnically homogenous society of small farmers and included all citizens in a social democracy, which led to enhanced health, housing, education, and wealth. There are grave doubts among many (besides the UNDP) that Guatemala can reform without structural changes in social exclusion, wealth, power redistribution, and demilitarization (Jonas 2000; Robinson 2000; Schirmer 1998).

Rights Go Together

There are both general connections between human rights and well-being and specific paths or sequences of policies that lead toward well-being worth consideration. To begin with the first approach, my assumption in chapter 1 can be affirmed as a finding: Respect for life integrity rights is positively related to achievement of subsistence rights. Although rights can be logically divided, their fulfillment hangs together; the classes distinguished—life integrity, freedom, and subsistence—are all positively related.

In this chapter, the evidence presented appears to corroborate my original explanations of why life integrity respecters live better and longer.

Virtuous Cycles Spiral Up and Vicious Cycles Spiral Down

Respect for life integrity is more than the absence of repression, violation, and fear; it is a precondition for an atmosphere in which citizens are more likely to trust than to fear each other. Thus, they are ready to participate as active citizens in public affairs. Trust and participation are ordinarily used as indicators of social capital.

We have independent evidence about the level of popular trust in eighty societies around the world through the World Value Survey

(WVS). The WVS asked questions such as "Would you say that most people can be trusted or that you can't be too careful in dealing with people?" beginning in 1981 (Inglehart and Norris 2003). Our analyses showed that the level of trust was significantly related to the level of governments' violation of life integrity in 1997: The greater the state violations, the lower was the mean level of trust. A similar relationship was found between life integrity violations in 1987 and citizens' level of trust in 1991 in these countries.

Respect for life integrity and for civil liberties increases the likelihood that formal democracies will become free states, liberal rather than illiberal democracies (see chapter 7 and Fein 1995). In free states, governments must enlist the support of their citizens by appeal, persuasion, and compromise and are impelled (if only to stay in power) to promote policies that they believe increase the well-being of their citizens. Citizens' health and economic security in turn advances economic productivity and state stability. Free states in which citizens enjoy civil liberties also enable citizens to appeal to the government and contend among themselves, proposing new paths. Such nonviolent ways to resolve conflict lead to greater cohesion among citizens from different classes, ethnic groups, and races, assuming that the group is not excluded from participation or rewards.

Social cohesion, in turn, deters state violations of life integrity by instilling in the rulers the sense that such violations will not be accepted by their citizens. State respect for life integrity reinforces norms of general respect, which lead to greater reciprocity and result in higher levels of social capital. Social capital also has structural roots or concomitants. Robert Putnam (1993), comparing states and regions within Italy, showed that equality—both civic equality and economic equality—and social capital were positively related. Thus, one might expect (following Putnam's logic) that highly unequal and discriminatory states would be less likely to be cohesive and to develop social capital, and more egalitarian and inclusive national communities would make the development of social cohesion and social capital more likely. Social cohesion also has other effects that lead to development. It makes better policy more likely by increasing the trust in government in less-developed countries, which enables their leaders to make decisions leading to economic reforms that could lead to short-term losses but long-term gains (Ritzen, Easterly, and Woolcock 2000).

However, economic development and productivity also depend on peace and freedom as well as respect for life integrity. Dictatorships and authoritarian states at low economic levels that rely on repression do not usually produce the security that favors growth; nor are they likely to put money in public health since their first concern in funding is for their survival. Gross violators (more likely to be not free and partly free states) are much more likely to be engaged in civil wars than respecters/NGV (discussed in chapter 7; see also Henderson and Singer 2000). States that kill, maim, and torture their citizens routinely in order to control them or to eliminate them do not produce cohesion; they produce fear. Fear induces people to distrust each other, deters their joining together freely, and is thus inimical to civil society.

The impact of the struggle for power is starkly exhibited in the poverty and economic decline in sub-Saharan Africa, especially the zone of violence described by Berkeley in Central Africa—including Liberia, Sudan, Congo, Rwanda, and Uganda in earlier years—in which the "mode of production was enrichment through looting" (Berkeley 2001, 54)—discussed in chapter 7.

Terror is an instrument for governments and contenders. The cycle of violations of life integrity leading to war and reinforced by war exacerbates poverty and underdevelopment, triggering economic regression. Although rebels use terror to extract diamonds, gold, and other portable resources, terror destroys the economy that most people depend on, because people cannot plough, harvest, produce, or invest when there is no personal security. As Thomas Hobbes put it more than 350 years ago:

> Whatsoever therefore is consequent to a time of Warre, where every man is Enemy to every man; the same is consequent to the time, wherein men live without other security, than what their own strength, and their own invention shall furnish them withall. In such condition, there is no place for Industry; because the fruit thereof is uncertain; and consequently no Culture of the Earth; no Navigation, nor use of the commodities that may be imported by Sea ... and which is worst of all, continuall feare, and danger of violent death; And the life of man, solitary, poore, nasty, brutish and short. (1961 [1651], 100)

Implications for the Future

Implications for the future need to take into account not only past policies but new challenges confronting states. Old challenges, such as the debt burden in developing countries, constraints on welfare posed by adjustment programs of the International Monetary Fund, demographic growth, inequities in the world system of exchange, and the impact of globalization, have been widely discussed. But discussion should also focus on how aid policies of the Western states and international organizations affect human rights and the impact of such policies on development, so as to avoid aid increasing the potential for gross violations of life integrity and genocide, as in Rwanda (Uvin 1998).

Showing how respect for life integrity and freedom enhances social and economic rights—for example, reduction of poverty and enhancement of health—in the contexts discussed might be an instrument to broaden our view of the link among democracy, development, and human rights. However, Jack Donnelly asserted (1999) that it is wrong to take for granted, as did the Vienna Declaration and Programme of Action (adopted by the 1993 World Conference on Human Rights), that "democracy, development and respect for human rights and fundamental freedoms are interdependent and mutually reinforcing" (1999, 608–609). Electoral democracy and free markets (the latter "an economic analog to a political system of majority rule without minority rights" [Donnelly 1999, 630] are means, not ends, and they are not enough. How to achieve these ends depends on strategy and contingent decisions. He continues to make the case for human rights as a priority.

> Those [rights-protective] regimes will be democratic. They are desirable, however, because we think that empowering the people is the best political mechanism we have yet devised to secure all human rights for all. Rights-protective regimes will also pursue economic development. But development is desirable as much for the resources it makes available to provide economic and social rights for members of disadvantaged groups as for the intrinsic values of the goods produced. (Donnelly 2003, 203)

How paths of development can be changed so that citizens of former dictatorships and failed states can have a better future in states that respect life integrity demands imagination: to draw not only on the past, but to learn to create free rights–respecting states. This demands creating inclusive communities and civil society organizations that enable people to develop trust, mutual helpfulness, and cooperation. In order for people in such states to survive and believe in a future worth working toward, this must be done with the help of the international organizations and states. Development ethicists concerned with state and individual capacities discuss the effects of globalization and democracy as dialogue (Crocker 2006). Perhaps citizens of affluent states might be moved by dialogue (or enlightened self-interest or solidarity) to commit greater resources in order to create a more self-sustaining and less dangerous world.

Note

1. First, I discriminated states that were usually respecters of life integrity from gross violators in 1987 and 1997 in the regions considered. This process was based on coding each state's practices from human rights reports (further discussed in chapter 7). In each year studied, countries were distinguished by whether (1) they had shown consistent respect for life integrity (ranks 0, 1), including among respecters countries that were not gross violators (NGV) and showed instances but not a general pattern of abuse (rank 2), or (2) whether they were gross violators (ranks 3, 4, and 5), collectively labeled gross violators. For simplicity, the first group is labeled "Generally Respect Rights" and the second is called "Gross Violators" in tables 8.1 through 8.3.

9
Conclusion and Implications:
What Can Be Done?

To intervene or not—this should always be a hard question. Even in the case of a brutal civil war or a politically induced famine or the massacre of a local minority, the use of force in other people's countries should always generate hesitation and anxiety. So it does today among small groups of concerned people, some of whom end up supporting, some resisting, interventionist policies....

I am going to focus on the arguments for and against "humanitarian intervention," for this is what is at issue in the former Yugoslavia, the Caucasus, parts of Asia, much of Africa.... The presumption against intervention is strong; we (on the left especially) have reasons for it, which derive from our opposition to imperial politics and our commitment to self-determination, even when the process of self-determination is something less than peaceful and democratic.... Still, nonintervention is not an absolute moral rule: sometimes, what is going on locally cannot be tolerated....

Yes, the norm is not to intervene in other people's countries; the norm is self-determination. But not for *these* people, the victims of tyranny, ideological zeal, ethnic hatred, who are not determining anything for themselves.... Whenever the filthy work can be stopped, it should be stopped. And if not by us, the supposedly decent people of this world, then by whom?

—Michael Walzer, *Arguing about War* (2004)

The question of how to arrest human wrongs—slavery, terror, geno-cide—is not only a local question but one involving international responsibility, as Walzer attests. There are many ways to deter and arrest wrongs without violence, which shall be explored herein, but we cannot avoid the question of intervention (discussed later).

In order to arrest human wrongs, we must first understand why they happen and how it is that many people ignore and justify these violations. What assumptions, interests, and power structures would have to change to eliminate such wrongs? The preceding chapters probed what one can learn from the past. This chapter also asks what victims, perpetrators, and people in other states can do to deter and check gross violations of life integrity, and why they should do so.

Although it is likely that the same types of violations considered herein will persist and recur, there are new actors with new scripts, strategies, tactics, ideologies, and networks, which inspire new forms of international terror. In the twentieth century, human rights were denied in the name of ideologies claiming rights for one group or nation and denying individual rights, exalting the state (fascism) or one class (communism). Rights are and have been denied for a variety of justifications: ideology, religion, nation (and national liberation), security, and group protection. In the beginning of the twenty-first century, terror was also imposed in the name of God (Allah) by Islamic extremists—although disowned by many believers in Islam.

To inquire into what has been shown herein, one must understand the underlying dilemmas groups and nations must resolve (discussed in chapter 1) that suggest why it is so hard to wrest human rights from other humans.

1. Who belongs? Who is included in the universe of obligation, the circle of persons with rights that must be respected? Some categories of included/excluded groups are: citizens/aliens, believers/nonbelievers (or believers in another religion who might be termed infidels), majority/minorities, dominant ethnic group(s)/other group, dominant race/other races, revolution-aries/antirevolutionaries, males/females, caste strata/below caste (untouchables). These are all types of respected and dis-respected groups in different societies.

2. Who rules? This question involves regime types, terms of obedience, and legitimacy as well as the presence or absence of civil and political rights that give people the power to decide who rules, check their rulers, and participate in making policy.

3. Who decides on the rules of exchange? Is labor free or co-erced—enslaved, bonded, trafficked? There are also the classic

controversies over the role of labor, landownership, and capital, as well as the right of labor to organize freely without state control. What part of the labor force is unfree? Is this lack of freedom sanctioned by the state or overlooked?

Denying and suppressing human rights serve to reinforce class, status, and power for some as well as to preserve their sense of meaning and group borders. The victims of slavery, terror, and genocide are all defined outside of the universe of obligation of the perpetrator; no duties are owed them. But the victims of each type of violation have very different origins and destinies.

Slaves are not organized, present no threat, and can claim no rights. In a minority of cases, that is, traditional servitude (in Mauritania and some cases in Southeast Asia), there are minimal obligations for sustenance. The susceptibility of certain peoples in many countries to becoming slaves rests on the teaching of contempt for such groups over generations. Women are particularly subject to becoming enslaved by trafficking because of both the culture of abasement of women and their emergence as a valuable commodity in international commerce—they can be sold (including by parents), traded, or volunteer, seeking better opportunities.

The victims of twentieth-century slavery come from the most varied points of origin. They might be outside (aliens) or inside the nation (citizens/residents); snatched, sentenced, enlisted, or born into servitude; conquered in war, serving in peace, or volunteering for a job abroad. They might be housed in camps, brothels, factory hostels, or private homes. They might be racially distinct or similar to their enslavers, keeping in mind that the classification and perception of race are defined locally. Mostly they are invisible, strangers below the social radar screen, only detected by international, state, and local human rights nongovernmental organizations (HRNGOs).

Their enslavers have been states, paramilitaries (allied with and opposing states), criminal networks, households, and private employers. States (and some paramilitaries) have distinct needs to control territory as well as opportunities and ideological agendas that private employers usually do not have. In some cases, they seize slave workers from nations and groups that challenge the legitimacy of their rule. Employers are ordinarily just interested in exploitation. Often, this is gross exploitation from an economic as well as a moral standard, comparing the profit enslaved trafficking women bring to their traffickers and brothel owners to the profits from ordinary commerce.

Conclusion and Implications: What Can Be Done?

Terror states subjugate whole classes and groups as well as potential dissidents, and on occasion individuals who are merely different (rather than deviant), such as some handicapped persons in Argentina. What is common among the states of terror discussed (Algeria 1954–1962, Argentina 1975–1979, Guatemala 1960–1996, Iraq 1968–2003) is that all but Argentina were ethnically divided societies (Argentina was politically polarized). A significant segment of the people did not accept or had contended in the recent past with the authority of the government. All these states experienced a legitimacy crisis.

The victims of terror were usually demonized and labeled as outside the nation when they were not ethnically distinct. The governments instigating rebellion (or that feared rebellion) were based on colonial rule (Algeria) and violent coups (Argentina, Guatemala, and Iraq). Who rules was the primary question in all four cases. Who are the people to which the regime must be accountable? was the underlying question. From the governments' vantage point and that of dominant elites within each nation, there was or had been a real threat. In Argentina, previous terrorism of the left and right was often cited as a reason many Argentineans welcomed the generals' coup in 1975.

Terror was a weapon of the government to suppress potential opposition and inhibit criticism; it could change the terms of exchange. Terror enabled governments in Guatemala and Argentina to repress unions and movements for social change, using selective disappearance and assassination. Other classes were enriched by the state in Argentina, and the great majority in Iraq became more affluent during Saddam Hussein's first decade in power.

Civil war, resurgent rebellion, and the threat of terrorism (present or recurrent) provided the justification presented to the international community for state counterterrorism: torture, disappearance and killing of suspects, and denial of the rule of law. The continued existence of regimes of state terror depended on the regional and international neighborhood as well as the domestic one. Latin America (and especially Central America) in the last century was largely under U.S. domination. U.S. policy after 1945 was in part a product of the polarization of the Cold War; anyone against our communist enemy must be our friend. In the Middle East and Africa, international opinion was also moved by post–World War II commitments to decolonization and self-determination.

The terroristic regimes of Argentina and Guatemala were initially supported by the United States, and Iraq's regime was reinforced by the Soviet Union—although by the late 1980s, virtually all Western states fortified Iraq in its war with Iran. In Algeria, French domination and counterterror were rationalized as a response to the terror of the Algerian Front for National Liberation (FLN), but support for maintaining Algeria as part of France (Algérie Française) was withdrawn by the French public; the price in domestic disorder was too high. Withdrawal of U.S. support for France in Algeria is believed to have also influenced French calculations.

Human wrongs can cause disorder and instability. Realists make the case that other states check gross violators based on their own national self-interest. Looking back to the first half of the twentieth century, one can observe how totalitarian states—Nazi Germany and the Soviet Union—were states of slavery, terror, and genocide. In the late twentieth century, Democratic Kampuchea and Sudan also employed slavery, terror, and genocide. Totalitarian states (Nazi Germany, the Soviet Union, Iraq, Democratic Kampuchea) are more likely than other states to be aggressors and start wars. States of terror are more likely than other states to become states of genocide, which virtually always occurs during war.

When opposition of ethnically and regionally distinct groups emerged—in Iraq among the Kurds, in Guatemala the Mayan Indians—these governments escalated from terror to genocide. There was no selection of victims who left relatives behind to mourn them; there was indiscriminate slaughter. But genocide of whole peoples also emerged by design or ideology rather than in retribution or reprisal in the twentieth century.

Theories of race—an Aryan master race in Nazi Germany, a transnational Turkic race in the Ottoman Empire, an indigenous race versus an alien Tutsi race in Rwanda—were elaborated to justify the slaughter of preselected victims. In the ongoing genocide in Darfur, the victims are usually identified by race.

Genocides since 1945 have often been a response to ethnic domination leading to the rebellion of a subordinated group, which, in turn, elicits a genocidal response from the state. Most states of ethnic exclusion and discrimination in Asia, Africa, and the Middle East between 1948 and 1988 produced rebellions that led to genocide and state-sponsored massacres (Fein 1993b).

States and international organizations should work to prevent and redress such discrimination and exclusion in order to annul the preconditions for rebellion, discrimination, and genocide. They should also avoid creating the conditions that lead to exclusive nationalism.

Exclusive nationalism is most likely to emerge from states in crisis and breakdown. These conditions incite ethnic entrepreneurs to arouse support and create unity by magnifying fears of the ethnic Other and thus justify eliminating them. Genocide is more likely to occur when states' legitimacy depends on their claim to represent one ethnic or religious group. "Who belongs?" is the question preceding and validating the answer to "Who rules?"

What was necessary for genocide to succeed was the lack of intervention by major powers. In World War I this could be attributed to the inability of the Allies to physically intervene and the policy of the Ottoman Empire's German ally, who veered from complicity to belated protest, only putting the brakes on to deter deportations from the metropolises of Constantinople and Smyrna. In World War II, Allied nonintervention could be attributed to the Allies' refusal to make rescue and deterrence of extermination of the Jews a war goal. In both wars, the Allies promised postwar judgment, a goal aborted and defeated after World War I by competing national interests but fulfilled by the Allies at Nuremburg in 1946 (Bass 2000). In Rwanda, the world community overlooked all opportunities to deter and check the genocide. The United Nations started prosecution of the *génocidaires* in 1996 by expanding the International Criminal Tribunal for War Crimes in the Former Yugoslavia to include Rwanda.

Between 1945 and 1995, the United Nations consistently avoided confronting genocide and genocidal massacres, in effect viewing them as the right of sovereign states, as Leo Kuper observed (1981, 161). What is new today is the commitment of the UN secretary-general to the "Responsibility to Protect" and the appointment of a Special Rapporteur for Genocide (with minimal staff), Juan Mendez, and aides to warn against it. However, the UN is continually foiled from taking effective action (action in Darfur is still in doubt as of this writing) to stop genocide by the unwillingness of member states to take risks and pay costs as well as the need for consensus within the UN Security Council.

There are few situations where identities of contending groups are simply those of oppressors and victims, few groups that are just "innocent victims," but there are many *implicated victims,* more on some sides in some situations. Significant voices in all these groups excluded (and continue to exclude) their Other (antagonist group) from the universe of obligation. They often demanded a monopoly of rule, for both the protection of their group and its expression as a nation-state. The demand for majority rule can also activate the fears of the minority, who might prefer separation if they are outnumbered. Gaining power is seen by many (in the minority and majority group) as a more important cause than wresting human rights. But getting power without protecting human rights can come back to haunt empowered groups as they re-create discrimination and rebellion by their rule.

Repairing the World: What Can Be Done?

Reconstruction and reform can come from within states and from without. It can come from below if citizens and leaders are persuaded that these might make their life better. Where societies are divided and disempowered groups are excluded and exploited, such groups and classes can mobilize nonviolent action when conditions make communication possible. The U.S. civil rights movement of the 1960s was an example of how an oppressed minority denied citizenship rights—members of whom were periodically threatened by lynching and murder—triggered support from the national majority against a regional ruling majority by using nonviolent action. Nonviolence has contributed to successful outcomes for oppressed groups and nations in a wide range of minority and national struggles in the twentieth century, including the United States (1959–1965), India (1920–1948), the Philippines (1983–1986), Poland (1980–1989), and Eastern Europe and Mongolia (1988–1989), cases documented by Peter Ackerman and Jack DuVall (2000).

Sometimes the victims are completely enslaved or disempowered minorities who cannot organize because they are unfree, isolated, and demoralized. How could we enable them to end slavery?

Ending Slavery

Looking back at the Nazi and Soviet uses of slave labor—both made possible by totalitarianism—it is clear that there was no possibility of reform in the face of absolute power. Only the overthrow of the system stopped German slavery and genocide in 1945. In the Soviet case, the contradictions within the Gulag and attempted reforms restricted the severity of labor camps after the death of Stalin in 1953. There is no evidence that the Loghai system in China of labor camps (masked as commercial enterprises) has been checked by reforms in China or by laws of the United States and other states against import of goods produced by prisoners.

Apart from China and North Korea (in which the enslaved are in prison camps), stationary slavery and bonded labor today are most apt to be prevalent in areas where they are sanctioned by religion, particularly Hinduism and Islam. This cannot be changed by law alone (as India demonstrates), but there is no evidence that it can be changed without effective legal sanctions. The continuation of slavery in states with free markets can usually be related to gross inequality between groups and classes, collusion and integration of economic and political elites, and the powerlessness and exclusion of the victims from the universe of obligation of the perpetrators and bystanders.

Such practices cannot be changed without domestic mobilization and domestic and international law, accompanied by international incentives and sanctions—carrots and sticks. Neither tradition, ideology, nor self-interest is likely to be challenged effectively from inside a state without international pressure.

Slavery in Muslim sub-Saharan Africa is illustrated herein by Sudan and Mauritania. In Sudan, it stems from government policy rewarding raiders, and it is perpetuated in Mauritania from custom (see chapter 2). Both HRNGO campaigns, which focus on slavery alone, and broader international efforts (involving Europe, the United States, and Africa) to liberate and rehabilitate slaves deserve consideration.

Bonded labor in India continues to exist after more than half a century in an electoral democracy, a predominantly Hindu culture, but a state that emerged from a secular independence movement with a liberal tradition and constitution. Indian leaders have for many years proclaimed concern for social justice and passed legislation not only to emancipate bonded laborers, but also to rectify past injustices by compensating them with land and job training. But India is also a country with high unemployment and little ability for illiterate landless laborers to escape.

The untouchables, or *dalits,* whose stigma is justified by Hinduism, are the class most likely to be victims of multiple gross violations of life integrity, including rape, police torture, lack of protection, and deprivation of equal rights (see chapter 2). But the greatest violence in daily life is their lack of free movement and control, bound to individual patrons or impersonal bonded labor.

Nongovernmental organizations that aim to emancipate the dalits, who are formally free in India (abolition of untouchability was written into the Indian Constitution), confront not only indifference within India but often ignorance and denial of responsibility by bystanders outside India, who credit the claim of the Indian government that this is a cultural or religious question, implying that the principle of freedom of religion enjoins its toleration—forgetting how caste degradation was repudiated by the founders of modern India. Neither constitutional guarantees nor affirmative action plans (for Scheduled Castes, e.g., dalits, and Scheduled Classes) have affected the majority of the dalits (Hooda 2001, 178–179).

To achieve their goals to emancipate the dalits, Indian groups need to legislate and implement laws not only wiping out bonded labor but giving compensation and rehabilitation to the dalits. The latter also requires expansion of economic opportunities so that dalits are able to get work, become self-supporting, and not go back to their previous employers or patrons. Women's cooperatives and microcredit NGOs also provide sources of employment that can help bonded laborers become free of debt.

International human rights and other groups can put pressure on the Indian government by giving bonded labor greater visibility, organizing consumer boycotts of export products made by bonded labor and preferential buying campaigns for fair-trade goods. They can also bring up questions about Indian practices in international fora, such as UN committees. Other governments and international lenders could make aid contingent on plans to emancipate and rehabilitate bonded laborers in the projects or areas they aid.

The exploitation of bonded and child labor in India (and elsewhere) might indeed create a self-reinforcing cycle; by enlarging the labor supply and diminishing the wage rate, unemployment increases and the price of free labor declines (Weiner and Noman 1995, 187). This relationship needs to be made explicit in order to persuade poorer classes and lower castes (who might fear competition with the dalits) that they would gain rather than lose by doing away with bonded labor and hyperexploitative child labor. There is disagreement among Indians (and others) over what kinds of labor are appropriate for children and should be tolerated.

Other types of slavery involve a range of countries in the global economy. The trafficking of persons in the international labor market is the greatest transnational cause of enslavement today. Sexual slavery and other trafficking are usually not visible to ordinary citizens, because they are a hidden and criminal enterprise. The pull of the international labor market in low-wage and disorganized countries with weak or failed states opens the incentives for women to volunteer or to be forced into the international sex trade. Ethnic networks at home and abroad recruit and sell slaves of the same ethnicity.

Debt bondage results from the obligations of trafficked women to pay back the money paid to their relatives who sold them, if their entry to the trade was not voluntary, and to reimburse the trafficker for his alleged costs of smuggling them across borders if they left their country voluntarily. Throughout Asia and Europe, women and girls who become forced prostitutes, drawn by international traffickers across borders, are not part of the society to which they are imported and are excluded from the political community.

Although not necessarily invisible in their home country, the sexually enslaved become invisible and stigmatized in the country to which they are imported. Often, they cannot go home again because of the stigma and fear of the response from parents and neighbors. Their debt will in many cases follow them, with the women usually having no means to pay it off except by returning to the sex trade.

Both effective criminal control and mobilization against trafficking often depend on local and international social movements.

Trafficked persons are drawn to work in both free and partially free states, states open to media and Western influences, in which bystanders have the ability to publicize, protest, and mobilize against their condition. Although only dictatorships have the capacity for large-scale enslavement of citizens and strangers in the twentieth century, authoritarian states (such as Sudan and Mauritania) instigate and tolerate slavery, and free and partly free states (e.g., Thailand, India, Israel, and Brazil) might overlook it in ranking their political priorities, effectively sustaining slavery.

These priorities can be changed. Studies of cross-border sexual slavery concur on two complementary strategies to stop it. First, states and donors should try to deter slavery by providing employment in their home countries to people who might otherwise volunteer for what is advertised as employment abroad. Second, eliminating the sex trade also means educating and penalizing families who trade their daughters for profit and enhancing the status of women, countering the teaching of abasement of females.

Strategies for change can include gender-conscious development, giving women other employment, stimulating the economy, and instituting more effective crime control. These changes depend not only on international state cooperation to stop trafficking but on local human rights groups that press governments to enact laws to punish traffickers rather than victims, to offer trafficked prostitutes sanctuary and support rather than prison and deportation, and to monitor patterns of importation, brothel and sweatshop ownership, and police corruption. HRNGOs from countries of origin can try to persuade people not to accept false offers of employment abroad and give them advice to protect themselves if they do. Other kinds of trafficking, which involve production of goods for domestic and international sale, suggest other strategies (previously discussed) of halting the sale of products of bonded labor.

Last, in many cases there is the problem of redress and rehabilitation. Slaves and bonded laborers must be rehabilitated and get alternate employment, land, and credit to provide for themselves. International aid to expand economic development must take into account what such countries are doing to end or sustain slavery. Donors can mandate conditions and provide incentives to emancipate slaves.

There are several ways people and organizations can check slavery. The more successful efforts have involved triggering focal points of the *triangle of impact*. The triangle of impact reinforces (1) protest of local HRNGOs with (2) responses of international or Western-based HRNGOs and those of governments and intergovernmental organizations and officials (such as the UN High Commissioner of Human Rights), which (3) press the government responsible for tolerating or overlooking slavery and trafficking to change. Thus, local social movements can foment official action abroad, using the fulcrum of more powerful states and organizations over less powerful states to move the latter.

This process has been reinforced by recent legislation of the U.S. government, now the hegemonic power. This legislation has been largely impelled by the organized evangelical Christian movement in the United States (Hertzge 2002). Such legislation includes the International Religious Freedom Act (1998), the Victims of Trafficking and Violence Protection Act (2000), and the Sudan Peace Act (2001).

Illustrations of the triangle of impact include the following:

1. In Israel, the documentation of the Israel Women's Network (1997) of extensive trafficking of women from former Soviet lands, which was tolerated by police and government, provoked little action until it was communicated by other human rights and Jewish women's NGOs in the United States. The effect of Human Rights Watch's and Amnesty International's condemnation and pressure on Israel from the U.S. government mobilized public criticism in Israel, enabling the Knesset to pass a law

(proposed for years) in 2000 making the practices that sustain trafficking illegal. In October 2006, a stronger law was passed by the Knesset that was said to be a response to U.S. pressure.

This is not a case of instant success; few campaigns produce instant success. Progress on implementation of the Israeli government's commitment consistently depends not only on state-to-state pressure but on the unremitting work of local Israeli HRNGOs, including Hotline for Migrant Workers, Physicians for Human Rights–Israel, and various NGOs representing feminists, sexual minorities, and ex-prostitutes.

The supply of women from the former Soviet Union ready to go to Israel, the vast majority knowing (by all accounts) that they will serve as prostitutes, might also be diminished by the efforts of local Russian organizations and the press to protect women from enticement. Publicized testimony of former prostitutes, such as a report in the *Moscow Times* and on CBS News in February 2003 that told of the experience of Inna from Moldova, smuggled through Egypt to Israel—rape, mistreatment, shame, depression, and contracting venereal disease—could deter others from enlisting for work abroad (Plushnick-Masti 2003; CBSNews.com, February 24, 2003).

2. Bonded laborers in Asia have been assisted by international nongovernmental organizations that target export industries to organize consumer boycotts of products made with child labor, such as carpets, by popularizing distinguishing symbols (i.e., Rugmark) for approved products.

Persuading other countries to end stationary slavery may be promoted by appealing to their own interests in development. Slavery and economic development do not mix well because development (where aided by international agencies and governments) must be visible. Visibility can cause shame among slaveholders and profiteers in reaction to protests by national and international HRNGOs and exposure by the media. Increasingly, development depends on global trade. The visibility of multinational companies engaged cannot be subject to the information-management techniques practiced in Uttar Pradesh (India) or Noukachott (Mauritania). Such companies are increasingly monitored by shareholders' movements and can be pressured by stockholder campaigns and consumer boycotts. The vision of imagined futures could affect the reconstruction of present inequality.

Chapter 9

Exposing Links—Democracy, Human Rights, and Causes of Conflict

After the breakup of the Soviet Union and decline of communist and alternate models of rule in the 1990s, there was an extension of electoral democracies from 1987 to the twenty-first century. Although human rights are often understood to be a concomitant of democracy, this inadequate perspective overlooked the practices of some contemporary democracies (see chapter 7). However, democracy for many advocates was viewed not only as an end in itself but an element stabilizing international relations. Because wars do not occur in the modern age between democratic nations, the diffusion of democracy was believed to be a strategy for enhancing world peace.

Just as wars between states would be less likely, it was also believed that there would be fewer causes of internal war in democracies. The organs and sites of repression and annihilation—secret police, concentration camps, prisons without oversight—should be eliminated or easily exposed, given free speech, assembly, and an independent judiciary. But elimination and exposure depend on a full liberal electorate guaranteeing individual human rights, regardless of who rules. Chapter 7 discusses the reasons why electoral democracy alone is not enough to protect human rights.

Liberal democracy depends on some preconditions. Severe inequality and large-scale social exclusion—whether based on ethnicity, class, or gender—are directly related to the failure of states to respect life integrity and move toward freedom and development. Poor states are more likely to produce tyrants who view the state as a method of enrichment and rely on repression to rule. But it is an unstable rule, for such tyrants and ethnocracies often produce their own opposition. Such rule is likely to sink state and society deeper into poverty.

States split by conflict along group lines are more likely also to be poor states and failed states. Both the military and rebels, often predatory militias greedy for loot, are likely to take over (or seek to overthrow) the state. In the last ten years, such militias have devastated poor African states—Liberia, Sierra Leone, Democratic Republic of Congo. Sierra Leone and Liberia were rescued from terror and anarchy (2003–2005) by military forces of the United Kingdom, the United Nations, and the Economic Community of West African States, respectively.

Gross violations of life integrity are the cause of major international problems that are often not seen as related: millions of refugees and displaced persons, famine, and malnutrition. Unplanned famines have been especially characteristic of communist states in the last seventy-five years of the twentieth century: for example, the Soviet Union, China, Ethiopia (under the Dergue), Democratic Kampuchea, and North Korea.

The lack of civil liberties and the repression of information (signifying the lack of civil liberties), which allowed states to deny and tolerate famine, now represent dangers not only to their own citizens but to public health and human security internationally. Jonathan Mirsky charged that "Communist China's long obsession with secrecy was one cause of the SARS (Severe Acute Respiratory Syndrome) crisis" because of its classification of infectious diseases as "highly secret," which caused officials to suppress and deny the incidence of SARS, allowing it to spread (2003, 42). Similarly, the repression of protest by whistle-blowers in Russia has impeded identification of nuclear and chemical problems that could lead to transnational environmental disasters; the denial of signs of bacteria and viruses by states in the Middle East and Balkans has spread diseases; the denial of HIV/AIDS in Africa spreads AIDS; and the repression of protesters in the Caribbean and Latin America who spoke up against stripping of forests inhibited international action against environmental damage, which could lead to global warming (Schultz 2001, chs. 4–7). These threats are seen by many as episodic and unpredictable. One predictable condition or necessity to live is adequate food.

I suggest several reasons for the substantive advantage demonstrated by rights respecters. Respect for life integrity and other human rights in free states is more likely to motivate people to cooperate and increase cohesion among citizens than are cruelty, repression, and gross violations of life integrity. Citizens who are not afraid of their government are more likely to participate and join together, more likely to cooperate with reforms, and better able to check government from bad policies. Cohesion also creates social capital, which might produce economic innovations and greater productivity. Specific policies of democratic governments that have been noted include investment in public health, which leads to longer life, better health, and greater productivity and income.

Social cohesion and social capital are less likely to be found and to improve life chances generally in societies with extreme inequality and ethnic discrimination. Exclusion makes states poorer and makes conflict and internal war more likely, which, in turn, lead to flight, famine, and decline in national productivity and income. Partly free or "illiberal" democracies that do not surmount the lack of social cohesion seem likely to remain gross violators and to remain poor.

The inclusion of all citizens—and protection of noncitizens' basic human rights—seems the sine qua non for effectively controlling who rules and who makes the rules of exchange. It is an enabling condition, necessary but not sufficient. Even when exclusion does not threaten political order, it has negative effects for the country as a whole.

For example, the untouchables in India do not threaten the stability of the government, but holding untouchables in contempt makes torture more tolerable and directly and indirectly diminishes human capital. The Indian public's disinterest in universal primary education has been attributed to the fact that the majority of Indians believe that outcastes and lower castes are destined to work with their hands and not their heads (Weiner and Noman 1952). The lack of basic literacy degrades the health and productivity of the whole Indian nation.

For development to work for all, respect for life integrity, civil liberties, democratic rule, and development must be pursued together. But electoral democracy is not enough without civil liberties and respect for life integrity.

Assistance for Democratization and Development and Foreign Aid

International aid for democratization in states experiencing regime changes was institutionalized in the last decade of the twentieth century, transferring resources and prescriptions from the developed West to the rest of the states. This could be considered a wise investment if it works, because fully free liberal democracies are most apt to be respecters of life integrity, more apt to experience economic growth than gross violators (see chapters 7 and 8) and, according to much research, do not go to war with other democracies. Yet most countries in transition did not become free states—the states most likely to protect life integrity—but "illiberal democracies" going nowhere (Czakaria 1997). Thus, the pattern of gross violations of life integrity found in 1987 was similar or worse in 1997.

How can this be understood when 1987–1997 was a decade of investment in international assistance for democratization? What many have not noted is that because of its extensive aid, the United States does not use legislation on the books for decades to protect human rights in countries where it can be assumed to have influence (discussed in the following section).

Thomas Carothers's assessments (1999, 2002) seem astute. At the beginning, there was little distinction between democracy and democratization—between the form, the end-goal, and the process. An inordinate stress was put on free elections as the means and measure of democracy. Western states and NGOs developed techniques to run, monitor, and legitimate elections as free and fair. But elections, necessary for regime change, accomplished less than expected. They did not eliminate routinized police and military violations of life integrity, transform civil-military power, change patterns of political and economic discrimination of ethnic groups, or alter the distribution of power, which entitles some and disempowers many. Often, elections offered very restricted choice and failed to produce popular support to sustain the new governments' legitimacy; nor did they sustain belief that government made a difference in the lives of most citizens.

Realist critics stress the pitfalls of "illiberal democracies" (Zakaria 1997), but reading them carefully implies that the challenges of democratization are better served by stressing a "human rights regime," William Schultz says, than by regressing to authoritarian regimes. "They end up, in other words, where the great human rights champions of democracy have been all along—with the conviction that democracy requires more than free elections; it also requires a culture of respect for fundamental human rights" (2001, 51).

The challenges to democratization come not only from resistance to change at the top (indicated by cronyism, patronage, and corruption), but also from the lack of support among the majority who do not see their life improved by the changes democratization programs impart: elections, political parties, NGOs, and media principally based on a detached urban elite. Yet local forces play the major part in whether democratization unfolds or regresses, as the failure of aid to deepen democracy in Russia and Albania (among other places) demonstrates. Rather than aiding dominant elites, democratization aid could be more effective by expanding the demand for and exercise of human rights, which would motivate more citizens to participate and to defend a democratic state.

Wresting human rights is ultimately done at home. The severity of ethnic and class conflicts is often a product of earlier discrimination that could have been resolved had life integrity and civil rights and liberties been respected. Unresolved conflicts and social exclusion undermine solidarity, making life worse for all. Solidarity is more likely to produce respect for life integrity and greater dividends in terms of human development, including economic growth, promoting a virtuous cycle.

To promote such development, my findings suggest democratization and development planners need to put more emphasis on preventing gross violations of life integrity and encouraging respect for human rights. Strategies to implement this might include:

1. aiding local communities and NGOs in order to promote social cohesion and participation, particularly in areas where women and certain classes and groups have been excluded, making continuation of such aid linked to respect for human rights;
2. providing models to poor countries of other countries that were also poor and in which greater democracy and development reinforced each other, perhaps by exchanges with such countries;
3. linking abolishment of slavery and forced labor with rehabilitation and aid;
4. enforcing laws against foreign aid to gross violators of human rights; and
5. creating new norms by judging past transgressors and the history of gross violations (see Hayner 2002).

International solidarity and aid will be needed to help poorer nations make these changes and solve economic and health problems at the same time. Some suggestions advanced include redressing trade rules to allow free markets for poorer countries, annulling debt, making free generic drugs available, and transferring billions of dollars to stop the spread of HIV/AIDS. States that respect life integrity and human rights are more likely than other states to use such transfers well.

Foreign aid is one means by which developed countries transfer resources to less-developed countries. By the year 2001, U.S. human rights legislation that stipulated conditions negating aid to gross violators of human rights (defined similarly to life integrity) had been on the books for forty years; in the 1990s, legislation monitoring religious freedom and global trafficking with potential sanctions was added. These standards began with the Foreign Assistance Act of 1961 (Section 116[d], barring economic assistance to gross violators of human rights unless such assistance benefited needy people, and Section 502[b] of the Foreign Assistance Act of 1961 [as amended, 22 U.S.C.A. 2304], banning military aid). The latter states:

1. The United States shall, in accordance with its international obligations as set forth in the Charter of the United Nations and in keeping with the constitutional heritage and traditions of the United States, promote and encourage increased respect for human rights and fundamental freedoms throughout the world without distinction as to race, sex, language, or religion....

2. Except under circumstances specified in this section, no security assistance may be provided to any country the government of which engages in a consistent pattern of gross violations of internationally recognized human rights. Security assistance may not be provided to the police, domestic intelligence, or similar law enforcement forces of a country ... the government of which engages in a consistent pattern of gross violations of internationally recognized human rights unless the President certifies in writing ... that extraordinary circumstances exist warranting provision of such assistance. (Steiner and Alston 2000, 1093–1095)

The last sentence in Section 502(b)2 has allowed U.S. presidents (both Republican and Democratic) to consistently thwart the intent of this act. Schultz observed that 44 percent of countries that received U.S. combat training in 1997 were nondemocratic, including gross violators; besides countries in Latin America these have included Turkey, Indonesia, Algeria, and Kenya (Schultz 2001, 138–140). The largest beneficiaries are in the Middle East.

Virtually all major states (including the five permanent members of the UNSC) have supplied arms to states with poor human rights records between 1999 and 2003 (Yanik 2006). If no requirement is enforced that such states stop specific practices—for example, torture, collective arrest and punishment, curbs on minorities' civil liberties and freedom of movement, and denial of equal protection under the law—what sanction or incentive is there for these countries to do so?

Although there can be no guarantee that foreign aid would be the lever to change countries' practices, giving foreign aid to gross violators can only discourage reform from within in states seeking to change when foreign powers reward rights violators.

Developed countries affect less-developed countries through their trade, technology, security, environment, migration, investment, and aid policies. The Center for Global Development and Foreign Policy developed an index ranking rich countries on a compound of these factors in 2004: Top-ranking countries (in order of rank) were the Netherlands, Denmark, Sweden, Austria, United Kingdom, Canada, and the United States (*Foreign Policy,* May–June 2004). Thus, richer countries can give positive incentives to poorer countries in many ways. Aid itself might do more harm than good if misspent, William Easterly (2006) maintains.

Prevention and Intervention against Terror and Genocide

The United Nations no longer views state sovereignty as absolving all state crimes and a warrant for genocide, as Leo Kuper observed that it did in the thirty-five years after World War II (Kuper 1981, 161). By the end of the twentieth century, the international community had begun to condemn genocide and state aggression, direct and indirect: for example, direct invasion, "ethnic cleansing," "population bombing," and state-sponsored terrorism. Justifications of humanitarian intervention have been around for decades, but in the last decade of the twentieth century more interventions were internationally mandated or approved than in the total of the preceding four decades of the United Nations. These included Iraq/Kuwait (1990–1991), Liberia (1992), Somalia (1992–1993), Rwanda (after the genocide in 1994), Haiti (1994–1995), Bosnia and Herzegovina (1993–1996), Albania (1997), Central African Republic (1997), Sierra Leone (1997), Yugoslavia/Kosovo (1999), East Timor (1999), and Sudan (2006) (Chesterman 2001). But the international community has not devised means to prevent the human rights violations and aggression that precipitated these interventions.

The failure by major powers and by the United Nations to intervene to deter *génocidaires* and stop genocide has been the norm in the twentieth century and the twenty-first century so far. It was particularly appalling in Rwanda (1994), because major states were warned in advance and the UN Genocide Convention implies a collective obligation to stop genocide. Similarly, in Darfur, Sudan, the UNSC has passed only ineffectual or unimplemented resolutions since 2004. Major powers on the UN Security Council (UNSC) checked potential timely intervention to stop genocide based on narrow conceptions of their self-interest.

Gross violations of life integrity, such as the massacres against Tutsis in Rwanda from 1991 to 1994, were warning signs of the potential for escalation to genocide. By not responding to warning signs, major patrons of Rwanda (such as France) and the United Nations in effect told the *génocidaires* that they could do whatever they wanted. When the genocide emerged in April 1994, the role of the United States, by then the only superpower, was critical in the UN's decision not to intervene (Leitenberg 1994). Power observed that there was a range of means short of physical intervention to deter and check genocide (2002, 382–385, 504). Yet the conversation on Rwanda and other genocides usually focuses on humanitarian intervention—physical intercession. The case for humanitarian intervention assumes that the universal obligation to defend the right to life—violated by genocide— invoked by "just war" theory is equally compelling or greater than the invocation of sovereignty embedded in the UN Charter; some legal scholars affirm its validity and others deny it any legal status (Chester-man 2001; Wheeler 2000; Riemer 2000; Harff 1991). Although there is disagreement among advocates of humanitarian intervention on who can authorize it, what causes should trigger it, what preliminary steps must be taken prior to use of force, how much force should be used to be effective, and what interveners must do afterward, there is general agreement that intervention against genocide and crimes against humanity fits within the UN Charter provisions and "just war" rationales for the use of force (Campbell 2001; Riemer 2000; Smith 2000; Harff 1991 and 1984; Walzer 1992).

Neal Riemer summed the criteria: (1) authorization by an appro-priate authority; (2) support of a just cause (such as to prevent or stop genocide); (3) use of force as a last resort; (4) "a [preliminary] prudent appraisal of the benefits and costs of intervention"; (5) "the expectation of a reasonable chance of immediate success in prevent-ing or stopping genocide"; (6) "humane and proportionate means ... in the interest of minimizing harm, especially to the innocents involved in the conflict"; and (7) "the reasonable chance of long-run success ... in putting into place a human-rights–respecting regime to ensure the ongoing protection of human rights" (Riemer 2000, 8–9). There is little agreement among critics about what is an appropriate authority and whether this requires UN sanction.

Advocates of humanitarian interventions often imply a disinter-ested intervener, but no successful intervener in post–World War II genocides has been disinterested: not India in East Pakistan (1971), Tanzania in Uganda (1979), or Vietnam in Democratic Kampuchea (1979). None of these interventions was approved by the United Nations. The neighboring intervening states were at war with the *génocidaire* state, impelled in part by its mass expulsions and aggres-sion. Nicholas Wheeler asserts that "India's, Vietnam's and Tanzania's actions *were all justifiable because the use of force was the only means of ending atrocities on a massive scale, and the motives/means employed were consistent with a positive humanitarian outcome*" (2000, 294).

Nor was the UN intervention in Bosnia in 1995 entirely disinterested. The North Atlantic Treaty Organization (NATO) was confronted not only with the threat of annihilation of Bosnia-Herzegovina but also of the dissolution of NATO and perils in disengagement if it failed to intervene. Neighboring states seldom intervene for purely humanitarian reasons against states of genocide; it is often because such states are aggressors and their neighbors have strategic reasons to disable them—to protect national borders and stem the flow of refugees as well as to prevent more suffering. War and intervention have repeatedly halted genocide: in Europe (1941–1945)—despite the disinterest of the Allies in halting genocide (Fein 1979), East Pakistan (1971), Uganda (1979), Cambodia (1979), and Bosnia (1995). Yet war has also enabled genocide to unfold in some of these and other places (Fein 1993b). So the links between war and genocide are tangled, and potential interveners must assess the possibilities of making the situation worse rather than better in calculating their justification and strategy.

Peoples at risk of genocide usually have to rely on interested, not disinterested, interveners. The costs a nation or nations are willing to pay depend not only on how they evaluate threats to them but on their values and ties with the people at risk as well as their interests. Ties might be an outcome of a shared colonial history, proximity, an ethnic diaspora in the intervening nation that relates to the people at risk, and common experiences in the past.

Kenneth Campbell makes the case for interested intervention by the United States, asserting that both the United States and the UN have misunderstood the strategic threat genocide represents in the twentieth century and have persistently used the wrong model (peacekeeping, which presumes neutrality) to check it.

> UN peacekeeping coordination and support can be improved significantly, but the strategy of peacekeeping is fundamentally alien to the nature of genocide and cannot effectively stop it ... without the threat of force to suppress ongoing genocide and to arrest its leading perpetrators, punishment will never be more than partially effective.... However, none so far have come forth with a strategic approach that accurately identifies the fundamental nature of genocide as a core threat to the international system.... My thesis is that the principal reason for the

international community's failure to stop contemporary genocide was US policymakers' misunderstanding of the strategic nature of genocide, and their failure to treat the prevention of genocide as a vital national interest. (Campbell 2001, 3)

Campbell considers the need for appropriate military doctrine, strategy, and tactics to stop genocide, arguing that the Weinberger-Powell doctrine (commonly understood to inhibit intervention) can be a useful guide. Further, he shows how the United States misread the preconditions for the Dayton Agreement in Bosnia, attributing inflated effects to airpower—leading to overreliance on it in Kosovo (1999)—and failed to understand the potential for public support to stop genocide.

The Cost of Nonintervention

The failure to stop genocide and ethnic cleansing leads to escalation and diffusion of conflict and boomerangs against the governments who refused to deter it, Bruce Jentleson points out (Hamburg 2002, 127–130). This effect is amply illustrated in the case of the Rwandan genocide, where the lack of prevention not only led to escalation and diffusion, but also vastly escalated the cost to the international community and to the Rwandan people. The cost of prevention (including stationing peacekeeping troops) in Rwanda is estimated to have been from 5 percent to 20 percent of the cost of international aid and funding the International Tribunal for War Crimes in Rwanda by 1996—that is, within two years from $5 to $20 was spent for every $1 that might have been spent in 1994 to check the genocide (Fein 2000a, 43–44).

Nor did this calculate the cost in economic terms and human suffering to surviving Rwandans. "Rwanda, which had climbed between 1976 and 1990 from the seventh to the nineteenth place from the bottom among least-developed countries, descended to become the second poorest country on earth in 1997" (Fein 2000b, 44). Further, the Rwandan genocide dynamics spilled over to Zaire as the *génocidaires* fled there, helping to destabilize that failed state, which became the Democratic Republic of Congo (DRC). The DRC has been torn by internal and international war since 1995—the first African international war—with neighboring states invading and looting it. It was a war marked by ethnic massacres, mass death of an estimated 3.3 million people attributed largely to malnutrition and untreated preventable diseases—for war undermined commerce, agriculture, health, and humanitarian assistance—and decline in the DRC's low standard of living. In terms of both international order and human rights, tolerating genocide is prohibitively destructive.

The high costs in human suffering, international stability, and money (income lost and dollars spent on remediation) are among the reasons why the question of humanitarian intervention—a right of states—was reframed by an International Commission as "the [international community's] responsibility to protect" citizens of sovereign states that cannot or do not exercise their responsibility to prevent mass murder, rape, and starvation of their citizens (International Commission on Intervention and State Sovereignty, December 2001).

Checking States of Terror

Like states of genocide, states of terror are often life-threatening, but the threat is restricted initially to perceived opponents of the state. States of terror are usually states lacking legitimacy, coming into power by force, in which one faction or elite in a divided society imposes its will on another group or class. Once terror states are established, they usually cannot be reversed by internal political processes unless the army/leader/colonial power yields their authority—sometimes hastened by defeat in war or international pressure.

Since citizens of terror states cannot protest openly and effectively, they must depend on international human rights organizations to press other states to inhibit the murder and repression of terror states. Such nonviolent action as that of the Mothers of the Plaza de Mayo in Argentina (1975–1979), who continually protested the disappearance of their children (see chapter 4), helped spread the word to the international community but did not themselves check the regime's policy of terror.

One way to press such states to change without physical intervention would be for other states to stop supporting states of terror and frankly recognize their lack of legitimacy. There are many economic and political sanctions to check such states—limiting access to credit markets and trade preferences, social and cultural boycotts, diplomatic pressure and nonrecognition—and incentives to dictators to step down and reinstate democratic rule. The strategies and tactics of preventive diplomacy have been advanced in the last decade (Hamburg 2002).

When states based on repression or counterterror are confronted with terrorist movements in opposition, movements that do or would terrorize or annihilate a segment of their population, it becomes strategically and politically difficult for outsiders to press for change and seek to safeguard the security of people from all groups, a sine qua non for a peaceful transition.

Iraq's Escalation from Terror to Genocide and Putative Threat

One incentive for states to check states of terror by applying sanctions and disincentives early might be the realization that such states are more likely to escalate to states of genocide and aggression against their neighbors than are other states. Iraq was the most recent case of a totalitarian state escalating from terror to genocide. Iraq went to war against its neighbors (Iran and Kuwait), committed genocide and crimes against humanity against its citizens, and defied international resolutions and sanctions to force it to eliminate its weapons of mass destruction. Yet there was no attempt by any state to check Iraq before its invasion of Kuwait, except for Israel's destruction of Saddam Hussein's French-built nuclear reactor in 1981, an act widely condemned by other states at the time. Nor were there any sanctions against the gassing of the Kurds in 1987–1988, using a prohibited weapon of mass destruction in the genocidal operation known as Operation Anfal (see chapter 6). Virtually all major states armed and fortified Iraq: France, the USSR, the United States, United Kingdom, and Germany.

Although since 1991 Iraq failed to fill the conditions for disarming its weapons of mass destruction (WMDs), several major powers on the UN Security Council (UNSC)—France, Russia, China—balked in the succeeding decade at executing the decisions of the UNSC, avid for more contracts and petrodollars. During this period, Saddam reframed the issue as that of suffering, starvation, and excess death of children, effects allegedly imposed on Iraq by the United States and UN. Yet "sanctions ... always exempted the importation of food and medicine." Iraq rejected "Oil-for-Food" agreements offered by the UN for five years and increased investment in weapons of mass destruction, using money that could have been used to improve the living standard of Iraqis (Leitenberg 2002).

Pressure by the United States to account for Iraq's WMDs led the UN Security Council to pass Resolution 1441 in 2002, but the UNSC did not agree to another resolution before the U.S.-led war against Iraq in 2003. The objectives of that war were first justified by the United States in terms of a novel preemptive security doctrine for self-protection against imminent or future use of WMDs. These were never found, although there was evidence earlier that Saddam was seeking to acquire nuclear weapons (Obeidi 2004). These justifications were elaborated by the U.S. agenda for "regime change," which implied that bringing democracy to Iraq would instigate democratization through the Arab Middle East—a domino effect. This justification met none of the rationales usually suggested for humanitarian intervention.

Evidence for the belated addition of charges of human rights violations as a justification for the war in Iraq was first voiced by UK spokesmen. Jack Straw, UK foreign secretary, in December 2002 cited gross violations of human rights and crimes against humanity—decades-old to recent acts—in order to show that Saddam Hussein's was a "regime of unique horror" (Hoge, December 3, 2002, A20; UK Foreign and Commonwealth Office 2002).

Such violations did motivate some liberal interventionists and former Iraqis to support the war. One of the latter, Kanan Makiya, made the case that the regime in Iraq was not only a criminal state but that the United States had a special obligation to remove it: "My position rests on the exceptional nature of Ba'athi totalitarianism in Iraq (and is therefore not extendable to all the nasty states that exist in the world). Moreover, it derives from the particular historical experience—dating back to the 1991 Gulf War—that binds the United States to Iraq. The outcome of that war, which left the dictator in place and precipitated one of the harshest sanction regimes of recent times, places an extraordinary moral responsibility upon the shoulders of the United States to finish that which it in a very important sense left unfinished" (Makiya 2003, 12).

The U.S.-led coalition's 2003 invasion and occupation of Iraq did not meet most criteria for humanitarian intervention. By this writing, the coalition intervention has not brought security to Iraq and its state of freedom appears unstable to many. Public discourse focused in 2006 on whether it has actually promoted international terrorism by diverting U.S. resources from Afghanistan. The brutal insurgency and communal conflict that have ensued (no end in sight at the time of this writing) can best be understood in terms of the history of communal violence in Iraq (see chapter 5).

Michael Walzer said in 2003 that he "would support a UN war to enforce inspection ... [but] would not support a U.S. war for 'regime change' (though I don't doubt that the Iraqi regime needs changing)"

(2003, 5). In 2006, he reiterated that "just war" theory did not justify intervention for regime change (democratization) and that Iraq (and the misuse of U.S. power) could have been checked by containment—"force short of war ... trade sanctions or a weapons embargo." He faulted Europe for not displaying the commitment that could have made the latter effective (Walzer 2006). Jean Elshtain disagreed, supporting the intervention and observing that the UN-endorsed "Responsibility to Protect" made it imperative to take into account not only the WMD question but the ongoing "culpable killing [of the regime] ... as many as eighty thousand Iraqi children per year were dying as a direct result of Saddam's 'gaming' of the oil for food and medicine program" (Elshtain 2006).

Many critics such as Walzer affirm that genocide and crimes against humanity are justifiable reasons for humanitarian intervention but do not support trying to impose democracy by intervention. The argument is also one about the realistic limits on the goals of foreign policy and the costs and unanticipated consequences of intervention. There are many countries that need change, the costs (to them and the interveners) and risks could be high, and the likelihood of success is unknown. Moreover, the threats they present to potential interveners vary.

There was a surfeit of early warning signs of massacre and genocide in Yugoslavia, Rwanda, and Darfur. Milton Leitenberg (2006) shows that the failure to intervene and stop these was not that of the United States and the UN alone, but of specific states and organizations: NATO and the European Union, the African Union and Arab and Muslim states.

Some opposition to humanitarian intervention stems from opposition to interventions in the past with no humanitarian intent, such as U.S. intervention in Latin America. States of terror in Latin America, in which the United States has been the dominant power for the past century, generally targeted their citizens but not other states. These terror regimes would have been easier to prevent and undermine than to overthrow. The United States was responsible for overturning an elected regime and putting a new regime in place in Guatemala in 1954, which instituted a general state of terror termed "counterterror"—beginning in 1966 and continuing for over two decades (see chapter 5). In the following decades, the United States failed to check terror states in Argentina and Guatemala, despite attempts during the presidential administration of Jimmy Carter (1976–1980). U.S. support for such regimes was part of a plan (Operation Condor) to defend continental security in Latin America against alleged subversion (see chapter 4). Such a plan was possible not because of "rogue elements" in the Central Intelligence Agency or the military but because of U.S. Cold War mentality and national security doctrine.

The use of international sanctions and other means of influence to delegitimate and bring down terror states has to be considered not only because terror states commit crimes against humanity, but also because terror states often become states of genocide and massive slaughter. These include Iraq and the Kurds (and later the Marsh Arabs) and Guatemala and the Mayans (victims of genocide among the estimated 200,000 dead)—see chapter 5. Further, certain terror states become aggressors or sponsors of aggression. Terror states that became aggressors or interveners or harbored perpetrators of crimes against humanity and genocide include (starting in the 1930s) Nazi Germany and pre–World War II Japan, the Soviet Union, Iraq, Indonesia, and Afghanistan.

The public focus shifted from state to nonstate actors after September 11, 2001, focusing on Al Qaeda. Terrorism was viewed by many as a response of extremist Islamic movements, which targeted not only the United States but also allies of the United States—the United Kingdom and Spain—leading to the death of thousands of innocent civilians of all faiths. Although "Terror in the Name of God" (Stern 2003) has been justified at different times and places by other faith communities, after 2001 it was predominantly justified in the name of Islam. Terrorists and suicide bombers committed crimes against humanity in the name of rage against the West and religion—although their justification is believed by some to be based more in Leninist theory than in Islamic texts (Bourumand and Bourumand 2002).

The major threat to liberal democracies in the West might not be the numbers killed but the distrust of majorities in these countries of their Muslim neighbors and the temptation of free states to violate their own values in the name of security. These abuses are not those of the United States alone. The abuses of the United States have so often been exposed that they need not be documented herein: imprisonment of suspects at Guantanamo without trial, torture in Abu Ghraib and Afghanistan, "extraordinary rendition" or the outsourcing of torture, and constrictions of the right to privacy in the U.S. Rulings by the U.S. Supreme Court affirming the applicability of international law to prisoners and by Britain's highest court (Law Lords) forbidding the use of evidence obtained by torture show the usefulness of divided powers in free states to protect liberty in times of conflict.

This presents a challenge to the West to prosecute and deter terrorists and yet maintain civil liberties and the rule of law. Wresting human rights will be a continuing struggle to overcome human wrongs and forge new solutions to our needs for justice and security.

Little progress has been made in the last decade to resolve the problems created by state terror and antistate terror. The need to wrest human rights and arrest human wrongs will continue to confront us. It is not just states that violate or overlook others' violations of human rights, but also people organized against the state (who might later take over the state). Further, it is sometimes the same people who demand one set of human rights (e.g., political rights, self-determination) who (when empowered) commit, aid, or abet human wrongs to punish their real or perceived enemies.

Bibliography

Ackerman, Peter, and Jack DuVall. *A Force More Powerful: A Century of Nonviolent Conflict*. New York: St. Martin's Press, 2000.

African Rights. *Facing Genocide: The Nuba of Sudan*. London, July 1995.

Ally, Jane. "Witness to a Slave Raid." Speech to the National Press Club, 1996.

Amnesty International. *Amnesty International Report 1976*. London: Amnesty International, 1976.

———. *Amnesty International Report 1998*. London: Amnesty International, 1998.

———. *Iraq: Victims of Systematic Repression*. London: Amnesty International, 1999.

———. *Amnesty International Report 2002*. New York: Amnesty International, 2002.

———. *Amnesty International Report 2003*. New York: Amnesty International, 2003.

———. *Amnesty International Report 2005*. New York: Amnesty International, 2005.

———. *Amnesty International Report 2006*. New York: Amnesty International, 2006.

Anderson, Martin E. *Dossier Secreto: Argentina's Desaparecidos and the Myth of the "Dirty War."* Boulder, CO: Westview Press, 1993.

Anyaoku, Emeka. "Cultures of Democracy: A Commonwealth Perspective." *The Roundtable* 357 (October 2000): 529–536.

Applebaum, Anne. *Gulag: A History*. New York: Doubleday, 2003.

Arat, Zehra F. "Diminishing the Scope of Human Rights and Democracy: A Critique of the U.S. Approach and Its Impact." A paper delivered at the Hinman Symposium on Democratization and Human Rights, State University of New York, Binghamton, September 24–26, 1998.

Arendt, Hannah. *The Origins of Totalitarianism.* Rev. ed. New York: Harcourt Brace, 1966.

Argentine National Commission on the Disappeared. *Nunca Mas: Report of the Argentine National Commission on the Disappeared.* Translated from the Spanish. New York: Farrar, Straus & Giroux, 1986.

Aronsfeld, C. C. "The Nazi Design Was Extermination, Not Emigration." *Patterns of Prejudice* 9, no. 3 (May–June 1975).

Atlantic Monthly. "Letters to the Editor." *Atlantic Monthly* (December 1999).

Bales, Kevin. *Disposable People: New Slavery in the Global Economy.* Berkeley: University of California Press, 1999.

———. "The Social Psychology of Modern Slavery." *Scientific American* 286, no. 4 (April 2002): 80–88.

———. *New Slavery: A Reference Handbook.* 2nd ed. Santa Barbara, CA: ABC–CLIO, 2004.

———. *Understanding Global Slavery: A Reader.* Berkeley: University of California Press, 2005.

Ball, Patrick, Paul Kobrak, and Herbert F. Spirer. *State Violence in Guatemala, 1960–1996: A Quantitative Reflection.* Washington, DC: American Association for the Advancement of Science/CIIDH, 1999.

Baram, Amatzia. *Building toward Crisis: Saddam Husayn's* [sic] *Strategy for Survival.* Washington, DC: Washington Institute for Near East Policy, 1998.

Barber, James David. "Rationalizing Torture: The Dance of the Intellectual Apologists." *Washington Monthly* (December 1985): 12–18.

Barrett, David B., George T. Kurian, and Todd M. Johnson. *World Christian Encyclopedia.* 2nd ed. New York: Oxford University Press, 2001.

Barro, Robert. "Determinants of Democracy." *Journal of Political Economy* 107, no. 6 (1999): pt. 2, S158–S183.

Bass, Gary Jonathan. *Stay the Hand of Vengeance: The Politics of War Crimes Tribunals.* Princeton, NJ: Princeton University Press, 2000.

Bates, Robert H. *Prosperity and Violence: The Political Economy of Development.* New York: W. W. Norton, 2001.

Batutu, Hanna. *The Old Social Classes and the Revolutionary Movements of Iraq.* Princeton, NJ: Princeton University Press, 1978.

Beah, Ishmael. "The Making, and Unmaking, of a Child Soldier." *New York Times Magazine* (January 14, 2007): 36–70.

Becker, Jasper. *Hungry Ghosts: Mao's Secret Famine.* New York: Free Press, 1998.

Bell-Fialkoff, Andrew. *Ethnic Cleansing.* New York: St. Martin's Griffin, 1999.

Bibliography

Berkeley, Bill. *The Graves Are Not Yet Full: Race, Tribe and Power in the Heart of Africa.* New York: Basic Books, 2001.

Biro, Gaspar. "Situation of Human Rights in the Sudan." Report by Special Rapporteur to United Nations Commission on Human Rights, February 1, 1994.

Bloom, David E., and David Canning. "The Health and Wealth of Nations." *Science* 287 (February 18, 2000): 1207–1209.

Borkin, Joseph. *The Crime and the Punishment of I .G. Farben.* New York: Free Press, 1978.

Bouluque, Sylvain. "Communism in Afghanistan." In *The Black Book of Communism: Crimes, Terror, Repression.* Edited by Stephane Courtois et al. Cambridge, MA: Harvard University Press, 1999, 705–726.

Bourumand, Ladan, and Roya Boroumand. "Terror, Islam, and Democracy." *Journal of Democracy* 13, no. 2 (2002): 5–20.

Boyden, Stephen Vickers. *Western Civilization in Biological Perspective, Patterns in Biohistory.* Oxford: Clarendon Press, 1987.

Brailovsky, Antonio Elio. "Forward." In Patrick J. Buchanan, "The Right Time for Torture." *Skeptic* (January/February 1977): 16–19.

Brass, Paul R. "The Partition of India and Retributive Genocide in the Punjab, 1946–47." *Journal of Genocide Research* 5, no. 1 (March 2003): 71–102.

Braylan, Marisa, et al. *Report on the Situation of the Jewish Detainees—Disappeared during the Genocide Perpetrated in Argentina.* Buenos Aires: Argentinian Jewish Community Centers Association (DAIA), 2000.

British Broadcasting Company. BBC News. 2001–2006.

Brockett, Charles D. "Sources of State Terrorism in Rural Central America." In *State Organized Terror: The Case of Violent Internal Repression.* Edited by Timothy Bushnell et al., 59–76. Boulder, CO: Westview Press, 1991.

———. *Political Movements and Violence in Central America.* New York: Cambridge University Press, 2005.

Broder, Jonathan. "An Excerpt: Inside Saddam's Court." *New York Times Magazine* (October 1, 2000): 41F.

Brown, David S. "Democracy, Colonization, and Human Capital in Sub-Saharan Africa." *Studies in Comparative International Development* 35, no. 1 (Spring 2001): 20–40.

Brown, Phyllida. "Violence and the Virus Infecting Women with AIDS." *Amnesty Now* (Summer 2004): 8–11.

Buchanan, Patrick J. "The Right Time for Torture." *Skeptic* 17 (January/February 1977): 16–58.

Bunch, Charlotte. "Women's Rights as Human Rights: Towards a Re-Vision of Human Rights." *Human Rights Quarterly* 12 (1990): 486–498.

Burkett, Elinor. "God Created Me to Be a Slave." *New York Times Magazine* (October 12, 1997): 56–60.

Burkhalter, Holly. "The Politics of AIDS." *Foreign Affairs* 83, no. 1 (January–February 2004): 8–14.

Burkhart, Ross E., and Michael S. Lewis-Beck. "Comparative Democracy: The Economic Development Thesis," *American Political Science Review* 8, no. 4 (December 1994): 903–910.

Burr, Millard. *A Working Document II: Quantifying Genocide in the Southern Sudan and the Nuba Mountains 1983–1998*. Washington, DC: U.S. Committee for Refugees, December 1998.

Burr, Millard, and Robert O. Collins. *Requiem for the Sudan: War, Drought and Disaster Relief on the Nile*. Boulder, CO: Westview Press, 1995.

Byrne, Malcolm. "Saddam Hussein: More Secret History." www/gwu.edu/ ~nsarchiv/NSAEBB/NSAEBB107.index.htm, December 18, 2003.

Caldwell, Gillian, Steven Gallster, and Nadia Steinzor. *Crime and Servitude: An Exposé of the Traffic in Women for Prostitution from the Newly Independent States*. Washington, DC: Global Survival Network, 1997.

Campbell, Kenneth J. *Genocide and the Global Village*. New York: Palgrave, 2001.

Cardenas, Sonia. "International Human Rights Pressure and Democratization: What's at Stake?" A paper delivered at the Hinman Symposium on Democratization and Human Rights, State University of New York, Binghamton, September 24–26, 1998.

Carothers, Thomas. *Aiding Democracy Abroad: The Learning Curve*. Washington, DC: Carnegie Endowment for International Peace, 1999.

———. "The End of the Transition Paradigm." *Journal of Democracy*, vol. 13, no. 1 (January 2002): 5–21.

CBSNews.com. "Sex Trade Flourishing in Holy Land." February 24, 2003.

Chalk, Frank, and Kurt Jonassohn. *The History and Sociology of Genocide*. New Haven, CT: Yale University Press, 1990.

Charny, Israel, ed. *Encyclopedia of Genocide*. 2 vols. Santa Barbara, CA: ABC-Clio, 1999.

Chesterman, Simon. *Just War or Just Peace? Humanitarian Intervention and International Law*. Oxford: Oxford University Press, 2001.

Chill, Julia, and Susan Kilbourne. "The Rights of the Girl Child." In *Women, Gender, and Human Rights: A Global Perspective*. Edited by Marjorie Agosin. New Brunswick, NJ: Transaction, 2001, 152–169.

Chirot, Daniel. *Modern Tyrants: The Power and Prevalence of Evil in Our Age*. New York: Free Press, 1994.

Chua, Amy. *World on Fire: How Exporting Free Market Democracy Breeds Ethnic Hatred and Global Instability*. New York: Doubleday, 2003.

Cingranelli, David L., and David L. Richards. "Respect for Human Rights after the End of the Cold War." *Journal of Peace Research* (September 1999).

Citizens' Commission on Bonded and Child Labour (India). *Freedom from Bondage/Citizens Commission on Bonded and Child Labour, First National Convention*. New Delhi: Indian Social Institute, 1995.

Clay, Jason. "Food as a Weapon." *ISG Newsletter* 1, no. 2 (Fall 1988): 8–10.

Clay, Jason W., and Bonnie K. Holcomb. *Politics and the Ethiopian Famine.* Cambridge, MA: Cultural Survival, 1986.

Cohen, Roger. "Ethnic Cleansing." In *Crimes of War: What the Public Should Know.* Edited by Roy Gutman and David Rieff. New York: W. W. Norton, 1999, 136–138.

Cohen, Stanley. *States of Denial: Knowing about Atrocities and Suffering.* Cambridge: Blackwell Publishers, 2001.

Collier, Paul, and Anke Hoeffler. "Greed and Grievance in Civil War." World Bank paper, October 21, 2001.

Collins, Robert. "Slavery in the Sudan in History." *Slavery and Abolition* 20, no. 3 (December 1999): 67–95.

Comission para el Esclarecimiento Historico/Commission for Historical Clarification (CEH). *Guatemala: Memoria del Silencio/Guatemala: Memory of Silence.* 9 vols. Guatemala City: Commission for Historical Clarification, 1999. See both Spanish and English versions at http://hrdata.aaas.org/ceh.

Commission on the Ukrainian Famine. *Report to Congress.* Washington, DC: U.S. Government Printing Office, 1988.

Cranston, Maurice. *What Are Human Rights?* New York: Basic Books, 1964.

Crocker, David A. "Ethics of Global Development: Agency, Capability, and Deliberative Democracy—An Introduction," *Philosophy and Public Policy Quarterly* 26, nos. 1–2 (Winter/Spring 2006): 21–27.

Crossette, Barbara. "U.N. Warns That Trafficking in Human Beings Is Growing," *New York Times,* June 25, 2000, p. 10.

Dadrian, Vahakn N. "The Secret Young Turk Ittihadist Conference and the Decision for the World War I Genocide of the Armenians." *Journal of Political and Military Sociology* 22, no. 1 (Summer 1994): 173–198.

Dahrendorf, Ralf. *Class and Class Conflict in Industrial Society.* Stanford, CA: Stanford University Press, 1959.

Daley, Suzanne. "France Is Seeking a Fine in Trial of Algerian War General." *New York Times,* November 29, 2001, A6.

Dallaire, Romeo. *Shake Hands with the Devil: The Failure of Humanity in Rwanda.* New York: Carroll and Graf, 2003.

Dauer, Sheila. "Indivisible or Invisible: Women's Human Rights in the Public and Private Sphere." In *Women, Gender, and Human Rights: A Global Perspective.* Edited by Marjorie Agosín. New Brunswick, NJ: Transaction, 2001, 65–82.

Davenport, Christian. "The Problem of Taming State Power through Democracy." A paper delivered at the Hinman Symposium on Democratization and Human Rights, State University of New York, Binghamton, September 24–26, 1998.

Davis, David Brion. *Slavery and Human Progress.* New York: Oxford University Press, 1984.

———. *In the Image of God: Religion, Moral Values and Our Heritage of Slavery.* New Haven, CT: Yale University Press, 2001.

Dedring, Jurgen. "Socio-Political Indicators for Early Warning Purposes." In *Early Warning and Conflict Resolution.* London: Macmillan Press, 1992.

Des Forges, Alison. *Leave None to Tell the Story: Genocide in Rwanda.* New York: Human Rights Watch, 1999.

de Waal, Alex. "What AIDS Means in a Famine." *New York Times,* November 15, 2002, A31.

———. "Counter-Insurgency on the Cheap." *London Review of Books* 26, no. 15 (2004), available online at www.lrb.co.uk/v26/n15/waal01.htm.

Dextehe, Alain. *Rwanda and Genocide in the Twentieth Century.* Translated by Alison Marschner. New York: New York University Press, 1994.

Diamond, Larry. "Economic Development and Democracy Reconsidered." *American Behavioral Scientist* 35, nos. 4–5 (March–June 1992): 450–499.

Diamond, Larry, and Marc F. Plattner, eds. *The Global Resurgence of Democracy.* Baltimore: Johns Hopkins University Press, 1993.

Dirks, Nicholas B. *Castes of Mind: Colonialism and the Making of Modern India.* Princeton, NJ: Princeton University Press, 2001.

Djilas, Milovan. *The New Class: An Analysis of the Communist System.* New York: Praeger, 1957.

Donnelly, Jack. *Universal Human Rights in Theory and Practice.* Ithaca, NY: Cornell University Press, 1989.

———. "Human Rights, Democracy and Development." *Human Rights Quarterly* 21, no. 3 (August 1999): 608–632.

———. *Universal Human Rights in Theory and Practice.* 2nd ed. Ithaca, NY: Cornell University Press, 2003.

Doorenspleet, Renske. "Democratic Institutions, Political Stability and Lack of Violence in New Democracies." A seminar presentation at the Belfer Center for Science and International Affairs, Kennedy School of Government, Harvard University, Cambridge, MA, March 13, 2003.

Doyle, Kate. "Death Squad Diary." *Harper's* (June 1999): 50.

Drescher, Seymour, and Stanley L. Engerman, eds. *A Historical Guide to World Slavery.* New York: Oxford University Press, 1998.

Drost, Pieter N. *The Crime of State.* 2 vols. Leyden: A. W. Sythoff, 1959.

Duff, Ernest, and John McCamant with Waltraud Q. Morales. *Violence and Repression in Latin America: A Quantitative and Historical Analysis.* London: Free Press, 1976.

Durkheim, Emile. *The Division of Labour in Society.* Translated by George Simpson. New York: Free Press, 1933 [1893].

Dutt, N. K. *Origin and Growth of Caste in India.* 2nd ed. Calcutta: Firma K. L. Mukhopadhyay, 1968–1969.

Dworkin, Anthony. "The Kissinger Factor and U.S. Policy on the International Criminal Court." www.crimesofwar.org/onnews/news-icc-us2.html (November 15, 2002).

Dworkin, Ronald M. *Taking Rights Seriously*. Cambridge, MA: Harvard University Press, 1978.

Easterly, William. *The White Man's Burden: Why the West's Efforts to Aid the Rest Have Done So Much Ill and So Little Good*. New York: Penguin Press, 2006.

Eckstein, Harry. *Division and Cohesion in Democracy: A Study of Norway*. Princeton, NJ: Princeton University Press, 1966.

Elman, Miriam Fendius, ed. *Paths to Peace: Is Democracy the Answer?* Cambridge, MA: MIT Press, 1997.

Elon, Amos. "Letter from Argentina." *New Yorker* (July 21, 1986): 74–96.

Elshtain, Jean Bethke. "Regime Change and Just War." *Dissent* (Summer 2006): 109–111.

Encyclopedia of World History. New York: Facts on File, 2000.

Etcheson Craig. *After the Killing Fields: Lessons from the Cambodian Genocide*. Westport, CT: Praeger, 2005.

Ezell, Walter. "Investigating Genocide: A Catalog of Known and Suspected Cases and Some Categories for Comparing Them." In *Remembering for the Future*, vol. 3. Edited by Y. Bauer et al. Oxford: Pergamon Press, 1989, pp. 2880–2892.

———. "Newspaper Responses to Reports of Atrocities: Burundi, Mozambique, Iraq." In *Genocide Watch*. Edited by Helen Fein, 87–112. New Haven, CT: Yale University Press, 1992.

Falcoff, Mark. "The Timerman Case." *Commentary* (July 1981).

Fanon, Frantz. *The Wretched of the Earth*. Translated by Constance Farrington. New York: Grove Press, 1963.

Farouk-Sluglett, Marion, and Peter Sluglett. *Iraq since 1958: From Revolution to Dictatorship*. New York: KPI, 1987.

Farrell, Michael B. "Global Campaign to Police Child Sex Tourism." *Christian Science Monitor*, April 22, 2004, available at www.csmonitor. com.

Feierstein, Daniel. "Political Violence in Argentina and Its Genocidal Characteristics." *Journal of Genocide Research* 8, no. 1 (2006): 1–20.

Fein, Helen. *Imperial Crime and Punishment: The Jallianwala Bagh Massacre and British Judgment, 1919–1920*. Honolulu: University Press of Hawaii, 1977.

———. *Accounting for Genocide: National Responses and Jewish Victimization during the Holocaust*. New York: Free Press, 1979.

———. *Lives at Risk: A Study of Life-Integrity Violations in 50 States in 1987, Based on the Amnesty International 1988 Report*. New York: Institute for the Study of Genocide, 1988.

———. "The Politics of Paranoia in Jonestown: Twentieth Century Totalitarianism in Microcosm." In *State Organized Terror: The Case of Violent Internal Repression*. Edited by V. Schlapentokh et al. Boulder, CO: Westview Press, 1991, 275–288.

———. *Genocide: A Sociological Perspective*. London: Sage, 1993a [1990].

———. "Accounting for Genocide after 1945: Theories and Some Findings." *International Journal on Group Rights* (1993b): 57–83.

———. "Revolutionary and Antirevolutionary Genocides: A Comparison of State Murders in Democratic Kampuchea (1975–1979) and Indonesia (1965–66)." *Comparative Studies in Society and History* (October 1993c): 794–821.

———. "More Murder in the Middle: Life Integrity Violations and Democracy in the World, 1987." *Human Rights Quarterly* 17, no. 1 (February 1995): 170–191.

———. "Genocide by Attrition 1939–1993: The Warsaw Ghetto, Cambodia and Sudan." *Health and Human Rights* 2, no. 2 (1997): 10–45.

———. "Editorial: Defense as a Moral Offense—A Justification for Preventive Genocide." *ISG Newsletter*, no. 21 (Summer/Fall 1998): 6.

———. "Gender and Genocide: The Uses of Women and Group Destiny." *Journal of Genocide Research* 1, no. 1 (Spring 1999): 43–64.

———. Civil Wars and Genocide: Paths and Circles." *Human Rights Review* 1, no. 3 (April–June 2000a): 49–61.

———. "The Three P's of Genocide Prevention: With Application to a Genocide Foretold—Rwanda." In *The Prevention of Genocide: Mission Impossible?* Edited by Neal Riemer. New York: Praeger, 2000b, 41–66.

Feitlowitz, Marguerite. *A Lexicon of Terror: Argentina and the Legacies of Torture.* New York: Oxford University Press, 1998.

Feldman, Noah. *After Jihad: America and the Struggle for Islamic Democracy.* New York: Farrar, Straus & Giroux, 2003.

Ferencz, Benjamin. *Less Than Slaves: Jewish Forced Labor and the Quest for Compensation.* Cambridge, MA: Harvard University Press, 1979.

Festinger, Leon. *A Theory of Cognitive Dissonance.* Stanford, CA: Stanford University Press, 1957.

Finnegan, William. "The Invisible War." *New Yorker* (January 25, 1999): 50–73.

Fiske, Susan T. "Stereotyping, Prejudice and Discrimination." In *Handbook of Social Psychology.* Edited by Daniel T. Gilbert, Susan T. Fiske, and Gardner Lindzey, 355–414. 4th ed. Boston: McGraw-Hill, 1998.

Flint, Julie, and Alex de Waal. *Darfur: A Short History of a Long War.* London: Zed Books, 2005.

Foreign Policy. "Ranking the Rich" (May–June 2004).

Forster, Jurgen. "The German Army and the Ideological War against the Soviet Union." In *The Policies of Genocide: Jews and Soviet Prisoners of War in Nazi Germany.* Edited by Gerhard Hirschfeld. London: Allen and Unwin, 1986, 15–29.

Foucault, Michel. *Discipline and Punish: The Birth of the Prison.* Translated by Alan Sheridan. New York: Pantheon Books, 1977.

Fowler, Jerry. "Evolution of Conflict and Genocide in Sudan: A Historic Survey." In *Darfur: Genocide before Our Eyes*. Edited by Joyce Apsel. New York: Institute for the Study of Genocide, 2005.

Fredrickson, George M. *White Supremacy: A Comparative Study in American and South African History*. Oxford: Oxford University Press, 1981.

Freedom House. *Freedom in the World 1997–1998*. New York: Freedom House, 1998.

Fukuyama, Francis. *The End of History and the Last Man*. New York: Free Press, 1992.

Garfield, Richard. "Estimating Changes in Mortality and Excess Deaths among Iraq Children from 1990–1998." Manuscript, Columbia University School of Public Health, December 27, 1998.

Gendzier, Irene L. *Frantz Fanon: A Critical Study*. New York: Pantheon Books, 1973.

Genovese, Eugene. *Roll, Jordan, Roll: The World the Slaves Made*. New York: Pantheon Books, 1974.

George, Alexander, and Andrew Bennett. *Case Studies and Theory Development in the Social Sciences*. Cambridge, MA: MIT Press, 2005.

Geras, Norman. *The Contract of Mutual Indifference: Political Philosophy after the Holocaust*. London: Verso, 1998.

Geretzny, Alfred G. *Mauritania*. New York: Praeger, 1967.

Germani, Gino. *Authoritarianism, Fascism, and National Populism*. New Brunswick, NJ: Transaction, 1978.

Godoy, Angelina Snodgrass. "Lynchings and the Democratization of Terror in Postwar Guatemala: Implications for Human Rights." *Human Rights Quarterly* 24, no. 3 (August 2002): 640–661.

Goffman, Erving. *Asylums*. Garden City, NY: Doubleday Anchor, 1961.

Goni, Uki. *The Real Odessa: How Peron Brought the Nazi War Criminals to Argentina*. London: Granta, 2002.

Gouldner, Alvin. "The Norm of Reciprocity: A Preliminary Statement." *American Sociological Review* 25 (April 1960): 161–177.

Guest, Ian. *Behind the Disappearances: Argentina's Dirty War against Human Rights and the United Nations*. Philadelphia: University of Pennsylvania Press, 1990.

Guroian, Vigen. "Collective Responsibility and Official Excuse Making: The Case of the Turkish Genocide of the Armenians." In *The Armenian Genocide in Perspective*. Edited by Richard G. Hovannisian, 135–152. New Brunswick, NJ: Transaction, 1986.

Gurr, Ted R. "The Political Origins of State Violence and Terror: A Theoretical Analysis." In *Government Violence and Repression: An Agenda for Research*. Edited by Michael Stohl and George Lopez. New York: Greenwood Press, 1986, 45–71.

———. *Minorities at Risk: A Global View of Ethnopolitical Conflicts*. Washington, DC: U.S. Institute for Peace, 1993.

————. "Attaining Peace in Divided Societies: Five Principles of Emerging Doctrine." *International Journal on World Peace* 19, no. 2 (June 2002): 27–51.

Gurr, Ted R., and Barbara Harff, eds. "Early Warning of Communal Conflicts and Humanitarian Crises." *Journal of Ethno-Development* 4, no. 1 (July 1994).

Gurr, Ted R., and James R. Scarritt. "Minorities at Risk: A Global Survey." *Human Rights Quarterly* 11, no. 3 (August 1989): 375–405.

Gutman, Matthew. "Pressured by U.S., Israel Battles a Burgeoning 'White Slave' Trade." *Forward* (June 28, 2002): 8.

Gutman, Roy, and Phillip Rieff, eds. *Crimes of War: What the Public Should Know.* New York: W. W. Norton, 1999.

Guzman, Jessie P., ed. "Lynching." In *Racial Violence in the United States.* Edited by Allen D. Grimshaw. Chicago: Aldine Publishing Company, 1969, 56–59.

Ha'aretz. www.haaretz.com/2004.

Hadenius, Axel. *Democracy and Development.* New York: Cambridge University Press, 1992.

Hamburg, David A. *No More Killing Fields: Preventing Deadly Conflict.* Lanham, MD: Rowman and Littlefield, 2002.

Hamm, Brigitte J. "A Human Rights Approach to Development." *Human Rights Quarterly* 23, no. 4 (November 2001): 1005–1031.

Haney, Craig, Curtis Banks, and Philip Zimbardo. "Interpersonal Dynamics in a Simulated Prison." *International Journal of Criminology and Penology* 1 (February 1973): 69–97.

Hannum, Hurst. "International Law and the Cambodian Genocide: The Sounds of Silence." *Human Rights Quarterly* 11, no. 1 (1989): 82–128.

Hannum, Hurst, and David Hawk. *The Case against the Standing Committee of the Communist Party of Kampuchea.* New York: Cambodia Documentation Commission, 1986.

Harff, Barbara. *Genocide and Human Rights: International Legal and Political Issues.* Denver, CO: University of Denver Monograph Series in World Affairs, 1984.

————. "Humanitarian Intervention in Genocidal Situations." In *Genocide: A Critical Bibliographic Review.* Vol. 2. Edited by Israel W. Charny, 146–153. New York: Facts on File, 1991.

————. "No Lessons Learned from the Holocaust?" *American Political Science Review* 97, no. 1 (February 2003): 57–73.

Harff, Barbara, and Ted Gurr. "Toward Empirical Theory of Genocides and Politicides: Identification and Measurement of Cases since 1945." *International Studies Quarterly* 37, no. 3 (1988): 359–371.

————. "Conceptual and Policy Issues in Early Warning Research: An Overview." *Journal of Ethno-Development* 4, no. 1 (July 1994).

————. "Genocide and Politicide in Global Perspective: The Historical

Record and Future Risks." In *Just War and Genocide: A Symposium.* Ottawa: Canadian Centre for Foreign Policy Development, February 2001.

Hawk, David. *The Hidden Gulag: Exposing North Korea's Prison Camps.* Washington, DC: U.S. Committee for Human Rights in North Korea, 2003.

Hayner, Priscilla B. *Unspeakable Truths: Facing the Challenge of Truth Commissions.* New York: Routledge, 2002.

Heinz, Wolfgang S. "Gross Human Rights Violations—A Search for Causes: Experiences in Argentina, Brazil, Chile and Uruguay." *PIOOM Newsletter* (Winter 1997): 20–24.

Henderson, Conway W. "Conditions Affecting the Use of Political Repression." *Journal of Conflict Resolution* 35, no. 1 (March 1991): 120–142.

Henderson, Errol A., and J. David Singer. "Civil War in the Post-Colonial World, 1946–1992." *Journal of Peace Research* 37, no. 3 (May 2000): 275–299.

Hentoff, Nat. Four-part series: "Farrakhan and the Slave Masters," "Slavery and the Wayward Press," "Journey into Outer Darkness," "How to Stop Slavery in Sudan." *Village Voice* (December 12 and December 19, 1995).

Herbert, Ulrich. *A History of Foreign Labor in Germany, 1880–1980: Seasonal Workers/Forced Laborers/Guest Workers.* Translated by William Templar. Ann Arbor: University of Michigan Press, 1990.

Herbst, Jeffrey. "How Rebels and Soldiers Fight in Africa." A seminar presentation, Center for International Affairs, Harvard University, Cambridge, MA, October 25, 2001.

Hertzge, Allen. "The Role of the Faith-Based Constituency in Preventing Genocide." Paper presented at Genocide Prevention, Morality, and the National Interest Conference Committee on Conscience, U.S. Holocaust Memorial Museum, Washington, DC, May 13, 2002.

Hey, Hilde. *Gross Human Rights Violations: A Search for Causes: A Study of Guatemala and Costa Rica.* The Hague: Martinus Nijhoff, 1995.

Hilberg, Raul. *The Destruction of the European Jews.* Chicago: Quadrangle, 1961.

Hobbes, Thomas. "Of the Natural Conditions of Mankind." In *Theories of Society,* vol. 1. Edited by Talcott Parsons et al. New York: Free Press of Glencoe, 1961 [1651], 98–100.

Hochschild, Adam. *King Leopold's Ghost.* New York: Houghton Mifflin, 1998.

———. *Bury the Chains: Prophets and Rebels in the Fight to Free an Empire's Slaves.* Boston: Houghton Mifflin, 2005.

Hoeffel, Paul Heath, and Juan Montalvo. "Missing or Dead in Argentina." *New York Times Magazine* (October 21, 1979): 45–80.

Hoge, Warren. "Britain Issues File on Iraq's 'Unique Horror'." *New York Times,* December 3, 2002, A20.

Hooda, Sagar Preet. *Contesting Reservations: The Indian Experiment on Affirmative Action.* Jaipur/New Delhi: Rawat Publications, 2001.

Horne, Alistair. *A Savage War of Peace: Algeria 1954–1962.* London: Papermac, 1987.

Horowitz, Donald L. *Ethnic Groups in Conflict.* Berkeley: University of California Press, 1985.

———. *The Deadly Ethnic Riot.* Berkeley: University of California Press, 2001.

Howard, Rhoda E. *Human Rights and the Search for Community.* Boulder, CO: Westview Press, 1995.

Howard, Rhoda, and Jack Donnelly. "Chapter 4: Human Dignity, Human Rights, and Political Regimes." In *Universal Human Rights in Theory and Practice.* Edited by Jack Donnelly, 66–87. Ithaca, NY: Cornell University Press, 1989.

Huggins, Martha K., Mika Haritos-Fatouros, and Philip G. Zimbardo. *Violence Workers: Police Torturers and Murderers Reconstruct Brazilian Atrocities.* Berkeley: University of California Press, 2002.

Human Rights Watch. *Iraq's Crime of Genocide: The Anfal Campaign against the Kurds.* New Haven, CT: Yale University Press, 1995a.

———. *Slaughter among Neighbors: The Political Origins of Communal Violence.* New Haven, CT: Yale University Press, 1995b.

———. *Slaves, Street Children and Child Soldiers.* New York: Human Rights Watch, September 1995c.

———. *Shattered Lives: Sexual Violence during the Rwandan Genocide and Its Aftermath.* New York: Human Rights Watch/Africa Watch, 1996.

———. *Owed Justice: Thai Women Trafficked into Debt Bondage in Japan.* New York: Human Rights Watch, 2000.

———. *Caste Discrimination: A Global Concern.* New York: Human Rights Watch, August 2001.

———. *"We Have No Orders to Save You": State Participation and Complicity in Communal Violence in Gujarat.* New York: Human Rights Watch, April 2002.

———. "Facts about Child Soldiers." New York: Human Rights Watch, 2006. http://www.humanrightswatch.org/campaigns/crp/facts.htm. Accessed March 9, 2006.

Human Rights Watch/Asia. *A Modern Form of Slavery: Trafficking of Burmese Women and Girls into Brothels in Thailand.* New York: Human Rights Watch, December 1993.

———. *Contemporary Forms of Slavery in Pakistan.* New York: Human Rights Watch, 1995.

Huntington, Samuel. *The Third Wave: Democratization in the Late Twentieth Century.* Norman: University of Oklahoma Press, 1991.

———. *The Clash of Civilizations?* Cambridge, MA: Olin Institute, 1993.

Inglehart, Ronald, and Pippa Norris. *Rising Tide: Gender Equality and Cultural Change around the World.* New York: Cambridge University Press, 2003.

International Center for Transitional Justice. "The Applicability of the United Nations Convention on the Prevention and Punishment of the Crime of Genocide to Events Which Occurred during the Early Twentieth Century." New York: International Center for Transitional Justice, 1993. See also http://zoryaninstitute.org/Table_of_Contents/genocide_docs_turksintor.htm.

International Commission of Jurists. *Torture and Intimidation in the West Bank: The Case of Al-Fara'a Prison.* Geneva: International Commission of Jurists, 1985.

International Commission on Intervention and State Sovereignty. *The Responsibility to Protect.* Canada: Department of Foreign Affairs and International Trade, December 2001. www.dfait-maeci.gc.ca/icisse/report2-en.asp.

International Military Tribunal. *Nazi Conspiracy and Aggression,* vol. 4. Washington, DC: U.S. Government Printing Office, 1946.

Jain, Mahaveer. *Bonded Labour: Justice through Judiciary.* New Delhi: Manak Publications, 1997.

Jerusalem Post. www.jpost.com, 1985–2007.

Johnson, Eric A. *Nazi Terror: The Gestapo, Jews and Ordinary Germans.* New York: Basic Books, 1999.

Jok, Jok Madut. *War and Slavery in Sudan.* Philadelphia: University of Pennsylvania Press, 2001.

Jonas, Susanne. "Democratization through Peace: The Difficult Case of Guatemala." *Journal of Interamerican Studies and World Affairs* 47, no. 4 (Winter 2000): 9–38.

Jonas, Susanne, et al., eds. *Testimony of the Permanent Peoples Tribunal on Guatemala.* San Francisco: Synthesis Publishers, 1984.

Karatnycky, Adrian. "Muslim Countries and the Democracy Gap." *Journal of Democracy* 23, no. 1 (January 2002): 99–113.

Keen, Donald. *The Benefits of Famine: A Political Economy of Famine and Relief in Southwestern Sudan, 1983–1989.* Princeton, NJ: Princeton University Press, 1994.

Kelman, Herbert C., and V. Lee Hamilton. *Crimes of Obedience: Towards a Social Psychology of Authority and Responsibility.* New Haven, CT: Yale University Press, 1989.

Kempadoo, Kamala, ed. *Trafficking and Prostitution Reconsidered.* Boulder, CO: Paradigm Publishers, 2005.

Kempadoo, Kamala, and Jo Doesma, eds. *Global Sex Workers: Rights, Resistance, and Redefinition.* New York: Routledge, 1998.

Kiernan, Ben. *The Pol Pot Regime: Race, Power, and Genocide in Cambodia under the Khmer Rouge, 1975–79.* New Haven, CT: Yale University Press, 1996.

Kirkpatrick, Jeane. "Dictatorships and Double Standards." *Commentary* (November 1979).

Bibliography

Kissi, Edward. "The Holocaust and Africa: Africa and the Holocaust." Kent Family Lecture at the Strassler Center for Holocaust and Genocide Studies, Clark University, Worcester, MA, March 13, 2002.

Klinghoffer, Arthur J. *The International Dimension of Genocide in Rwanda.* Basingstoke, UK: Macmillan, 1999.

Krain, Matthew. "State-Sponsored Mass Murder: The Onset and Severity of Genocides and Politicides." *Journal of Conflict Resolution* 41 (1997): 331–360.

Kramer, Mark. "Introduction." In *Redrawing Nations: Ethnic Cleansing in East-Central Europe.* Edited by Philipp Ther and Ana Siljak. Lanham, MD: Rowman and Littlefield, 2001.

Kuper, Leo. *Genocide: Its Political Use in the Twentieth Century.* New Haven, CT: Yale University Press, 1981.

Kurzman, Charles. "Despotism, Democracy and Economic Development." Paper presented at the Eastern Sociological Society, New York City, March 18, 1993.

Lacy, Marc. "African Women Gather to Denounce Genital Cutting." *New York Times,* February 6, 2003, 3.

Landesman, Peter. "A Woman's Work." *New York Times Magazine* (September 15, 2002): 18.

Langbein, John H. *Torture and the Law of Proof: Europe and England in the Ancien Regime.* Chicago: University of Chicago Press, 1976.

Langguth, A. J. "Torture's Teachers." *New York Times,* June 11, 1979, A19.

Leaning, Jennifer. "The Human Impact of War in Darfur." In *Darfur: Genocide before Our Eyes.* Edited by Joyce Apsel. New York: Institute for the Study of Genocide, 2005, 60–70.

LeBlanc, Lawrence J. "The United Nations Genocide Convention and Political Groups: Should the United States Propose an Amendment?" *Yale Journal of International Law* 13, no. 2 (1988): 268–294.

———. *United States and the Genocide Convention.* Durham, NC: Duke University Press, 1991.

Legett, George. *The Checka: Lenin's Political Police.* Oxford: Clarendon Press, 1981.

Leitenberg, Milton. "U.S. and UN Actions Escalate Genocide and Increase Costs in Rwanda." In *The Prevention of Genocide: Rwanda and Yugoslavia Reconsidered.* Edited by Helen Fein. New York: Institute for the Study of Genocide, 1994, 33–42.

———. "International Sanctions: The Experience of the United Nations and Iraq." A paper prepared for the Conference on Peaceful Use of Biotechnology and the Convention on Biological Weapons, June 26–27, 1998, International Center for Genetic Engineering and Biotechnology, Trieste, Italy.

———. "Saddam Is the Cause of Iraqis' Suffering." *ISG Newsletter,* no. 28 (Winter 2002): 4–14.

————. "Book Review: Beyond the 'Never Agains,'" *Institute for the Study of Genocide Newsletter* 37 (Winter 2006): 12–16.

Lemarchand, René. "Disconnecting the Threads: Rwanda and the Holocaust Reconsidered." *Journal of Genocide Research* 4, no. 4 (December 2002): 499–518.

Lemkin, Raphael. *Axis Rule in Occupied Europe.* Washington, DC: Carnegie Endowment, 1944.

Lerner, Gerda. *The Creation of Patriarchy.* New York: Oxford University Press, 1986.

Lerner, Melvin J. *The Belief in a Just World: A Fundamental Delusion.* New York: Plenum Press, 1980.

Levin, Michael. "The Case for Torture." *Newsweek* (June 7, 1982): 13.

Levine, Mark. "Creating a Modern Zone of Genocide: The Impact of Nation and State Formation on Eastern Anatolia 1878–1923." *Holocaust and Genocide Studies* 12 (Winter 1998): 398–433.

Lewis, Anthony. "Abroad at Home: Accomplice to Terror." *New York Times,* March 22, 1981, E19.

Lewis, Bernard. *Race and Slavery in the Middle East.* New York: Oxford University Press, 1990.

Lewthwaite, Gilbert A., and Gregory Kane. "Spotlight on Slavery." Three-part series. *Baltimore Sun,* June 14–18, 1996.

Lipset, Seymour M. *Political Man: The Social Bases of Politics.* New York: Anchor Books, 1963.

————. "The Social Requisites of Democracy." *American Sociological Review* 49, no. 1 (1994).

Locke, John. "Second Treatise of Government (1690)." In *The Human Rights Reader.* Rev. ed. Edited by Walter Laqueur and Barry Rubin. New York: New American Library, 1989.

Lovejoy, Paul E. *Transformations in Slavery: A History of Slavery in Africa.* 2nd ed. Cambridge: Cambridge University Press, 2000.

Machel, Graça. *Impact of Armed Conflict on Children.* New York: United Nations Department of Public Information, UNICEF, 1996.

Mahmud, Ushari Ahman, and Suleyman Ali Baldo. "Human Rights Violations in the Sudan, 1987." Abridged and translated by the Anti-Slavery Organization. Available at www.anti-slavery.org.

Makiya, Kanan. *The Republic of Fear: The Politics of Modern Iraq.* Al-Khalil, Samir (pseud. Kanan Makiya). Berkeley: University of California Press, 1989.

————. *The Republic of Fear: The Politics of Modern Iraq.* Updated ed. Berkeley: University of California Press, 1998.

————. "Symposium: War and Iraq." *Dissent* (Winter 2003): 12.

Malamud Goti, Jaime. *Game without End: State Terror and the Politics of Justice.* Norman: University of Oklahoma Press, 1996.

Mandami, Mahmood. *When Victims Become Killers: Colonialism, Nativism, and the Genocide in Rwanda.* Princeton, NJ: Princeton University Press, 2001.

Manz, Beatrice. *Paradise in Ashes: A Guatemalan Journey of Courage, Terror and Hope.* Berkeley: University of California Press, 2004.

Maran, Rita. *The Ideology of Torture in the French-Algerian War.* New York: Praeger, 1989.

Marchak, Patricia. *State Terrorism in Argentina in the 1970s.* Montreal: McGill-Queens University Press, 1999.

Margolin, Jean-Louise, and Pierre Rigoulot. "Communism in Asia: Between Reeducation and Massacre." In *The Black Book of Communism: Crimes, Terror, Repression.* Edited by Stephane Courtois et al.; translated by Jonathan Murphy and Mark Kramer. Cambridge, MA: Harvard University Press, 1999, 517–635.

Markusen, Eric, and Samuel Totten. "Investigating Allegations of Genocide in Darfur: The U.S. Atrocities Documentation Team and the UN Commission of Inquiry." In *Darfur: Genocide before Our Eyes.* Edited by Joyce Apsel. New York: Institute for the Study of Genocide, 2005, 48–59.

Marshall, Phi, and Susu Thatun. "Miles Away: The Trouble with Prevention in the Greater Mekong Sub-Region." In *Trafficking and Prostitution Reconsidered: New Perspectives on Migration, Sex Work and Human Rights.* Edited by Kamala Kempadoo. Boulder, CO: Paradigm Publishers, 2005, 43–63.

Massing, Michael. "Does Democracy Avert Famine?" *New York Times,* March 1, 2003, p. A19.

May, Rachel. *Terror in the Countryside: Campesino Responses to Political Violence in Guatemala, 1954–1985.* Athens: Ohio University Center for International Studies, 2001.

McCamant, John. "Domination, State Power, and Political Repression." In *State Organized Terror: Tragedy of the Modern State.* Edited by Timothy Bushnell et al. Boulder, CO: Westview Press, 1991, 41–58.

McCann, James A., and Mark Gibney. "An Overview of Political Terror in the Developing World, 1980–1991." In *Human Rights and Developing Countries.* Edited by David L. Cingranelli. Greenwich, CT: JAI, 1996 [1993], 15–27.

McClintock, Michael. *The American Connection.* Vol. 2: *State Terror and Popular Resistance in Guatemala.* London: Zed Books, 1985.

——. *Instruments of Statecraft: U.S. Guerrilla Warfare, Counter-Insurgency, and Counter-Terrorism, 1940–1990.* New York: Pantheon, 1992.

——. "What Can Governments, International Organizations, and Non-governmental Organizations Do Now to Prevent Genocide." In *Ever Again?: Evaluating the United Nations Genocide Convention on Its 50th Anniversary and Proposals to Activate the Convention.* Edited by Orlanda Brugnola, Helen Fein, and Louise Spirer. Institute for the Study of Genocide: ISG Working Paper, 1999, 70–80.

McKinley, James C., Jr. "UN Tribunal Convicts Rwandan of '94 Genocide." *New York Times,* September 3, 1998, A1.

McMillan, Alistaire. *Standing at the Margins: Representation and Electoral Reservation in India.* New Delhi: Oxford University Press, 2005.

McSherry, J. Patrice. "Operation Condor, Deciphering the U.S. Role." www. crimesofwar.org/special/condorhtml (2001).

Mehta, Gita. *Snakes and Ladders: Glimpses of India.* New York: Nan A. Talese/ Doubleday, 1997.

Mellibovsky, Matilde. *Circle of Love over Death.* Translated by Maria and Matthew Proser. Willimantic, CT: Curbstone Press, 1997.

Melson, Robert. *Revolution and Genocide: On the Origins of the Armenian Genocide and the Holocaust.* Chicago: University of Chicago Press, 1992.

Merry, Salley Engle. *Human Rights and Gender Violence: Translating International Law into Local Justice.* Chicago: University of Chicago Press, 2006.

Messer, Ellen. "Food Wars: Hunger as a Weapon of War in 1994." In *The Hunger Report 1995.* Edited by Ellen Messer and Peter Uvin, 19–48. Leiden, Netherlands: Gordon and Breach Publishers, 1996.

Midlarsky, Manus. *The Killing Trap: Genocide in the Twentieth Century.* New York: Cambridge University Press, 2005.

Milgram, Stanley. *Obedience to Authority: An Experimental View.* New York: Harper and Row, 1974.

Milner, Wesley T., Steven C. Poe, and David Leblang. "Security Rights, Subsistence Rights, and Liberties: A Theoretical Survey of the Empirical Landscape." *Human Rights Quarterly* 21 (1999): 403–443.

Minogue, Kenneth. "The History of the Idea of Human Rights." In *Human Rights Reader.* Edited by Walter Lacquer and Barry Rubin, 3–16. New York: New American Library, 1989.

Mirsky, Jonathan. "How the Chinese Spread SARS." *New York Review of Books* (May 29, 2003): 42.

Moeller, Robert G. *War Stories: The Search for a Usable Past in the Federal Republic of Germany.* Berkeley: University of California Press, 2001.

Moore, Barrington. *Social Origins of Dictatorship and Democracy: Lord and Peasant in the Making of the Modern World.* Boston: Beacon Press, 1966.

Moore, Mick. "Democracy and Development in Cross-National Perspective: A New Look at the Statistics." *Democratization* 2, no. 2 (Summer 1995): 1–19.

Morrison, George, et al., eds. *Black Africa: A Comparative Handbook.* 2nd ed. New York: Paragon House, 1980.

Motro, Helen Schary. "Equality Soldiers in Israel: Protecting Women from Sex Slavery and Harassment." *Lilith* (Fall 2000): 20–22.

Naimark, Norman M. *Fires of Hatred: Ethnic Cleansing in the Twentieth-Century Europe.* Cambridge, MA: Harvard University Press, 2001.

National Security Archives. Argentina: 65 documents. http://www.gwu. edu/~nsarchiv.

———. Guatemala: 74 documents. www.gwu.edu~nsarchiv/latin_america/ Guatemala.html.

Natsios, Andrew S. "The Politics of Famine in North Korea." *United States*

Institute of Peace Special Report. Washington, DC: United States Institute of Peace, August 2, 1999.

———. *The Great North Korean Famine: Famine, Politics, and Foreign Policy.* Washington, DC: United States Institute for Peace, 2002.

New Israel Fund. *NIF News,* October 3, 2006: 2–3. Available at www.news@nif.org.

Newsweek. "Slavery." *Newsweek* (May 4, 1992): 8–15.

New York Times, 1980–2007.

Nielsen, Francois. "Sociobiology and Sociology." In *Annual Review of Sociology* 20 (1994): 272–273.

Nisbet, Robert A. *The Sociological Tradition.* New York: Basic Books, 1966.

Nussbaum, Martha. "Genocide in Gujarat." *Dissent* (Summer 2003): 15–23.

Obeidi, Mahdi, and Kurt Pitzer. *The Bomb in My Garden.* Hoboken, NJ: John Wiley, 2004.

O'Donnell, Guillermo. "Democratic Theory and Comparative Politics." A paper presented at the annual meeting of the American Sociological Association, Chicago, August 6, 1999.

Omvedt, Gail. *Dalits and the Democratic Revolution.* New Delhi: Sage, 1994.

Opperman, Martin. *Sex Tourism and Prostitution: Aspects of Leisure, Recreation, and Work.* Elmsford, NY: Cognizant Communication Corporation, 1998.

Osei-Hwedie, Bertha A. "Successful Development and Democracy in Africa: The Case of Botswana and Mauritius." *Il Politico* 65, no. 1 (January–March 2000).

Osiel, Mark. *Mass Atrocity, Ordinary Evil, and Hannah Arendt.* New Haven, CT: Yale University Press, 2001.

Ovadia, Ezra. *The Withdrawal of Rights.* Dordrecht: Kluwer Academic Publishers, 2002.

Pal, R. M. "Groups at Risk: Caste and Communal Violence in India." *ISG Newsletter,* no. 13 (Fall 1994): 4–6.

Patterson, Orlando. *Slavery and Social Death.* Cambridge, MA: Oxford University Press, 1982.

Penn, Michael L., and Rahel Nardos et al. *Overcoming Violence against Women and Girls: The International Campaign to Eradicate a Worldwide Problem.* Lanham, MD: Rowman and Littlefield, 2005.

Peters, Edward. *Torture.* New York: Basil Blackwell, 1985.

Physicians for Human Rights (PHR) Denmark. "Zimbabwe 2002: Post Presidential Elections—March to May 2002." http://www.phrusa.org/healthrights/phr_den052302/html.

Plushnick-Masti, Ramit. "Israel Tackles Trafficking of Women Sex Slaves." *Moscow Times,* February 21, 2003, www.iabolish.com/news/press-coverage/2003/tmt02-21-03.htm.

Poe, Steven C., and C. Neal Tate. "Repression of Human Rights to Personal

Integrity in the 1980s: A Global Analysis." *American Political Science Review* 87, no. 4 (December 1994): 853–872.

Poe, Steven C., C. Neal Tate, and Linda Camp Keith. "Repression of the Human Right to Personal Integrity Revisited: A Global Cross-National Study Covering the Years 1976–1993." *International Studies Quarterly* 43 (1999): 291–313.

Pohl, J. Otto. *Ethnic Cleansing in the USSR, 1937–1949.* Westport, CT: Greenwood Press, 1999.

Ponchaud, Pierre. *Cambodia Year Zero.* Translated by Nancy Amphoux. Harmondsworth, UK: Penguin, 1978.

Portes, Alejandro, and Patricia Landot. "Social Capital: Promises and Pitfalls of Its Role in Development." *Journal of Latin American Studies* 32 (2000): 529–547.

Potash, Robert. "The Army, Civil Society, and the Transition in Argentina, 1983–1988." A talk at the Center for the Study of Latin America, Harvard University, April 7, 1998.

Pourgerami, Abbas. "The Political Economy of Development: A Cross-National Causality Test of Development-Democracy-Growth Hypothesis." *Public Choice* 58, no. 2 (August 1988): 123–141.

———. "The Political Economy of Development: An Empirical Examination of the Wealth Theory of Democracy." *Journal of Theoretical Politics* 3, no. 2 (April 1991): 189–211.

Power, Samantha. *"A Problem from Hell": America and the Age of Genocide.* New York: Basic Books, 2002.

Prakash, S. S. *Bonded Labour and Social Justice.* New Delhi: Deep and Deep Publishers, 1990.

Pritchett, Land, and Lawrence H. Summers. "Wealthier Is Healthier." *Journal of Human Resources* 31, no. 4 (1996): 841–867.

Prunier, Gerard. *The Rwanda Crisis: History of a Genocide.* New York: Columbia University Press, 1995.

———. *Darfur: The Ambiguous Genocide.* Ithaca, NY: Cornell University Press, 2005.

Przeworski, Adam, et al. *Democracy and Development: Political Institutions and Well-Being in the World, 1950–1990.* Cambridge: Cambridge University Press, 2000.

Putnam, Robert, with Robert Leonardi and Raffaella Y. Nannetti. *Making Democracy Work: Civic Traditions in Modern Italy.* Princeton, NJ: Princeton University Press, 1993.

———. Seminar presentation on Social Capital. Department of Government, Harvard University, 2001.

Rapaport, Louis. "Crying for Argentina." *Jerusalem Post* (International Edition), August 23–29, 1981, 12–15.

Rawls, John. *A Theory of Justice.* Cambridge, MA: Harvard University Press, 1971.

Reeves, Eric. "Darfur: Genocide before Our Eyes." In *Darfur: Genocide before Our Eyes*. Edited by Joyce Apsel. New York: Institute for the Study of Genocide, 2005, 26–42.

Response 2002 (Simon Wiesenthal Center). "Europe: An Intolerable Climate of Hate." *Response* 3, no. 2 (Summer 2002): 2–6.

Richard, Amy O'Neil. *International Trafficking in Women to the United States: A Contemporary Manifestation of Slavery and Organized Crime*. Washington, DC: Center for the Study of Intelligence, November 1999.

Riemer, Neal, ed. *Protection against Genocide: Mission Impossible?* Westport, CT: Praeger, 2000.

Rittner, Carol, John K. Roth, and James M. Smith, eds. *Will Genocide Ever End?* St. Paul, MN: Paragon House, 2002.

Ritzen, Jo, William Easterly, and Michael Woolcock. "On 'Good' Politicians and 'Bad' Policies: Social Cohesion, Institutions and Growth." Washington, DC: The World Bank Policy Research Working Paper #2448, September 2000.

Robinson, William I. "Neoliberalism, the Global Elite, and the Guatemalan Transition: A Critical Macrosocial Analysis." *Journal of Interamerican Studies and World Affairs* 42, no. 4 (Winter 2000): 89–107.

Rodriguez, Junius P., ed. *The Historical Encyclopedia of World Slavery*. Santa Barbara, CA: ABC–CLIO, 1997.

Rohter, Larry. "Argentine Default Reopens 'Dirty War' Wounds." *New York Times*, March 12, 2002.

Rosenthal, Morton M. "A Survey of Anti-Semitism in Argentina." *Jewish Advocate* (January 5, 1978).

Rotberg, Robert, ed. *When States Fail: Causes and Consequences*. Princeton, NJ: Princeton University Press, 2004.

Rousseau, Jean-Jacques. "The Social Contract (1762)." In *The Human Rights Reader*. Rev. ed. Edited by Walter Lacquer and Barry Rubin. New York: New American Library, 1989, 69–74.

Rubenstein, Richard. *The Cunning of History*. New York: Harper and Row, 1975.

Rubin, Barnett E., and Paula R. Newberg. "Appendix: Statistical Analysis for Implementing Human Rights Policy." In *The Politics of Human Rights*. Edited by Paula R. Newberg. New York: New York University Press, 1980. 268–283.

Rudé, George F. E. *The Crowd in History: A Study of Population Disturbances in France and England, 1730–1848*. New York: Wiley, 1964.

Rummel, R. J. *Lethal Politics: Soviet Genocide and Mass Murder since 1917*. New Brunswick: Transaction, 1990.

———. *Death by Government*. Rutgers, NJ: Rutgers University Press, 1994.

Saeedpour, Vera Beaudin. "Establishing State Motives for Genocide: Iraq and the Kurds." In *Genocide Watch*. Edited by Helen Fein. New Haven, CT: Yale University Press, 1992, pp. 59–69.

Sanford, N. C. Comstock, et al., eds. *Sanctions for Evil*. San Francisco, CA: Jossey-Bass, 1971.

Sawyer, Roger. *Slavery in the Twentieth Century*. New York: Routledge and Kegan Paul, 1986.

Scheffer, David. "Presentation to Panel Two: The Responsibility to Protect." In *Preventing Genocide—Threats and Responsibilities: Proceedings of the Stockholm International Forum 2004*. Stockholm: Regeringskansliet, 2004, 131–133.

Schirmer, Jennifer. *The Guatemalan Military Project: A Violence Called Democracy*. Philadelphia: University of Pennsylvania Press, 1998.

Schlesinger, Stephen, and Stephen Kinzer. *Bitter Fruit: The Story of the American Coup in Guatemala*. Rev. ed. Cambridge, MA: Harvard University Press, 2005.

Schmeidl, Susanne. "From Root Cause Assessment to Preventive Diplomacy: Possibilities and Limitations of the Early Warning of Forced Migration." A doctoral dissertation presented to the Graduate School of the Ohio State University. Ohio State University, 1995.

Schmeidl, Susanne, and Howard Adelman, eds. *Synergy in Early Warning: Conference Proceedings*. Toronto, ON: York University, 1997.

Schmitter, Philippe C., and Terry Lynn Karl. "What Democracy Is … and Is Not." In *The Global Resurgence of Democracy*. Edited by Larry Diamond and Marc F. Plattner, 39–45. Baltimore, MD: Johns Hopkins University Press, 1993.

Schulz, William F. *In Our Own Best Interest: How Defending Human Rights Benefits Us All*. Boston: Beacon Press, 2001.

Sen, Amartya. *Development as Freedom*. New York: Knopf, 1999.

Simmel, Georg. *Conflict and the Web of Group Affiliations*. Translated by Kurt Wolff and Reinhard Bendix. New York: Free Press, 1955.

Simon, Jean-Marie. *Guatemala: Eternal Spring, Eternal Tyranny*. New York: W. W. Norton, 1987.

Simpson, Christopher. *Blowback: America's Recruitment of Nazis and Its Effects on the Cold War*. New York: Collier Books, 1989.

Simpson, John. *The Disappeared and the Mothers of the Plaza*. New York: St. Martin's Press, 1985.

Slack, Alison T. "Female Circumcision: A Critical Appraisal." *Human Rights Quarterly* 10 (1988): 437–486.

Smith, Michael Joseph. "On Humanitarian Intervention." In *Protection against Genocide: Mission Impossible?* Edited by Neal Riemer, 123–140. Westport, CT: Praeger, 2000.

Snyder, Jack. *From Voting to Violence: Democratization and Nationalist Conflict*. New York: W. W. Norton, 2000.

Spirer, Herbert. "Estimation of Killing Rates in Guatemala, by Ethnic Group and Region." Unpublished memorandum to Helen Fein, July 17, 1999.

Staub, Ervin. *Positive Social Behavior and Morality.* Vol. 1. New York: Academic Press, 1978.

———. *The Roots of Evil: The Psychological and Cultural Origins of Genocide and Other Forms of Group Violence.* Cambridge: Cambridge University Press, 1989.

Steiner, Henry, and Philip Alston. *International Human Rights in Context.* 2nd ed. Oxford: Oxford University Press, 2000.

Stern, Jessica. *Terror in the Name of God: Why Religious Militants Kill.* New York: Ecco, 2003.

Stockholm International Forum. *Preventing Genocide: Threats and Responsibilities.* Stockholm: Regeringskansliet, 2004.

Szymborska, Wislawa. *View with a Grain of Sand.* Translated by Stanislaw Baranczak and Clare Cavanaugh. San Diego, CA: Harcourt Brace, 1995.

Tertullian. *Christian and Pagan in the Roman Empire: the Witness of Tertullian.* Edited by Robert D. Sidner. Washington, DC: Catholic University of America Press, 2001.

Thomas, Dorothy Q., and Michele E. Beasley. "Domestic Violence as a Human Rights Issue." *Human Rights Quarterly* 15 (1993): 36–62.

Tilly, Charles. *Coercion, Capital and European States, AD 990–1990.* Cambridge, MA: Basil Blackwell, 1990.

Timerman, Jacobo. *Prisoner without a Name, Cell without a Number.* Translated by Toby Talbot. New York: Knopf, 1981.

Tocqueville, Alexis de. *Democracy in America.* Translated by Henry Reeve. New York: Oxford University Press, 1946.

Toynbee, Arnold. *The Treatment of the Armenians in the Ottoman Empire, 1915–1916.* London: His Majesty's Stationery Office, 1916.

UK Foreign and Commonwealth Office. *Saddam Hussein: Crimes and Human Rights Abuses.* London: Foreign and Commonwealth Office, November 2002.

UN Development Programme. *Human Development Report 1993.* New York: Oxford University Press, 1993.

———. *Arab Human Development Report 2002.* New York: UN Development Programme, 2002.

———. *Human Development Report 2002.* New York: Oxford University Press, 2002.

———. *Human Development Report 2005.* New York: UN Development Programme, 2005.

U.S. Committee for Refugees. *World Refugee Survey 1997.* Washington, DC: United States Committee for Refugees, 1997.

U.S. Congress. Senate Committee on Foreign Relations. Second Session of the 104th Congress. H.R. 4036 (1996).

———. *Slavery throughout the World: Hearing before the Committee on Foreign Relations, United States Senate, One Hundred Sixth Congress, second session, Sept. 28, 2000.* Washington, DC: U.S. Government Printing Office, 2001.

U.S. Department of State. *Country Reports on Human Rights 1979.* Washington, DC: U.S. Government Printing Office, 1980.

———. *Country Reports for Human Rights Practices for 1980.* Washington, DC: United States Department of State, 1981.

———. *Country Reports for Human Rights Practices for 1993.* Washington, DC: USDOS, 1994.

———. *Trafficking in Persons Report June 1994.* Washington, DC: U.S. Department of State, 1994.

———. "Mauritania." *Country Reports on Human Rights Practices for 1994.* Washington, DC: U.S. Government Printing Office, 1995.

———. *Country Reports on Human Rights Practices for 1997.* Washington, DC: U.S. Government Printing Office, 1998.

———. "Mauritania." *Country Reports on Human Rights Practices for 1999.* Washington, DC: U.S. Government Printing Office, 2000.

———. *Victims of Trafficking and Violence Protection Act 2000: Trafficking in Persons Report July 2001.* Washington DC: U.S. Department of State, 2001.

———. *Victims of Trafficking and Violence Protection Act 2000: Trafficking in Persons Report June 2002.* Washington, DC: USDOS, 2002.

———. *Trafficking in Persons Report.* Washington, DC: USDOS, 2005.

———. *Country Reports for Human Rights Practices for 2005.* Washington, DC: USDOS, 2006.

———. *Victims of Trafficking and Violence Protection Act 2000: Trafficking in Persons Report June 2006.* Washington, DC: U.S. Department of State, 2006.

Uvin, Peter. *Aiding Violence: The Development Enterprise in Rwanda.* Hartford, CT: Kumarian Press, 1998.

Van Aggelen, J. C. "Review: The Right to Life in International Law." *American Journal of International Law* 80 (1986): 742.

Vandenberg, Martina. *Trafficking in Women to Israel and Forced Prostitution.* New York: Israel Women's Network, November 1997.

Van den Berghe, Pierre. *Race and Racism.* New York: Wiley, 1967.

———. *The Ethnic Phenomenon.* New York: Elsevier, 1981.

Van der Dennen, J., and V. Falger, eds. *Sociobiology and Conflict: Evolutionary Perspectives on Competition, Cooperation, Violence and Warfare.* London: Chapman and Hall, 1990.

Van Schaak, Beth. "Limits of the United Nations Genocide Convention and Contemporary Jurisprudence." In *Ever Again?: Evaluating the United Nations Genocide Convention on Its 50th Anniversary and Proposals to Activate the Convention.* Edited by Orlanda Brugnola, Helen Fein, and Louise Spirer. Institute for the Study of Genocide Working Paper, 1999, 41–51.

Verbitsky, Horacio. *The Flight: Confessions of an Argentine Dirty Warrior.* Translated by Esther Allen. New York: New Press, 1996.

Vidal-Naquet, Pierre. "Preface." *Reason of State.* (Preface of the author to the edition of 2002 first published in 1962 by the Committee Maurice Audin.) Translated from the French by Algeria Watch. www.algeria-watch. org; http://64.233.179.104/translate_c?hl=en&sl=fr&u.

Wall, Irwin M. *France, the United States and the Algerian War.* Berkeley: University of California Press, 2001.

Waller, James. *Becoming Evil: How Ordinary People Commit Genocide and Mass Killing.* Oxford: Oxford University Press, 2002.

Wallerstein, Immanuel M. *The Modern World-System.* Vol. 2. New York: Academic Press, 1980.

Walter, E. V. "Violence and the Process of Terror." *American Sociological Review* 29 (April 1964): 248–257.

Walzer, Michael. *Just and Unjust Wars: A Moral Argument with Historical Illustrations.* 2nd ed. New York: Basic Books, 1977.

———. "How Should the Left Respond to a U.S. War against Iraq?" *Dissent* (Winter 2003): 4–5.

———. *Arguing about War.* New Haven, CT: Yale University Press, 2004.

———. "Regime Change and Just War." *Dissent* (Summer 2006): 103–108.

Weber, Max. "Politics as a Vocation." In *From Max Weber: Essays in Sociology.* Edited by H. H. Gerth and C. Wright Mills. New York: Oxford University Press, 1946.

Wechsler, Lawrence. *A Miracle, a Universe: Settling Accounts with Torturers.* New York: Pantheon Books, 1990.

Weiner, Myron, and Omar Noman. *The Child and the State in India and Pakistan.* Karachi: Oxford University Press, 1991.

Weldon, S. Laurel. *Protest, Policy, and the Problem of Violence against Women: A Cross-National Comparison.* Pittsburgh, PA: University of Pittsburgh Press, 2002.

Werth, Nicholas. "A State against Its People: Violence, Repression, and Terror in the Soviet Union." In *The Black Book of Communism: Crimes, Terror, Repression.* Edited by Stephane Courtois et al.; translated by Jonathan Murphy and Mark Kramer. Cambridge, MA: Harvard University Press, 1999, 33–268.

Wheeler, Nicholas J. *Saving Strangers: Humanitarian Intervention in International Society.* Oxford: Oxford University Press, 2000.

Whitaker, Ben. *Revised and Updated Report on the Question of the Prevention and Punishment of the Crime of Genocide.* New York: United Nations, 1985.

Wilson, Edward O. *On Human Nature.* Cambridge, MA: Harvard University Press, 1978.

Wood, Michael. "Destruction of the Marsh Arabs' Habitat in Iraq: Saddam's Latest War." *ISG Newsletter,* no. 12 (Spring 1994): 2–5.

Woods, Kevin, James Lacey, and Williamson Murray. "Saddam's Delusions: The View from the Inside." *Foreign Affairs* 85, no. 3 (May–June 2006): 2–26.

World Bank. *World Development Report 1998.* New York: Oxford University Press, 1998.

Bibliography

Yanik, Lerna K. "Guns and Human Rights: Major Powers, Global Arms Transfers, and Human Rights Violations." *Human Rights Quarterly* 26, no. 2 (May 2006): 357–388.

Yashar, Deborah J. *Demanding Democracy: Reform and Reaction in Costa Rica and Guatemala, 1870s–1950s*. Stanford, CA: Stanford University Press, 1997.

Zakaria, Fareed. "The Rise of Illiberal Democracy." *Foreign Affairs* 76, no. 6 (November/December 1997): 22–43.

Zweifel, Thomas D., and Patricio Navio. "Democracy, Dictatorship, and Infant Mortality." *Journal of Democracy* (April 2000): 99–114.

Index

Index

Index

Index

Index

Index

Social change, 10, 93
Social cleansing, 163, 177
Social cohesion, 206; lack of, 224; life chances and, 223; promoting, 226; respect for, 190
Social contracts, 12, 181
Social death, 19, 23
Social demands, rise of, 164
Social development, 121, 192
Social psychology, 15, 16
Social rights, 4, 5, 208
Social unrest, 44, 137
Societies, questions/assumptions underlying, 10–14
Sociobiology, 15, 16
Socioeconomic reform, 180, 189
Soldiers, child, 27
Solidarity, 11, 103, 225, 226
SOS Esclaves, Mauritania and, 36
Soustelle, Jacques, 71, 72
Soviet Union: breakup of, 173, 222; slave labor and, 26, 216; terror by, 62, 63, 214
Special Rapporteur on Human Rights in Sudan, 33
Speech, freedom of, 162, 186
Speke, John Hanning, 140
Spirer, Herbert, 99
SPLA. *See* Sudanese People's Liberation Army
Stalin, Joseph, 65, 216
Standard of living, 121, 184, 192, 233
State killers, 98, 133
State terror, 65, 69, 81, 86, 117, 121, 237; instruments of, 61; supporting, 118–119; victims of, 119, 132
State violations, underlying causes of, 170–177
State violence, 103, 108–109; collective violence and, 151–152; minorities and, 164; security and, 3; victims of, 90
Straw, Jack, 234
"Study of Assassination, A," 94
Submarino, 67
Sub-Saharan Africa, slavery in, 217
Subsistence rights, 5, 14, 21, 205
Sudan: genocide in, 133; independence of, 30; slavery in, 28–33, 42n1, 57, 217
Sudanese Christians, persecution of, 33
Sudanese civil war, 148; famine/genocide and, 31; slavery and, 27, 28
Sudanese government. *See* Government of Sudan
Sudanese People's Liberation Army (SPLA), 30, 148

Sudan Peace Act (2001), 33, 220
Suez Canal, nationalization of, 73, 104
Suicide, 7, 8
Sunnis, 105, 116
Supplementary Convention on the Abolition of Slavery, the Slave Trade, and Institutions and Practices Similar to Slavery (1956), 23–24
Suttee, 7
Szymborska, Wislawa, 60

Talabani, Jalal, 112
Taliban, 162, 172
Tate, Neal, 167
Terrible violators, 167, 169, 175
Terror, xv, 3, 31, 211, 213; accounting for, 16–21; antistate, 69, 237; checking, 80, 123, 210, 228–231, 232, 237; class bargaining and, 121; collective, 61, 69, 71, 74; communism and, 62; context of, 69; denial of, 122; dictatorships and, 123; economic growth and, 68; emergence of, 61, 62–63, 68; exchange relationships and, 21; exclusion and, 19–20; fascism and, 62; genocide and, 90, 119, 214, 233; government type and, 68; instilling, 17; institutionalization of, 14; intervention against, 228–231; Islamic, 76; justifying, 66, 69, 87, 236; mass participation in, 61; obligation and, 212; persistence of, 117–123; political, 68; rationalization of, 18; reactionary, 96; restrictions on, 19; rubber, 25; state, 61, 65, 69, 81, 86, 117, 118–119, 121, 132, 237; structure of, 109; threat of, 213; use of, 63, 65, 75, 90, 174; victims of, 213; violence/fear and, 118; as weapon, 74, 118, 213
Terror states, 61; checking, 123, 232–233, 235, 236; collaboration in, 122; crimes against humanity and, 236; ethnic division in, 213; genocide and, 132, 137, 236; human rights organizations and, 232; subjugation by, 213; U.S. support for, 213–214
Tertullian, Emperor, 61
Teyeb, Moctar, 36
Thailand: prostitution in, 50–51, 52; sex work in, 50–51; trafficking in, 50–51
Thatun, Susu, 50
Thesis of National Stability, 102
Tiananmen Square, 168
"Ticking bomb" case, torture and, 74
Tillon, Germaine, 75
Timerman, Jacobo, 64, 78, 83, 85

Index

Index

United Nations: estimates by, 192; *génocid-aires* and, 146, 215, 228– 229; genocide and, 156, 157, 230; Iran-Iraq War and, 112; Mauritania and, 36; peacekeeping by, 230–231; Rwanda and, 139, 156; Tutsis and, 140–141; UDHR and, 2

Universal Declaration of Human Rights (UDHR), 2, 4

Universal human rights, 4, 7; notion of, 1, 8; violation of, 10

UN Rapporteur on Rwanda, 143

UN Resolution 688, 115

UN Resolution 1441, 233–234

UN Security Council (UNSC), 124n2, 228; arms/human rights and, 227; Darfur and, 150, 215; ethnic cleansing and, 152; genocide and, 157; GOS noncooperation and, 150; Iraq War and, 117; Rwanda and, 145, 146; sanctions by, 117; WMDs and, 233

UN Special Rapporteur on Violence against Women, 32; trafficking and, 45, 47

UN Sub-Commission on Prevention of Discrimination and Protection of Minorities, 34

UN Verification Mission in Guatemala, 101

UN Working Group on Contemporary Forums of Slavery, 33

UNSC. *See* UN Security Council

Untouchables, 58, 163, 211, 217; caste relations and, 38; contempt for, 224; disadvantages for, 37; disrespect for, 187; exclusion of, 12

Urbanization, 34, 70

U.S. Agency for International Development (USAID), 101, 114

USAID. *See* U.S. Agency for International Development

U.S. Army School of the Americas, 77, 80

U.S. Atrocities Documentation Team, Darfur and, 150

U.S. Department of State (USDS), 80, 167; country ranking by, 44; Guatemalan Army massacres and, 100; Mauritania and, 35, 36; Policy Planning Council of, 95; prostitution/Israel and, 53; reports by, 51, 100, 101; Rwanda and, 145–146; trafficking and, 28, 54

U.S. Department of State (USDOS) Country Reports on Human Rights, 100

USDOS. *See* U.S. Department of State

U.S. National Endowment for Democracy (NED), 101

U.S. Senate Foreign Relations Committee, 36, 150

Vaky, Viron: counterterror and, 95–96

Varna, 37, 57

Vicious cycles, virtuous cycles and, 205–207

Victimizers: children as, 26–27; victims and, 18, 20, 68

Victims, 96; blaming, 15; bystanders and, 18; control of, 18; exclusion of, 19; genocide, 19, 132, 137; hatred of, 15; implicated, 215; innocent, 215; preselected, 135; random, 82; selecting, 18, 20; victimizers and, 18, 20, 68

Victims of Trafficking and Violence Protection Act (2000), 220

Videla, Jorge Rafael, 84, 89

Vienna Declaration of the World Conference on Human Rights, 9, 208

View with a Grain of Sand (Szymborska), quote from, 60

Vigilance committees, 71

Violence, 3, 17, 178; collective, 151–152; escaping, 153; physical, 189; rural collective, 102; social trauma and, 102; state, 90, 103, 108–109, 151–152; triggering, 16

Virtuous cycle, 21, 184, 191, 196, 226; vicious cycles and, 205–207

Volksgemeinschaft, 63

Von Wernich, Christian, 88

Voting rights, 2, 163

Vuelo, 67

Wage labor, 13

Waller, James, ancestral shadow and, 15; on Milgram research, 15

Walzer, Michael, 210; on human wrongs, 211; on intervention, 211; on justifying genocide, 235; on war/regime change, 234–235

War crimes, 9, 31, 79, 102, 112, 126, 132, 150, 156, 185; alleged, 178; genocide and, 134; justifying, 76; trials for, 125, 222

Wars: genocide and, 137, 230; international laws of, 75; internal/external, 110–114

Warsaw Ghetto, 133

Washington Post, on Kirkuk oilfields, 111

Wealth, 205; competition for, 176; life integrity and, 179

Weapons of mass destruction (WMDs), 115, 234, 235; disarming, 233; monitoring, 117

Weber, Max, 12, 90

Weinberger-Powell doctrine, 231

Index

About the Author

Helen Fein is Director of the Institute for the Study of Genocide in New York and an Associate of the Belfer Center for Science and International Affairs of the Kennedy School of Government at Harvard University. She is the author of two award-winning books: *Accounting for Genocide* (Free Press 1979), winner of the Sorokin Award of the American Sociological Association, and *Genocide: A Sociological Perspective* (Sage 1991, 1993), winner of the first PIOOM award in Amsterdam.

Made in the USA
Columbia, SC
23 September 2017